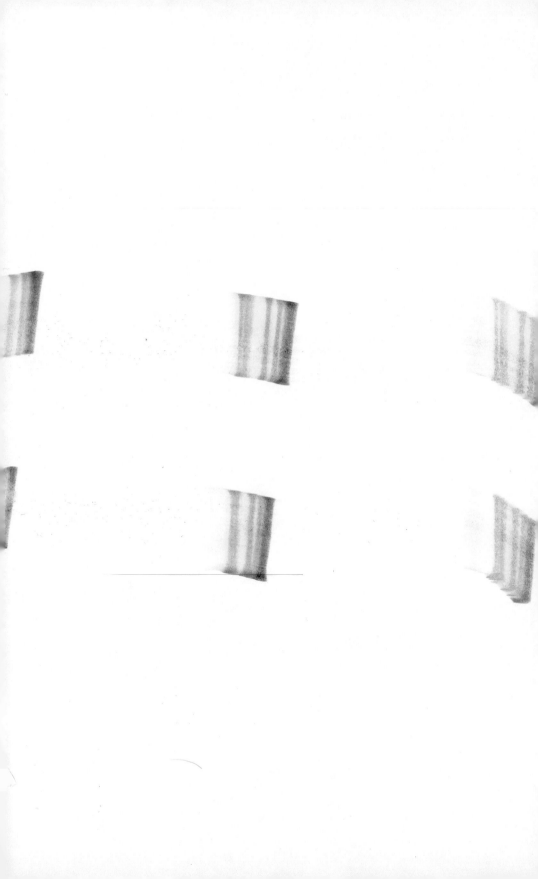

Executive's Guide to
E-Business

Executive's Guide to
E-Business

FROM TACTICS TO STRATEGY

Martin V. Deise
Conrad Nowikow
Patrick King
Amy Wright

JOHN WILEY & SONS, INC.

New York • Chichester • Weinheim • Brisbane • Singapore • Toronto

Library of Congress Cataloging-in-Publication Data:

Executive's guide to e-business: from tactics to strategy/Martin Deise [. . . et al.].
      p.   cm.
   Includes bibliographical references.
   ISBN 0-471-37639-6 (cloth : alk. paper)
   1. Electronic commerce.   I. Deise, Martin.
   HF5548.32.E97   1999
   658.8′00285′4678—dc21
   99-042978

Printed in the United States of America.

10   9   8   7   6   5   4   3

Contents

Foreword

With predictions that worldwide e-business spending will surpass $7 trillion by 2004, e-business is growing at an explosive rate. The rules have changed, and businesses are faced with a do-or-die proposition: become part of the new economy or perish amid competitive forces.

Powerful as it is, e-business is both an opportunity and a problem. The opportunity is clear. As a means of growing existing market share, entering new markets, forging alliances with business partners, and taking the all-important customer relationship to a new and unprecedented level, e-business is an unparalleled tool. The daunting problem for most executives, however, is deciding where to begin and how to follow through.

Not surprisingly, the magnitude of e-business implications has spawned a slew of books on the subject. Most, however, tell only half the story—the business-to-consumer (B2C) half. These are of limited use to executives preparing to chart an e-business course for their companies. It is the business-to-business (B2B) aspect that is at the core of what today's "e-xecutives" need to know.

Executives need to assess where they fit in the marketplace today—and, more importantly, where they want to be tomorrow. They should ask themselves: What kind of e-business should I have and how long should I stay there? How do I build the right technology infrastructure? How do I manage "e-shock" among my managers and other employees? How do I form and then manage the business partnerships I will need to provide seamless and superior customer service? How do I manage the competition?

Executive's Guide to E-Business: From Tactics to Strategy not only answers these questions, but does so with a clarity that is unprecedented in books of this kind. Imposing order on an unruly subject, the authors present us with a new—and refreshingly original—e-business model. Consisting of four "snapshots" across the e-business "panorama," the model moves from the tactical to the strategic, and, along the way, provides detailed information about the space that, at any given time, a company can occupy in the world of e-business. The authors then tell us how to maximize the opportunities of owning that space and how to minimize the risks.

Unlike some others, this book does not dwell on pie-in-the-sky theories or vague abstractions. The authors, PricewaterhouseCoopers consultants, give readers—both those just starting to contemplate e-business and those already well on their way as "e-nabled" companies—plenty of concrete, practical advice, solidly grounded in their extensive experience helping e-companies to succeed.

At PricewaterhouseCoopers, our consultants have worked with the world's largest companies, as well as with leading new entrants and Internet startups, to help them navigate e-business challenges, plan and implement e-business strategies, and gain a competitive edge. We know what the critical success factors are, and we help clients avoid the pitfalls.

Becoming an e-business winner is no easy task. And while this book cannot perform that task for you, it can certainly make it much easier. I highly recommend *Executive's Guide to E-Business: From Tactics to Strategy.* Read it. Learn from it. Keep it on your desk. I think you will find it indispensable as you take your own company forward on the path to e-business success.

Scott Hartz
Global Managing Partner
PricewaterhouseCoopers Management Consulting Services

Acknowledgments

Four names appear on the cover of this book, but, in fact, many individuals contributed to its contents. Writing a thought-provoking book on the subject of e-business requires a significant amount of research, analysis, and creativity, and we could not have done it alone.

Our book reflects the collective experience of many talented PricewaterhouseCoopers professionals gained during the performance of several hundred e-business-related client projects. While each of these individuals provided invaluable help, the authors particularly acknowledge the contributions of our colleagues Naj Rahman, Doug Baird, William Guyton, Naveen Lamba, Tim Wood, John King, Michael Gabbay, Colleen Wesling, Ed Berryman, and Grant Norris for their insight and dedication.

We would also like to thank Bob Van Saun and Tony Olender for acting as sounding boards and for providing an environment for testing many of the concepts discussed in this book.

In addition, we are grateful to Jack Dunleavy for encouraging us to write this book. We also cannot overestimate the value added by our production/editing team, including Doug Regan, who managed this project and kept it on track; Dan Gallaugher, who created our graphics; Jon Zonderman, whose editorial skills helped give our ideas structure and clarity; and Gene Zasadinski, whose final editing and attention to detail brought the manuscript to a higher level. We would also like to thank Sheck Cho, our editor at John Wiley & Sons, and his team for their tireless efforts on our behalf.

Finally, and most important, we want to thank our families and close friends for supporting us during many long nights and weekends spent writing our manuscript. We thank them for their understanding and patience. We could not have completed this book without their help.

Martin V. Deise
Conrad Nowikow, Ph.D.
Patrick King
Amy Wright

About the Authors

Martin V. Deise

A recognized authority on e-business, Martin V. Deise advises executives from global organizations, dot.com companies, and e-market ventures on e-business strategy and industry-transforming business models. As former program director for PricewaterhouseCoopers' E-Business Central Team in the Americas, he led the development of the organization's global e-business framework, which provides the foundation for its service offerings and thought leadership. His team was responsible for defining PricewaterhouseCoopers' consulting practice's e-business strategy, service offering, and infrastructure capabilities. He currently oversees a team of e-business strategy, process, organization, and technology professionals who provide leading-edge thought and end-to-end implementation capability for clients in the high-tech, consumer, industrial products, and telecom industries. Mr. Deise has authored numerous articles on e-business and is a frequent speaker at conferences and seminars.

Conrad Nowikow, Ph.D.

With more than 20 years of experience helping companies with all aspects of information technology, Conrad Nowikow is a founding member of PricewaterhouseCoopers' global e-business team, where he develops strategies, business processes, and information technology tools that support enterprises migrating to e-business. For the past five years, Dr. Nowikow has focused on defining interactive media and e-commerce strategies for major banking, high-tech manufacturing, telecommunications, information technology, and media clients. A sought after speaker at technology and business conferences, he is regularly quoted in the press and significant industry publications on e-business and technology matters. The leader of PricewaterhouseCoopers' e-procurement practice in Europe, Dr. Nowikow is a coauthor of *e-Supply Chain: Revolution or E-volution,* published by Euromoney.

Patrick King

Formerly head of PricewaterhouseCoopers' e-business consulting practice in Europe, Patrick King has worked on both sides of the Atlantic to develop e-business strategies that take advantage of the massive changes and opportunities emerging from this new business paradigm. Having been among the few consultants involved in e-business since its early stages, he possesses a keen insight into the unique challenges posed by the e-business revolution. A leading thinker and strategist on the impact of e-business across industries, Mr. King is a key member of Pricewater-houseCoopers' global e-business strategy development team. He frequently speaks on the subject of e-business futures at major conferences and summits throughout Europe.

Amy Wright

As head of the e-business practice for PricewaterhouseCoopers in the eastern United States, Amy Wright is responsible for bringing e-business strategies and solutions to clients in all industries, ranging from large global organizations to pure-play start-ups. Her strategic focus is the result of experience forming marketplace initiatives, trade exchanges, and portals and bringing organizations together to form partnerships that will serve the market as communities across the entire value chain. A leading force behind PricewaterhouseCoopers' firmwide transformation to an e-business, Ms. Wright is currently supporting that effort by driving cultural change and developing new go-to-market approaches, training and recruiting programs, tools, and methodologies. As a key member of the organization's global e-business strategy development team, she actively negotiates select equity and alliance partnerships and collaborates with other partners across geographies and industries to integrate clients, technologies, and solutions into end-to-end value propositions.

Introduction

A New E-Business Model

Today, whenever executives gather, the topic of e-business—its impact and its opportunities—is sure to surface. Such conversations are likely to center on start-ups and other competitors grabbing market share through innovative e-business strategies; the paramount importance of customers and the way companies relate to them; cost/benefit considerations driving investment in enabling technologies; the impact of e-business on brand and other public perception issues; the future of traditional products and services as many become commodities; strategic alliances and partnerships; and the fate of bricks-and-mortar businesses.

The range of possible subjects that e-business engenders is, in itself, telling. Clearly, e-business notions are reshaping commerce as we know it, turning old notions upside down and requiring completely fresh approaches. Consider just a sampling of what has changed: A few years ago, the cost of information handling was comparatively high, and for some companies, prohibitively so. Today, the Internet has driven that cost down dramatically, making it possible for commercial enterprises to turn the tables on competitors. In other situations, competitors may find themselves working together as partners, with each entity leveraging the other's special competencies. Speed, agility, and flexibility have become top priorities. And the supply chain (the work done once the sale is made) has given way in importance to the value chain (the end-to-end series of steps in the process from identifying to satisfying a customer's need). Access to new markets and additional segments of existing markets has become easier than ever before. Among e-businesses, service, quality, agility, and reach have gone up, while price, fulfillment time, and time to market have gone down, significantly enhancing the ability to provide value to customers while taking the competitive lead.

And the pace of change continues to accelerate. In just the last year, we have witnessed the emergence of new competitors, new business models, and new customer attitudes about doing business on-line. The Internet phenomenon is truly global; the question no longer is *whether* on-line business will survive, but, rather, *what will be left* of traditional business once e-business reaches its full potential. Current estimates indicate that in a few years, e-business will generate trillions of dollars. Just five years ago, the amount generated was insignificant.

As the notion that "e-business is business" gains wider acceptance, executives are realizing that technology alone cannot save the day. Business strategy, planning, organization, finance, law, and risk management are once again front and center as more organizations confront their e-business options. In fact, a growing number of early adopters—dot.coms and traditional companies alike—have gone back to the drawing board to rechart their course into the digital economy. This emphasis on planning, coupled with high economic stakes, has been largely responsible for putting e-business on the radar screens of senior executives everywhere.

During the past year, increasing numbers of senior executives have gotten the message. Some of these individuals may be technically savvy personally; others may be technologically challenged. All, however, understand the following critical insights:

○ *E-business is no longer optional;* it is not the latest fad destined to blow over during the next 30 to 60 days. While the underlying technology will most certainly change, e-business will continue to make its presence felt and become the standard mode of operating, not only in financial services, publishing, and retail, where we have already seen rapid and profitable advancement, but everywhere business is conducted. The sweeping dimensions of e-business's impact has led to an inescapable conclusion: Executive vision and leadership are critical to success in e-business.

○ *E-business is fundamental* to business strategy and process execution in the twenty-first century. Experienced practitioners know that e-business cannot be viewed as an independent development that runs alongside the traditional business, even though initial efforts may start out that way. Those who fail to embrace e-business fully and to change the existing organization at its core are missing a huge opportunity and, more importantly, are vulnerable to competitors who will most certainly exploit their weakness.

○ *The time for e-business action is now,* especially for companies with assets already in place and customers waiting to be served. First-mover advantages aside, organizations that fail to begin the transition to e-business in the near term will find, over time, that their options are increasingly limited and their costs overwhelmingly prohibitive. It has often been said that time is money. That truism has not changed. However, with e-business, there is less time but more money for firms that act.

Although many conclusions can be drawn from these sweeping changes, one seems particularly clear and compelling: Companies that expect to prosper in an e-business ("e-nabled") environment can no longer rely on business models that have their roots in thinking that originated more than a century ago, and that, until e-business exploded on the scene, remained virtually unchanged and unchallenged. Traditional notions about brands, advertising, distribution, and customers are now being challenged by new concepts of value. Executives must reexamine such notions or risk failure.

Today's most savvy organizations have already entered the e-business continuum. Some engage in e-commerce, which is the purchasing or selling of goods and services on the Internet. Others are leveraging a variety of technology tools combined with new services and information sources to obtain better knowledge of customers and markets, reduce costs, and fuel dramatic increases in value. Still others have made a further leap into e-partnering, integrating so effectively with other companies that they go to market as a collective. Regardless of their place on this continuum, companies that have embraced e-business are implicitly following a new model that drives value creation in the digital age. This model is based on new concepts of business strategy; a special regard for the impact of new organizational forms, technology, and business processes on bottom-line results; and an acute appreciation of the need not only to satisfy customers, but to *delight* them as never before.

In this book, we present this model of e-business as a tool for executives and practitioners who are responsible for positioning their organizations for success in the new millennium.

THE CASE FOR A NEW MODEL

Since the industrial revolution, businesses have used the same basic model to compete in the marketplace, a model based on carving out a section of the industry value chain and providing a value-added product, service, or product/service combination in a particular niche. Today, the impact of e-business demands that this model change.

Why? One compelling reason is the effect of e-business on shareholder value. Business leaders are finding a direct connection between their organization's level of e-business maturity and measures of their ability to provide customer value and build shareholder wealth. There is debate about the reason for this correlation. Most argue that companies

that operate as e-businesses enjoy improved revenue and margins, others
that the e-business label is simply a valuation hype. Regardless, there
is no disagreement on the result: Companies that successfully embed
e-business thinking into their strategy and e-business practices into
their operations are held in high regard by the financial markets and
deliver superior shareholder value.

As a result, companies today are assertively searching for new ways
to embrace e-business. But how can its power be exploited fully? One way
is to envision a new organizational model in which one views a company's
adopting of e-business principles as a series of snapshots within a continuous panorama of increasing e-business sophistication (Figure I.1).
Such a model defines the context of the e-nabled world. There, business
strategy changes far faster than in the past; a company that does not become fast and flexible will ultimately fail; and nothing is built to last, not
strategies, systems, or organizations.

In this new world, company leaders must discover fresh ways to identify and deliver unique value through employees, partners, and other
assets at their disposal. They must become collaborative in practice
and holistic in thinking. Their people must regularly work across functional, departmental, and divisional lines, operating across organizational boundaries in collaboration with people from other organizations.
Support systems must also bridge these traditional barriers, offering information and insights that all can share. All participants must learn to
live in an atmosphere of "concurrent business engineering."

Figure I.1   E-Business Panorama

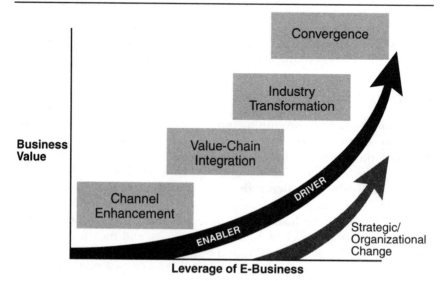

Such a world mandates a new model that corporate leaders can use to define where they are and where they are headed. The model must provide them with a common language with which to understand the dynamics of e-business and its impact on businesses and industries. It must encourage companies to use e-business to redefine corporate strategy rather than merely as a tool to reengineer and improve processes. The model must also enable leaders to determine when their business and/or industry is moving from incremental change to radical, "disruptive" change.

To be sure, process change is important in the context of e-business growth. In snapshot one (channel enhancement) and snapshot two (value chain integration) process change is an important consideration. But process change is a means, not an end. By the time a company is into the third snapshot of our e-business model (industry transformation), the benefits of internal process change have been exhausted, and options hinge on redefining the elements of an industry value chain that a company controls. Ultimately, in the fourth snapshot (convergence), some companies will realize that they can transcend their traditional industry boundaries, though their ability to do so will have as much to do with the relevant regulatory environment, their strategic alliances, and the qualities of existing multienterprise governance as with reengineering processes and value networks.

Accompanying each of the snapshots are a host of business considerations that each company needs to address (such as tax, legal, and organizational effects), various options for using e-nabling technology, and a number of possible strategic "plays."

In each consecutive snapshot, the complexity of strategic and organizational change necessary to achieve success increases along with the size of potential payoffs. In addition, as one moves across the panorama from left to right, the types of plays companies can undertake change from being purely tactical to being far more strategic in nature.*

In the first snapshot (channel enhancement), the plays are largely tactical, incrementally building efficiency and value into established constructs. In the second snapshot (value chain integration), the plays begin to become transformative and significant to the organization's bottom line. Within the last two snapshots (industry transformation and convergence), the plays are highly transformative and strategic, offering order-of-magnitude impacts.

As a company moves from left to right in the panorama and utilizes e-business more strategically, the degree of both business and

---

*Strategy is required at *every level* even though the bottom-line impacts are indeed smaller in the earlier stages. Not having a well thought out strategy early on may severely impact later options, leading to additional organizational retooling costs, or total organizational failure.

organizational risk it faces also increases. Managing such risk requires more than just technology. Leveraging e-business is far less about technology than it is about equipping the people who use it with the skills they need to make their business lives more productive and to enhance their contributions to corporate wealth.

NEITHER A HIERARCHY NOR DISCRETE STEPS IN A SERIES

The model presented here is not necessarily sequential; nor are individual stages mutually exclusive or static. We show the four snapshots in Figure I.1 as overlapping each other. A photographer constructing a panorama from a series of discrete snapshots creates some overlap so as not to end up with gaps. Likewise, our panoramic model suggests that activities, ways of operating, and strategies formed in any one snapshot may continue on into the next. The boundaries are, in fact, indistinct.

Some companies will move through the panorama one snapshot at a time to arrive at the final one; others will not. In fact, we argue that some companies will skip certain stages, leapfrogging over the consecutive movers, while others will land in and remain in one particular spot in the spectrum for a longer period of time. Still others will find a permanent home in the indistinct areas between snapshots, effectively combining the characteristics of each. Business and industry conditions, competition, and customer demand will, to some degree, determine within which snapshots companies in each industry can legitimately work and still survive.

Over time, all industries will move toward a state of convergence driven by customer demand for a small number of trusted relationships. Sooner or later, to survive, all companies will need to operate within the frame of the fourth snapshot—or perhaps, within that of a future snapshot that is today outside the range of our current e-business lens.

MOVING THROUGH THE E-BUSINESS PANORAMA

Whether as a guide to clarify issues or as a tool to formulate strategy, our model serves as a type of decision tree to help companies define whether to move one step at a time or to leapfrog from one strategic position to the next. In either case, e-nabled companies can expect to achieve improvements in three basic areas: relationship management, revenue enhancement, and cost reduction, though in different ways in different snapshots within the panorama.

Snapshot One: Channel Enhancement

Within the channel enhancement snapshot, companies use e-business technology as an enabler to modify existing business processes and in

---

**DECISION ONE: WHERE TO START—
BUY SIDE OR SELL SIDE?**

In the channel enhancement snapshot, companies decide whether they will use the Internet to enhance their sales channels or improve the efficiency of their buying process.

Those that engage primarily in business-to-consumer commerce will likely give priority to the sell side to generate increased revenue, better manage customer relationships, and, lastly, to reduce costs. This is especially true for dot.com companies that typically have negligible supply chains and that are driven by a need to rapidly gain market share.

Companies that engage primarily in business-to-business commerce will tend to give priority to reducing the costs of selling, buying, or both. Increased revenue and enhanced customer relationships are bonuses. Business-to-business e-commerce includes the creation of e-procurement systems for buying nonproduction goods and electronic channels to link distribution networks together more tightly.

---

some cases to create new ones targeted at improving business performance. Within this snapshot, companies employ e-business technology primarily for information sharing and e-commerce—the marketing, selling, or buying of products and services over the Internet—essentially enabling a new channel to market.

Snapshot Two: Value Chain Transformation

As the level of Internet competence and confidence grows, companies search for the next major step in e-business leverage. Many focus on identifying and analyzing the relationship between themselves and their business partners. Specifically, companies focus on leveraging e-business as a vehicle for value chain integration. They examine approaches for integrating their value chains and their information systems with the value chains of suppliers, logistics providers, distributors, and retailers to maximize efficiencies and reduce costs.

In a mature state, value chain integration allows companies to share real-time planning, cost, and production data between enterprise resource planning (ERP) systems, thereby allowing for the creation of a fully e-nabled *extraprise*, a term we use to characterize an extended enterprise consisting of the company and its value chain partners.

**DECISION TWO: WHO ARE YOUR STRATEGIC
PARTNERS AND HOW WILL YOU LINK TO THEM?**

In the late 1990s, leaders of e-business connected their company
processes and systems to those of customers and strategic suppliers. To be competitive moving forward, companies will have to
expand their thinking from the corporate entity to the extended
enterprise, including their network of strategic partners. Collaborative design, planning, and forecasting, and sharing knowledge
with strategic partners will migrate the value chain to a go-to-
market value network.

In the e-business world, executives will have to choose strategic
suppliers to ally with and determine how to interconnect their business processes and systems. As an alternative or supplementary strategy, executives will have to decide whether to outsource processes to
strategic partners for better efficiency and reduced cost. Those companies that try to go it alone will likely be blocked from participating in the networked economy.

As part of this analysis, some businesses take steps to seize the advantage afforded by the low cost of moving data, and to revisit the idea of
outsourcing noncore business processes throughout the value chain.

Snapshot Three: Industry Transformation

E-business is creating ways for companies to maximize shareholder value
by completely transforming their industries. As the lines between businesses become less pronounced, companies will find ways to work together that leverage each other's core competencies.

The term *going to market* will no longer be defined as the way a company enters the marketplace. Rather, it will characterize the way an integrated group of companies creates a set of cascading values to transform
the marketplace into a network of value providers.

Companies with a core competence in knowledge management will
thrive in this third snapshot. They will use business partners that have
created best-in-class processes in the physical world and others that build
and run the best value networks to transform the economic base and the
operating mechanics of their industries.

DECISION THREE: KNOWLEDGE-BASED OR PHYSICAL COMPANY?

The Internet will pose a huge threat to traditional companies. While such companies ponder their future directions, agile intermediaries will use the Internet to insert themselves between traditional companies and their customers. These intermediaries can be start-ups with no history, companies horizontally integrated with an organization's value chain looking for new growth opportunities, and/or competitors racing to get to a market first.

Where the second snapshot of the e-business panorama melds into the third is the point at which companies make the conscious effort to orient their strategies toward becoming knowledge-based (knowco) or physical goods-based (physco) companies. The term "orient" is important. Knowcos and physcos occupy opposite ends of a spectrum. Most companies will continue to have capabilities resident in both knowco and physco strategies but, in the new economy, will redirect investment and competitive posturing toward one strategy or the other.

A company orienting toward a knowco strategy will consider outsourcing much of its capital intensive production-related processes, freeing up capital to focus on the parts of their business that differentiate them in the marketplace. Knowco-oriented companies will tend to focus on building brand, capturing "ownership" of the customer-end market relationship, and investing in knowledge-based core competencies such as marketing and product or service development. They will become proficient at managing customer and supplier information and will put the major focus of their e-nabling technologies on the customer-end market connection, possibly even facilitating or aggregating customer knowledge for other companies.

Companies wanting to orient their business around a knowco strategy will rely on the Internet to help them get close to customers, using data collection and mining to develop unique customer offers; to outsource nonstrategic parts of their business; and to manage relationships with physco business partners.

Physco-oriented companies will drive their business strategies to become the best provider of products and services to knowco-oriented companies, which own the customer relationship. In essence, they will become hubs of processing expertise. Their success will be based on speed, quality, and delivery. They will understand that they are serving companies that own the customer-end

(continued)

**DECISION THREE: KNOWLEDGE-BASED
OR PHYSICAL COMPANY?** (*Continued*)

market relationship and will orient their strategies, processes, systems, and organization accordingly. A critical success factor for physco-oriented companies will be their ability to link electronically to knowco companies to plan, manage, and transact business at e-speed. Their differentiation in the marketplace will be based on their ability to provide service value to knowcos, to effectively manage capital (plant and equipment), and to build efficient best practices. Many of today's bricks and mortar production businesses will orient toward physco strategies.

Having entered the new millenium, many companies are on the cusp of a dilemma: Do they remain physcos? Do they try to reinvent themselves as knowcos? Or do they split themselves up into two or more parts, some remaining physcos and others becoming knowcos?

Snapshot Four: Convergence

Convergence is not necessarily just an e-business phenomenon. In theory, convergence could occur in the complete absence of e-business. However, the continual decline of the cost of moving information makes convergence easier—and cheaper—to accomplish.

Convergence is the coming together of companies in different industries to provide goods and services to customers. It is as much a function of industry deregulation and globalization as it is of e-nabled business models.

A supermarket's offering retail banking services is one example of convergence. Others are the emergence of software providers as "infomediaries" and the coalescing of many services and products in those segments of the utility industry that are being deregulated. The Internet is fueling more convergence by providing customers a one-stop shop for all of their products and services. Companies that capture customer loyalty and that can provide a one-stop shop for a customer market will be positioned for enormous growth.

Take, for example, America Online (AOL) and Time Warner. What motivated their recent merger? Both companies have access to millions of loyal customers, and both are very profitable. Their merger objectives were based on long-term strategy. Executives from AOL and Time Warner realize that both companies can contribute to providing the consumer total convergence of services through what many believe will be the next generation of personalized information services. AOL brings industry-leading knowledge of Internet services, software, and content, and a personalized channel for customers. Time Warner contributes a wealth of content, including books, movies, and music, and a cable television pipeline to consumers. Together, the two have the knowledge to construct a new world of personalized and interactive media services delivered right to consumers' homes. Most analysts agree that neither company can achieve this alone.

For another example, look at the many utility companies that are moving from a single company model, where an electric utility generates and sells electricity, to a two-company model, where one entity operates as a generating company and the other as a sales company. The sales companies compete for customers not only on the price of the electricity they transmit, but on the other value-added services they provide, such as selling natural gas, connecting customers to electric (or gas) appliance manufacturers and installers, or aggregating utility bills onto single monthly statements.

THE ULTIMATE E-NABLED LANDSCAPE

Virtual business networks will be the ultimate result of an e-nabled economy. In this world, individual businesses will become more focused and nimble. Industries will become more diffuse and volatile, defined only by interconnecting marketplaces and portals. As an industry becomes increasingly fragmented, more companies will attempt to become knowledge intermediaries. Corporate leaders will focus only on their company's core competencies and will seek other players, the portals, to take their problems—their noncore activities—away.

The dominant feature of this landscape is the network of interconnecting electronic markets. These e-markets will be differentiated by services they offer. Some will be strongly aligned to a particular industry. Ultimately these vertical e-markets will define the industry of their participants. Other e-markets will work across industries, offering best-in-class process execution. Businesses will link into multiple e-markets, as well as directly with each other, to acquire the products or services they need or to connect to their customers.

As company leaders look to create an e-business strategy and define their unique value proposition, they must focus on how they can respond to other companies in their value chain or e-market when those companies say, "Take my problem away."

THE E-BUSINESS CHALLENGE

Understanding how one company can take another's problems away while maintaining a viable place in the virtual world of the future requires keeping in mind some basic rules:

○ E-business employs "disruptive technology." While it can improve and enhance business, it can also disrupt the value chain by changing the way players within it interact.

○ E-business success *is not* about technology; it *is* about organizational change management and about people working in new ways, both within their company and with extraprise partners in value networks. It is also about using technology to enhance existing relationships and create new ones.

○ In the digital world, the company that owns the customer relationship and the customer knowledge is king. Companies must determine if they are (or can become) the party in the value chain that owns the customer relationship. Whatever a company's position, leadership must not only know what it knows, but know what it does not know. It must also be able to find and create networks with partners who can fill that knowledge gap.

○ Companies will constantly be creating new services based on their digital assets (information and processes). Some intermediaries (particularly those that define best practices) will emerge within the value chain; others will be forced out. Old and new intermediaries will fight for position. (Together, this set of strategies is known as *disintermediation, reintermediation,* and *counterintermediation.*)

○ Commoditization of products and services will move farther and farther up the value chain (a process of rolling commoditization) until, ultimately, everything upstream of customer contact will be a commodity. This means companies will continually be fighting to become knowledge or network masters. Companies that fail to do so will face life as low-margin commodity producers.

○ While rolling commoditization will squeeze companies from upstream in the value chain, customers will continually use knowledge technology to squeeze margins from the downstream end. Confronting rolling commoditization, intermediaries, and increasingly knowledge-enabled customers, even network and knowledge masters will be hard pressed to maintain competitive advantage for long periods of time.

○ All of this will lead to an environment where business strategy must be more flexible than ever before; where companies may need to dis-integrate over time, forming small, nimble knowcos to fight for position close to the customer, maintain physical competencies in a core physco, and pass off noncore activities to extraprise partners who are experts in these competencies.

*   *   *   *

The e-business world will become increasingly complex. Our model acknowledges that complexity by raising many questions and suggesting numerous implications for companies engaged in—or about to engage in—e-nabled business. In the remainder of this book, we take a more detailed look at each of the four snapshots that make up the e-business model. We also examine the effect of each on organizations and people and, where appropriate, the implications for information systems and technology.

1

Snapshot One:
Channel Enhancement

To date, in a business-to-consumer (B2C) e-business context, the word *channel* has meant a connection from a seller to the buyer. But in an e-nabled business-to-business (B2B) context, it is also useful to think of a *buy channel* for the acquiring company. We propose this concept because a channel implies management and control, and with Web-based technologies, a company can control far more effectively how its employees buy as consumers of indirect goods and services. Today, the company that wants to behave as one consumer, can.

The opportunities indicated in first snapshot in the e-business panorama (Figure 1.1) are almost all tactical. There, a company leverages e-business to improve processes in both the buying and selling channels. The degree of risk is minimal, and the degree of organizational change is relatively low for the company as a whole. (For those who work in purchasing and marketing, however, the degree of change can be quite high.)

In the e-nabled B2B world, channel enhancement means using Internet technology to enhance sales by adding an electronic sell channel, and using the same technology to enhance the corporate buyer's ability to buy as one consumer (e-procurement). Whether as a buyer or a seller, or as both, channel enhancement is where most large companies start their e-business endeavors. The seller is trying to push products through the sell channel at the same time the buyer is trying to maintain control of its corporate information and control what comes into the company through the buy channel.

In the e-nabled B2B world, channel enhancement is a battle between the two parties—seller and buyer—for control of the channel, especially when the buyer is a large company. Control of the channel

1

Figure 1.1   Snapshot One: Channel Enhancement

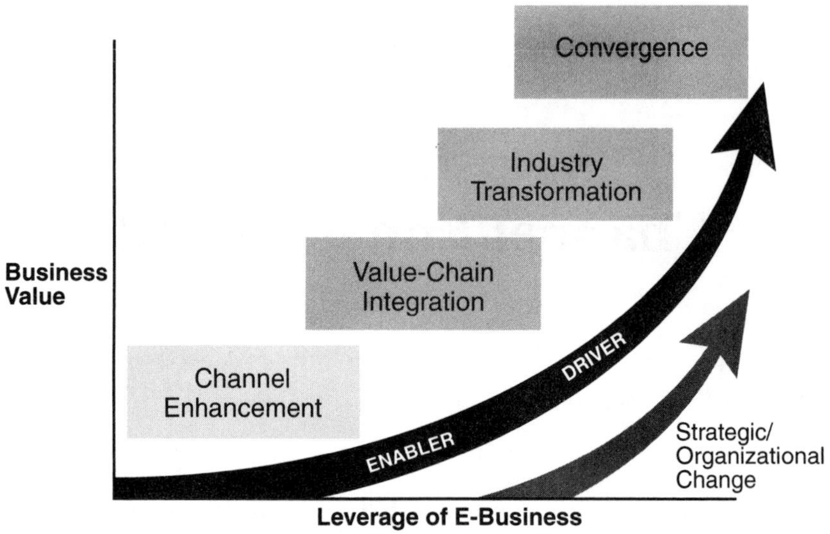

means control over terms of the transaction, as well as over information about the buyer's needs and desires.

In this snapshot, both the e-nabled sell channel and e-procurement are point solutions. On the sell side, the effort becomes truly all-encompassing only if the sell channel is integrated into the company's ERP system (enterprise resource planning applications, the computer programs that store data about the company's internal operations) to e-nable the purchasing of production. On the buy side, companies can, for the first time, use electronic catalogues and workflow systems to manage their indirect spending.

Within this first snapshot, business change is process oriented, that is, incremental rather than radical. Channel enhancement efforts are tactical rather than strategic. A company can add a sell channel without changing its basic business model and all of the required technology is readily available. If, however, a company truly expects to increase customer loyalty, customer service, or sales via this new channel, then new processes must be put in place to manage the channel.

VALUE PROPOSITIONS FOR SELLERS AND BUYERS

Channel enhancement results from gathering and managing knowledge about buying patterns on both sides of the channel. Sellers use this knowledge to craft products and services into customer-specific offerings, so-called markets of one. Buyers use this knowledge to negotiate better deals. By lowering costs, automation of the buying process benefits both sides.

Enhancing both the sell and nonproduction buy channels are the simplest forms of e-business, what we refer to as e-commerce. E-commerce is, for the most part, an efficiency play rather than an effectiveness play, focusing on cost reduction, extending a company's reach to a larger customer group, and speeding up time to market. Starting a Web site, putting product and service catalogues on the site, and using the site for customer support are all cost reduction exercises.

Most large companies will benefit more from a Web-enabled buy channel than they will from a Web-enabled sell channel. A 10 percent savings in the cost of indirect procurement can represent a 50 percent increase in profits, equivalent to that from a 50 percent increase in sales. As you read this chapter, envision your company as either the Web-enabled seller or the Web-enabled buyer, or both. Remember that everything you are trying to do to your suppliers, your customers are also trying to do to you.

On the sell side, effectiveness is enhanced in the case of products that must be configured; allowing the customer to configure on-line helps the seller reduce inventories and produce "just-in-time for customer" production. On the buy side, effectiveness is enhanced through getting individuals to comply with prenegotiated contracts.

In short, for the most part, channel enhancement in B2B has more to do with redesigning internal processes, creating an environment of standardization, and reducing costs than it does with absolute revenue increase and with integrating a company with other entities. This, of course, is very different from the "pure play" B2C Internet retailers, whose focus is entirely on revenue growth (or more accurately, customer capture). But, as many of the dot-coms are discovering, the back-end process and systems integration are necessary components of a long-term strategy for sustainable growth.

ENHANCING THE SELL CHANNEL

Figure 1.2 illustrates the traditional way people think about channels, that is, as sell channels and as opportunities for increasing both efficiency and effectiveness in demand management.

Opportunities include increasing revenue by creating an electronic sell channel; reducing the costs of selling and customer service through automation and process redesign; seizing the advantage of being an early adopter of Web-enabled push technology within any particular competitive market (although that is rapidly evaporating); and using sell channel

Figure 1.2   Traditional Sell Channel

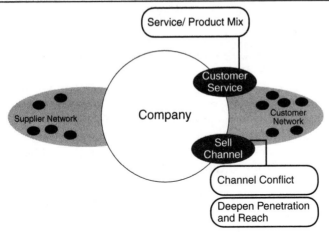

enhancement as a laboratory for the kinds of corporate behavior changes that need to take place in order to engage in more complex e-business and e-partnering relationships.

This strategy, however, posits a number of potential problems. The biggest problem is channel conflict (cannibalizing your other sell channels rather than really attracting new business.) Others include low return on investment (ROI); difficulty integrating Web-selling technology with legacy systems and even with newer ERP systems; and the issue of *scalability*.

Scalability refers to the ability of the channel to handle increasingly large volumes. Early adopter companies that put in a Web-based sell channel started simply by taking orders off the Web and rekeying them into the order-entry system, as if the order were taken by phone, fax, or in a face-to-face meeting. But at a point where about 10 percent of a company's present volume comes through the Web-based sell channel, it becomes necessary to focus on integrating the channel with the company's ERP system, because maintaining two separate processes becomes increasingly expensive, and increasing through-put actually begins to destroy value. Therefore, at this point, the Web-enabled sell channel needs to become more than just hype.

Companies serious about e-business can move forward in one of two ways. They either try to migrate their current sales model into a direct Web-enabled channel, or they use Web technology to strengthen their distribution network.

Whichever direction a company goes in, the greatest potential for new revenue results when the Web-enabled sales channel allows entry into markets in which it does not have a physical presence. Moving out from a saturated U.S. market, companies that have not been actively selling in Europe and Asia have been able to create new markets through their Web-enabled sell channel. Victoria's Secret, for example, was successful in this regard. The increased global visibility generated by a highly successful virtual fashion show led to more sales volume, better recognition, and new overseas markets.

Global Markets

Electronic communications creates de facto global markets. Many companies are using e-business to begin selling into countries and regions where the cost of having sales staff on the ground is prohibitive, or where the amount of potential business does not justify hiring sales staff. However, the level of actual business transacted is still relatively low, due to legal, cultural, tax, language, regulatory, and other barriers that impede shipping goods between countries. Internet-enabled companies are moving at a much faster pace in North America than in most of the rest of the world. While eStats reported in June 1999 that North America (Canada, United States, and Mexico) lost it majority share of the world's Internet user population in the first quarter of 1999, the company predicts that the United States will maintain its leadership in the volume of e-business transactions until at least 2003.

Serving global markets also involves many complex business decisions, including the cost of international customer service and warranties. Currently, perhaps the largest issue is the lack of assurances between buyers and sellers. In a purely electronic relationship, sellers need assurances that buyers can pay; buyers need assurance that sellers can deliver. This issue represents a major opportunity for the underwriters of these transactions.

As companies in North America and certain hot spots in the world flock to the Internet to conduct business, polarization will grow between those countries where e-business is a major component of most companies' operations, and countries where most companies don't utilize e-business technology.

It is already evident that the economies of countries in which companies use the Internet for business will grow far more rapidly than countries in which companies do not. Unfortunately, this also means that companies operating in countries without widespread support for Internet technology—due to infrastructure, business climate, or cultural issues—will fall behind.

For the near term, this gap in capability will create a competitive disadvantage. In the longer term, the widespread demand for conducting business over the Internet will drive most companies to adopt this new technology. However, first-mover advantage will have been lost for these organizations, resulting in a long-term negative impact on their country's economy.

Fear of conducting business on the Internet seems to be disappearing. Most major companies have moved from the fear stage through the curiosity stage—asking how they can leverage the technology for competitive advantage—and are now in the "we must participate" phase. A key driver has been the explosion of market valuation of businesses tied to the Internet, where shareholder value has skyrocketed like never before.

Additionally, the media has tracked the growth of the Internet as if it were a juicy political scandal. Every night the television news covers yet another story about the Internet or an Internet-related company. All of this publicity surrounding the Internet has led to more and more people of all ages accepting the Internet as a means of communicating, researching, and buying and selling.

Businesses, especially in the United States and in some Western European countries, are expanding their communications infrastructures and acquiring Web-based software applications. This business investment is preparing companies—from mom-and-pop stores to large industrial organizations—to do business in a fundamentally different way, requiring a change not just in technical perspective, but more importantly, in business culture.

Outside of the United States, pockets of countries are readily embracing the Internet. Canada, the United Kingdom, the Nordic countries and other countries in Western Europe, are rapidly developing communications infrastructures and creative new applications for the Internet. North American businesses wishing to expand into these regions of the world find a climate of readiness to do business via the Internet. In these countries, the Internet is now an accepted way of selling products and services. Customers have moved beyond the need for face-to-face meetings in order to transact business. In mid-1999, Cisco announced that it had increased the percentage of European business done over the Internet from 12 percent to 91 percent in just 18 months and believed the total would be nearly 95 percent by year-end.

However, in those countries where the Internet has not yet been widely accepted, Internet-savvy businesses must temper their expectations about customers and suppliers actually using this tool. Where brand recognition is lacking, true expansion in these new markets will require more than just creating a Web site.

From Markets to Communities

Telecommunications is a two-way street: Companies and their business partners use telecommunications to satisfy their customers; customers use it to define their collective needs and desires for various products and services.

The ability to collect and analyze vast quantities of customer data and turn it into useful customer knowledge allows companies to define their customers in a new way. Customers are no longer simply part of market segments; rather they are members of communities who share similar product interests.

By tying into such communities, companies receive feedback on current products and services, as well as assistance with research and development of new products and services. A company that has a natural affiliation with a customer community can aggregate customer knowledge on behalf of other companies that do not.

Smarter e-businesses will actively try to create or promote such communities—both in B2B and (famously) B2C. The current explosion in "portal" sites reflects the growing importance of communities. In the B2B world, the ultimate manifestation of "community" is when it "becomes the industry" (Snapshot Three). The e-business evolution snapshots will soon be as relevant to communities as they currently are to companies. Early examples will focus on buying and selling (Snapshot One); more sophisticated strategies will soon follow.

Sell-Side Value Proposition

Despite these advantages, it is still difficult to convince a chief financial officer looking at investment decisions that getting into sell-channel enhancement will increase revenue enough to cover the costs of technology and organizational change management (especially when a "serious" Web channel might easily cost $10 million to develop). Because an increase in revenues is difficult to measure as compared to the revenues realized by other channels to market, there must be other bases to the value proposition:

○ Enhancing the sell channel through technology will lower costs. For example, an enhanced sell channel is a cost-effective way to deal with customers, especially for companies in industries such as high technology products and electronics, where goods need to be configured and where the customer base is comfortable using computers.

○ Like ERP, an e-nabled sell channel is increasingly becoming part of the price of admission into the competitive world of twenty-first century business. In 1997 and 1998, using new technology provided some competitive advantage; but beyond 2000, any first-adopter advantage will have disappeared in most industries. Increasingly, an e-commerce sell channel is becoming a must.

○ An e-nabled sell channel allows for much more efficient collection and aggregation of customer information. Companies are increasingly realizing that customer information is a valuable asset. Knowing what customers buy, why they buy it, and what they buy in conjunction with it, can help a company develop new product configurations and effective pricing for markets of one.

Components of an E-nabled Sell Site

There are seven components of an e-nabled sell site:

1. Catalogue
2. Merchandising
3. Configurator
4. Shopping cart
5. Tax calculation
6. Shipping/Logistics
7. Payment system.

Catalogue. Catalogues and other content-management systems are used to present customers with information about goods and services offered for sale, bid, or auction. Some catalogue applications are designed to manage large numbers of individual items; search capabilities in such catalogues help buyers quickly navigate to and find the items they want.

Other applications are designed to emphasize merchandise presentation and special offers, much as a retail store is physically configured to encourage impulse or add-on buying. As with other aspects of e-commerce, it is important to match catalogue design and functionality to a company's business goals. Although there are many e-commerce catalogue software packages to choose from, only one may be appropriate for a particular company.

E-catalogues typically provide more information about products than paper catalogues. For example, along with traditional product attributes such as item numbers or stock-keeping units (SKUs), item description, and unit price, an e-catalogue may provide links that allow customers access to other information such as a photograph of an item, product or engineering specifications, or even a video demonstration.

E-catalogues may contain additional features, including cross- and up-selling capabilities, real-time inventory status, incentive pricing structures, and personalization features.

Many e-commerce packaged applications provide capabilities for catalogue creation and maintenance. Vendors that provide e-catalogue software and services include Actinic, Aspect Development, Harbinger, Mercado, and Requisite Technology.

Merchandising. Merchandising, sales promotion, or affinity programs such as frequent-flyer and buyer rewards are becoming common in e-commerce. Typically, they are initiated through a seller's catalogue or Web site. Some promotions occur beyond that site, however.

For example, electronic coupons can be distributed via e-mail to customers to encourage repeat purchasing. Direct mail campaigns can be implemented via e-mail.

Software packages to assist that function include e2 Software's Sales-Office and Revnet's UnityMail. Another vendor, Responsys, markets a service called Interact, which manages on-line direct marketing campaigns.

Configurator. If the product being sold has simple features (few or no conflicts between features within the product, few variable components, and straightforward pricing), then a simple catalogue may be sufficient to store the product's attributes. A book, for example, qualifies as such a product.

However, if the product's feature set is large, maps to a broad range of customer requirements, is composed of many interconnected elements—some of which are incompatible with each other—and is priced accordingly, then it is unlikely that a catalogue will be sufficiently flexible to model the various product lines and options.

Examples of such products include networking or telecommunications equipment, high-end servers, desktop computers, cars, or mutual fund investment opportunities. For such products, a configurator is the foundation that provides the needed customer-facing functionality.

A configurator is special-purpose software that allows users to define a product that meets given criteria or needs and whose features and options can be combined to work together. Configurators also may compute the price of an assembled item, calculate payments, or compare the difference between leasing and buying or buying and repairing.

A configurator's rule-based or constraint-based logic guides a user through the order process for complex products. E-commerce configurators promote unassisted selling, sometimes called customer self-service, through an intuitive Web interface.

Calico Commerce and Trilogy Software are two leading configurator producers. Calico's eSales Suite is a set of Java-based applications that guide customers through the purchase process. One of the modules, eSales Configurator, permits customer requirements and product attributes to be matched automatically and products and services to be configured accurately. It also provides the opportunity to up-sell and cross-sell by suggesting complementary products and options.

Trilogy Software's SC Config, a component of its Selling Chain Suite, is used primarily by distributors and resellers to deliver quotes based on several product variables. SC Config can also evaluate product options that would best meet a customer's needs. Trilogy Software's Selling Chain Suite consists of selling applications such as SC Catalogue, SC Commission, SC Pricer, and SC Promotion.

Shopping Cart.   In the physical retail world, consumers use shopping carts to wander the aisles of stores and hold their purchases. The shopping cart (shopping basket or shopping bag) is a convenient metaphor for the e-nabled world.

The electronic shopping cart, a concept pioneered by Open Market, holds a record of the selections a buyer is considering for purchase until the buyer is through shopping and ready to complete the purchasing process. At any point in the process, the buyer can review items in the cart, remove items, or change the quantity of a particular item.

Some shopping carts can remember the buyer's selections between sessions; this capability is known as a *persistent* shopping cart. A buyer can leave the Web site and still be at the same point in the shopping process when he or she returns.

Tax Calculation.   E-commerce sell channels usually rely on integrated third-party tax-calculation software to determine local, state, or other taxes they are required to collect. A niche software industry has developed to provide automated tax calculations and track tax responsibilities of merchants in the United States. Several vendors of automated tax compliance products are expanding into the international Internet e-commerce market, providing software with international tax calculation, audit, and reporting capabilities.

Perhaps the best-known example of such a product developer is Taxware International Inc. This company has built a comprehensive international tax solution that can integrate with either storefront or back-office systems and can be embedded or interfaced with commerce servers or other seller systems.

Shipping/Logistics.   In many order-processing systems, the shipping charge is set at a fixed fee based on the number of items purchased, shipment weight, or the price of the order. With the connectivity of the Web and the interoperability of discrete systems, shipping charges can be precisely determined in real time, and a tracking number can be assigned to the shipment at the time the order is placed.

An example of such a solution is TanData's Progistics Merchant module, which provides global shipping charges in real time, validation of destinations served by major carriers and associated transit times and tracking numbers for each package. It can also use the seller's prenegotiated rates from the carrier.

Payment System.   Currently, payment in most B2C e-commerce is via credit card. In B2B, the equivalent for low value items is the purchasing card (p-card). Credit card payment systems are common add-on components to e-commerce systems.

Typically, these modules implement Secure Sockets Layer (SSL) or Secure Electronic Transaction (SET) as security standards. Companies hosting e-commerce sites also can choose to outsource the payment function.

iCOMS and Paymentech are two vendors that offer payment-handling services. Other vendors, such as CyberSource, provide fraud detection software or services.

Commerce Platforms

One set of vendor offerings for an e-nabled sell channel, commonly referred to as commerce platforms, provides software, a framework, and tools for developing e-commerce capabilities. Commerce platforms are intended primarily for e-commerce sites that require a great deal of customization and flexibility.

These platforms make it easier to develop e-commerce applications such as feature-rich catalogues or ordering systems. They provide a well-defined set of application program interfaces (APIs), as well as integration of common modules that e-commerce applications require, such as payment methods or shipping logistics. However, implementing these platforms requires a high level of technical and programming expertise.

Commerce platforms include components for building and maintaining a commerce site. These components can include a catalogue, order taking and payment functions, security, programming methods to create and manage an interactive session, and basic site management tools. Leading commerce platforms include IBM's Net.Commerce, Microsoft's Site Server Commerce Edition, Sun/Netscape's Commerce-Xpert, and Oracle's Internet Commerce Server (ICS).

Sell-Side Packaged E-Commerce Applications

Purchasing and implementing a packaged sell-side e-commerce application is an alternative to developing a customer application using an e-commerce platform or tool kit. As the number of companies using the Web to sell their products has grown, an opportunity has been created for software vendors to sell packaged applications.

These applications typically include many of the sell-side components already discussed. The line dividing packaged applications from platform or tool kit products ultimately is arbitrary because the distinctions are a matter of degree rather than a difference in kind.

Numerous software packages or suites of preintegrated solutions are available for companies that do not want to build their own e-commerce solutions. These package vendors may target specific market segments, such as small-to-mid-sized retailers, or Internet service providers that, in turn, may host the software applications, hardware, and network infrastructure, leasing it to their customers.

Today's packaged sell-side e-commerce applications span a broad range, from basic products to full-featured offerings. However, the market generally can be segmented into entry-level and high-level packages.

Entry-level packages offer easy setup (using vendor-provided templates for basic design and wizards for configuration) and include basic catalogue and merchandising functionality. They may be limited in their personalization capabilities, the degree to which they can be customized or extended with custom programming, and their scalability. These packages are designed for rapid implementation and are inexpensive, with prices as low as $500; the most expensive in this category run to about $25,000.

Further customization or integration of entry-level products requires programming. Many vendors offer an expanded, more expensive, developer's version of the package, which can be used to develop additional functionality around the core. A significant number of products are available in this area, with new ones appearing, it seems, weekly.

High-end packages typically offer enhanced capabilities in one or more major functional areas, such as personalization, merchandising, EDI capabilities, or transaction management. They also implement a full set of APIs that can be used to provide integration with a company's ERP system. These packages offer a higher degree of scalability. Major providers of this type of software include BroadVision, ConnectInc.com, iCat, IBM, Inex, Intershop, InterWorld, Mercantec, Microsoft, Netscape, and Open Market.

E-Selling Process

Customers of an e-nabled sell channel engage in three activities: e-browsing (the desktop equivalent of window shopping), e-buying, and e-customer service.

E-Browsing. E-browsers visit the selling company's Web site, where basic corporate and product information is published. The more sophisticated Web sites publish an e-catalogue of products and services.

Corporate Information Sites. Corporate information sites have a limited value proposition. Not having one, however, is a business negative. This should be the entry point to the corporate information infrastructure.

Product and Services Catalogues. Product and service catalogues are a customer service/convenience issue. They allow browsing for customers who do not wish to use a paper equivalent. They are unlikely to totally replace the paper product in the near term, so they are mostly an additional cost in the hope of gaining the business of customers who use the Internet to search and research products and services. At a point in the future, some people will ask that paper catalogues stop being mailed to them.

Catalogue sites are mostly focused on end consumers and small businesses. Corporations hold catalogues internally that are aggregated from all of their suppliers. Data sheets and service catalogues are held and maintained publicly for both B2C and B2B e-business.

Intermediary Sites. A lot of browsing also takes place on intermediary sites. Electronic markets harken back to the farmer's market in the town center or village square, where supply from many sources comes together with demand from many consumers at a convenient location.

Virtual communities, not "owned" in the traditional sense, are another emerging nontraditional intermediary. *Portals* are positioned as a familiar interface or guide to the Internet, but in the end may serve as the ultimate intermediary to most e-commerce activities for consumers, and even for some small- and medium-sized companies.

Chemdex.com is a commercial example. Chemdex procures life science-related products for enterprises and university researchers. At the corporate end of the scale, heavy-duty business hubs will come to redefine whole industries by acting as exchanges for the principal goods and services needed within that industry. The recent announcement of a combined hub from Ford, GM, and DaimlerChrysler points the way.

E-Buying

E-buying occurs when the customer actually makes a purchase from the Web site. In order to do this, the selling company needs to have electronic

---

REUTERS

Reuters supplies the global business community and news media with a wide range of products, including real-time financial data, transaction systems, access to numerical and textual historical databases, news, graphics, still photos, and news video.

Reuters developed a customer self-service tool that integrates with the company's information products and provides on-line access to order processing, billing, and customer-support applications. This tool is an important component of the new Reuters B2B operating model. It e-nabled direct communication among the company, customers, and information providers.

The tool is based on open Internet technology standards and is available via a browser or via system-to-system communication. The solution achieves three goals.

1. It defines a new business model, moving from an administrator-to-administrator model to a user self-service model, integrating between Reuters' product delivery and administration.

2. A fully electronic order-processing and product-fulfillment system extends Reuters' business operations into the customer and supplier environments.

3. It implements an extensible technical solution. On-line product catalogues, electronic invoicing, on-line order processing, and customer management are incorporated to increase speed of order processing and product fulfillment. Reconciliations and discrepancies are reduced. Reuters' hands-on involvement in customer and product administration is reduced. All this leads to increased customer satisfaction and better client relationships.

---

transaction processing capability. Order status and delivery tracking also falls into the e-buying section of sell channel enhancement.

The E-Selling/Buying Scenario. The typical e-selling/buying scenario consists of seven steps (Figure 1.3):

1. Provide product information/catalogue
2. Configure solution
3. Determine cost

Figure 1.3   Typical E-Selling/Buying Scenario

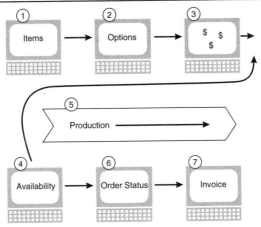

4. Check delivery availability

5. Process order

6. Provide order status

7. Invoice.

ENHANCING THE CUSTOMER SERVICE CHANNEL

E-customer service involves automating as much of the help desk as possible, through the use of Web or telephone call-center technology that takes customers through simple menus to solve most problems. They only have to speak with a customer service representative to resolve problems that require a significant degree of expertise.

Service is one of the biggest issues in the e-commerce space. In their evaluation of electronic merchants' performance, on-line buyers surveyed by rating service BizRate.com ranked "level and quality of customer service" last.

In order to implement e-customer service successfully, a company must begin utilizing data warehousing and data mining technology. The importance of data mining and data warehousing increases if a company moves to the right along the e-business panorama. For the present discussion, the following definitions are sufficient.

A *data warehouse* is a special-purpose database of already indexed, partitioned, and aggregated operational data, extracted from a company's databases. By effectively organizing data from various databases, the data warehouse provides an orderly accessible repository of known facts and related data that are used as the basis of inference and knowledge discovery.

Data warehousing allows a company to engage in *data mining,* the search for universal relationships and patterns that exist in a company's database, but are not apparent in a company's vast amounts of continuous transaction and relationship processing activities. Data mining is used to search through vast quantities of historical data to identify trends and opportunities.

While data warehousing and data mining are often thought of as tools for selling, customer-service data is one of the most important sources. By understanding the post-sale customer relationship, a company can learn about how it needs to design, build, and service its product and conduct the sales and service transactions in order to improve customer satisfaction.

E-nabled Customer Service

The Web can be used to provide personalized and responsive service specific to a particular customer—an individual, a family, or a company. Internet technology provides on-line support and service that enhances the "faster, better, cheaper" model of Internet buying. The Internet approach to customers is highly egalitarian and responsive. It nurtures trust and a personalized response with the customer during the sale and afterwards.

The self-service channel model offers companies the opportunity for relatively low-variable transaction costs. As activity through the e-nabled sell channel increases, sales and support-service costs begin to decline rapidly.

Already, some e-nabled customer and field-service applications give customers access to databases that only company employees could previously use. Customers need to get better, more timely, and more precise information about products and suppliers. Internet technology can provide a way for customers to get real-time data about products, availability, and pricing.

The Internet can be used to set up different Web sites that allow customers to interact with the company at many times throughout the sales and receiving cycle, including:

○ *Content sites,* which provide customers with basic information about the company, its products, and services.

○ *FAQ sites,* which provide answers to frequently asked questions about the company and its products and services.

○ *Knowledge-base sites,* which have knowledge bases that can be searched for answers. Such a site may have a knowledge base of service calls and solutions; customers may be able to correct simple problems without initiating a service call.

○ *Trouble ticket sites,* which allow customers to submit trouble tickets to initiate a service call.

○ *Interactive sites* that facilitate interaction with customers. These sites allow customers access to corporate databases and systems.

Cisco Systems lets customers discuss problems with each other, and they often find solutions through group self help. This puts customers and service engineers in the same community.

Interactivity and Personalized Service

Customers want to encounter a system that is highly effective, responsive, and flexible. Internet technology allows a high degree of interactivity so the customer can easily create, edit, send, confirm, and track orders.

Customers also wish to receive personalized service. E-commerce applications are customizable to accommodate specific customer needs, nuances, and interests, as well as to set up particular accounts, special terms, and tailored conditions.

Personalization involves tailoring a Web site's presentation to individuals or groups based on profile information, demographics, or prior transactions. Unlike a broadcast channel such as print, television, or radio, where most consumers receive the same content, each Web user has an individualized channel to a company's on-line presentation.

Personalizing a site may be done for business or merchandising purposes. Users of a B2B catalogue, for example, may see different prices, based on the volume discount negotiated by the user's company. In addition to custom pricing, preapproved product configurations and other prenegotiated packages of goods and services can be displayed.

If supply-chain efficiencies and new ways of executing sales and fulfillment represent significant changes in the cost base of e-business, personalization is where much of the added value is located. E-business leverages two fundamental forces in commerce by combining supply-side commoditization of products or services with demand-side customization.

To balance adding value through personalization while maintaining the cost base associated with commodity-based companies, e-business seeks to add information content to a transaction. The goal is to develop a personalized experience coupled with rapid order fulfillment. In this way, a customer may reap an actual or perceived bonus that adds value to transactions involving goods and services, which by all rights should be moving toward commoditization.

Personalization techniques include *clickstream data* (data on browsing behavior), which comes into a Web site from an unknown user and can be compared with patterns of clickstream behavior from previous visits to the site. Outputs from this are used to guide the creation of targeted Web pages.

Additionally, a data warehouse repository containing this data can be analyzed using data mining pattern-recognition software to devise the rules that govern which message to offer the anonymous prospect, how to counter points of resistance, and when to attempt to close a sale.

Collaborative filtering takes advantage of previous decisions made by other people with whom an individual shares common characteristics to help a company select information likely to be relevant to that individual. Collaborative filtering applications collect observations of user preferences and make recommendations based on user taste and preference correlation. Amazon.com, perhaps the best-known user of this technology, bases its recommendations to buyers of any given book on the preferences of previous buyers of the same book.

Rules-based systems match user profile data to a predefined set of rules or assumptions. A content-matching engine is the means by which these rules are used to identify content to be received by profiled users. Several different types of rules can be applied effectively.

Case-based personalization software translates user-supplied free-form text into a query that can be run against a database. This software often is used to automate query-handling interactions.

Call Centers

Call centers are the main point of contact for customers. Call center representatives:

- Resolve issues or refer problems to the next level of service provider
- Provide more information about products and services
- Make recommendations to customers about the products or services that best suit their needs
- Track calls and monitor progress on customer requests and problems
- Generate reports for root cause analysis.

Web-based customer service technology has evolved to include Internet telephony and alternatives such as interactive text chats and call-back requests.

The use of Internet protocol (IP) telephony in Internet call centers allows customers to speak directly with a call center agent while using the browser to access the company's Web site. Frequently integrated into a preexisting call center, it is comprised of several core technologies.

IP telephony can be used in call centers when, for example, a user is on a corporate Web site and requests technical support. The user clicks on a call button displayed on a page. The call button is a hypertext link that activates the IP telephony software that then connects the user with a call center agent.

Some call buttons might first ask for a customer's ID. This data allows the call center agent to access the customer's history, which products the customer is using, and what problems the customer has encountered previously. Allowing the call center agent to access the customer account history also enables the agent to sell upgrades or new products based on the customer's purchasing history. Computer-telephone integration (CTI) technology enables this capability and is available as a feature of high-end customer relationship management (CRM) software packages.

As an alternative to IP telephony, customers with two telephone lines can supply their secondary phone number to a merchant. While online, the customer can submit a request for support and expect a call on the secondary line. Callbacks are also used in situations where the customer is protected by a firewall that does not permit IP telephony.

For customers using slower connections, customer service representatives are using Web-based text chats. Customers can request support via the Web and then correspond in real time with the customer service representative. Some software products allow for escorted browsing, in which the agent escorts the customer through Web pages containing information relevant to the customer's query.

The agent and customer move from Web page to Web page in synch with one another. This technology likely will shorten the resolution time of any given query and make customers more self-sufficient in the future.

By supporting these customer service communication channels, the major telecommunications providers such as AT&T, MCI, and Sprint have become players in this software arena. Vendors including eFusion, Ericcson, and Sitebridge currently offer customer relationship management IP telephony packages.

These solutions allow more calls to be handled at call centers without additional personnel. Also, these solutions improve customer satisfaction because calls are processed and routed more rapidly.

Field Service

Field service deals with that part of customer service where qualified representatives of a company are sent to the customer's site to resolve problems. Calls from the call center are forwarded to field service when the problem can not be resolved by the call center.

E-nabled field service helps a firm's representatives by providing them with up-to-date customer and product information, including design documents and repair manuals via the Internet. Field service representatives can check on outstanding customer queries, view their active service calls, and even update the status of accounts while traveling.

For customer-facing applications, field service is being adapted to allow customers to serve themselves. For example, customers can go to the field service Web site and see what they need to do to set up a product, perform a test, and trouble shoot.

Cisco Systems has saved millions of dollars on Web-initiated customer service requests, and customer service productivity has increased dramatically. The company, a large supplier of networking products, provides customer service through Cisco Customer Connect (CCO), an e-nabled system that serves as the starting point for the vast majority of the company's customer service cases, greatly reducing the number of calls handled by technical assistance centers. In addition, the company's Open Forum, an on-line troubleshooting service, uses the Cisco Web site as the first level of escalating unsolved problems.

Sun Microsystems, a global provider of work stations, has created SunSolve service, allowing customers to download product documentation, receive the latest product advisories and specifications, and communicate with other users. It also provides answers to product questions. Another feature, Catalyst Catalogue, maintained by vendors, lists compatible third-party software. Finally, SunSoft Try and Buy allows users to download evaluation software and temporary demo licenses. Using this e-customer service, Sun saves millions of dollars annually in software mailing costs and achieves significant savings annually in telephone support.

Internet-Enhanced Dealer Service

Harley-Davidson does not expect consumers to buy motorcycles over the Internet, but the company does expect dealers to take advantage of the technology. Like many companies, Harley-Davidson is using e-business to enhance its existing dealer channel and help dealers provide better customer service.

Dealers use the Harley-Davidson extranet, H-DNET, to check recall status, order parts and accessories, and rapidly process reimbursements for warranty repair work. These transactions, which used to be performed either with paper and pen or through a proprietary client-server DOS-based software package called Talon, can now be processed on a Web browser.

Customer-Facing E-Mail

Companies that establish a Web presence are often surprised by the large volume of incoming e-mail they receive. The growth of e-mail as a form of customer interaction often outstrips companies' ability to handle it. In 1998, approximately 1.9 billion e-mail messages were sent each day. Pioneer Consulting estimated that this number grew to 4 billion by the end of 1999. This problem is compounded by the lack of an e-mail equivalent to the automated-call-director systems used by call centers to route calls to customer service representatives (CSRs).

In response to this challenge, several vendors are offering packaged applications specifically designed to handle customer-facing e-mail. A typical customer-facing e-mail package includes the following:

- The ability to receive incoming e-mail messages and route them to the appropriate destinations
- A work-flow mechanism for moving incoming messages through the series of steps necessary to generate a response
- Some type of knowledge-based or rules-based system, capable of creating or suggesting an appropriate response to each message
- A case management system that allows incoming e-mail messages that are continuations of previous interactions to be associated with the history of that interaction
- A set of tools for managing the process of responding to e-mail and for use in configuring and administering the e-mail system.

In its simplest form, a customer-facing e-mail package can be seen as a hybrid of a work flow system that manages the process of responding to e-mail messages, combined with a knowledge-based system that manages the content used in those responses.

ENHANCING THE BUY CHANNEL

By early 1999, companies had resigned themselves to the fact that they had to have an e-commerce sell channel in order to be perceived by customers as part of the modern world. Yet for many companies, those sell channels were not really producing much increased revenue. They were, however, reducing costs. And companies love to reduce costs.

This cost-reduction mindset caused corporate executives to think about how to cut costs on their nonproduction buying, an area that had long been overlooked and which was widely thought to be impossible to manage effectively.

Dedicated electronic data interchange (EDI) has been used for about two decades for the electronic exchange of information about production material purchases, but buying nonproduction-related goods and services (indirect procurement, also called goods-not-for-resale) has continued to be a pen-and-paper free-for-all, with individual employees having wide discretion to make their own purchases of low- and even moderate-priced goods and services. Could technology help them in any way? The answer is a definite yes.

Figure 1.4 positions the new concept of an indirect procurement buy channel in a company's value network.

Early efforts at managing indirect procurement focused on process cost reduction because, although most companies have no real solid handle on how much they spend on indirect procurement, financial managers do understand that there is a process cost problem in indirect procurement. Small orders do cost as much to process as larger orders. But before e-business solutions, tackling the problem meant creating a rigid set of procurement rules that would alienate employees and probably, for the most part, be ignored anyway.

E-Procurement Value Proposition

In roughly descending order of savings, the three value propositions for moving to e-procurement are: employee compliance with prenegotiated contracts, improved leverage with suppliers, and process improvement.

Our experience shows that compliance can be worth twice the reduction attained by leverage and up to 10 times the reduction from process enhancement. Knowledge is the key to making compliance and leverage possible and so worthwhile. Knowledge of established contracts, shared with individual buyers throughout the company, leads to better compliance. And knowledge of what buyers are actually spending on each supplier's products can be leveraged in the next round of negotiations.

For many companies, indirect procurement can represent as much as 30 percent of the company's annual revenues, an amount easily comparable

Figure 1.4   Indirect Procurement Buy Channel

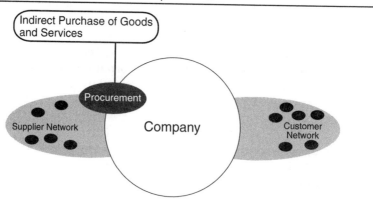

to the amount spent on direct procurement. Most companies, however, don't have the capacity to measure the amount accurately, explaining why, until recently, this area has been overlooked as nonstrategic. For many companies, issuing a single purchase order can cost more than $100. This cost, which can be substantially avoided, can add up to hundreds of thousands, or even millions, of dollars a year. And process cost reduction is typically the least important value of e-procurement!

Savings in this area go straight to the bottom line. As noted earlier, a 10 percent reduction in indirect procurement cost can result in a 50 percent increase in profit margin. In order to achieve an equal impact, a company would have to either increase sales by 50 percent, reduce overhead by 20 percent, or significantly reduce head count.

Indirect procurement involves more than just commonplace, small, low-cost, bland, or generic items such as office supplies, furniture, and computers. Indirect goods are the buying organization's commodity goods and include industry-specific items. For example, for telecommunications companies, network switches are indirect goods; for oil refineries large condensers that cost millions of dollars are indirect goods; for companies that operate gasoline stations, retail station fascia and signs are indirect goods.

Historically, purchasing cards (P-cards) were the indirect procurement instrument of choice because the issue was seen as one of process and paper elimination, not leverage. This offered consolidated billing, a large reduction in paperwork, and minimum management overhead. Unfortunately, such efforts were often poorly implemented, resulting in a mushrooming of the supplier base (contrary to best practice) and actually addressed the least important of the available value propositions underlying the bringing of indirect procurement under control.

Because indirect procurement is a true cross-industry problem, with a huge market opportunity for a good solution, independent software vendors have rushed into this space over the past couple of years. Internet startups have been slowly followed by ERP vendors, who by and large initially missed the significance of the Internet and its related technology as a new way to solve old problems.

A large percentage of indirect items and services can be put in a catalogue that is demand driven at the individual level and that mimics a consumer buy in the way it is carried out. Today, using packaged technology combining electronic catalogues and work flow distributed over corporate intranets, large companies in particular have realized that indirect procurement can now be effectively managed.

A one-time investment of $5 to $20 million—half spent on technology and half on organizational change management—to enhance the buy channel can yield yearly savings of up to 10 percent of the organization's spending on indirects. Controlling the channel as the buyer can lead to

Figure 1.5   Standardization of Indirect Procurement

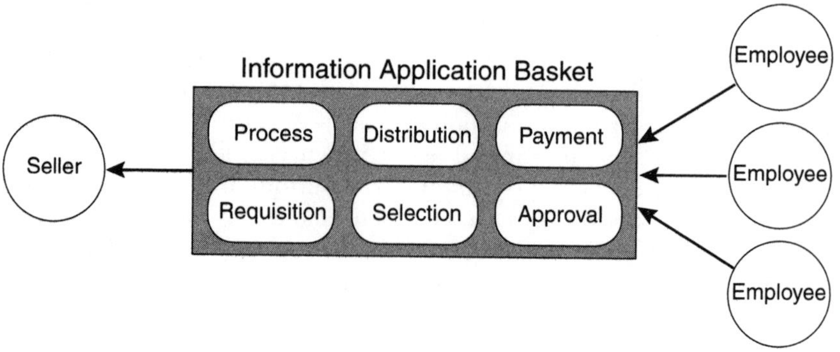

ongoing reductions in the price of goods, as the spending is leveraged and the volume concentrated among a smaller supplier base.

For some companies, this investment pays for itself literally in a matter of weeks; for any global 500 company, the payback should be less than six months. It is estimated that, by 2002, most of the global 500 companies will have installed such systems, at a total cost of about $5 billion. This investment is expected to yield annual savings of $7.5 billion.

Indirect procurement is similar to consumer purchasing because in most large corporations, individuals are allowed to make buying decisions for many, if not all, indirect items—everything from stationary to computers and office furniture. Technology allows the standardization of indirect procurement and will be the stepping off point for many large organizations moving into e-business (Figure 1.5).

E-Procurement Scenario

The e-procurement scenario is the flip side of the e-selling/buying scenario in the e-selling channel discussed earlier in this chapter. The full e-procurement cycle has 12 steps (Figure 1.6):

1. *Identify a need.* A company employee identifies a need for a particular product, service, or even a digital product.

2. *Sign on to an electronic procurement application.* The employee gains access to a browser-based procurement application that includes a user profile. The profile allows the user to access catalogues, items, and services retrieved from a digital library and authorized for use.

3. *Access authorized buying catalogues.* The employee's user profile, in conjunction with business rules and authorizations residing

Figure 1.6   Full E-Procurement Cycle

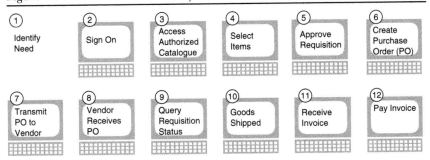

on the e-procurement application server, allows the employee access to only those catalogues required to perform his or her job. The electronic catalogue allows the user to perform complex searches and to configure the desired item for specific purposes. The content of the catalogue itself is created by the sourcing process operated by the company's procurement organization and supported by product usage information reports generated by the e-procurement system.

4. *Select an item from the catalogue and create a requisition.* Once the employee selects the desired item from the catalogue, a requisition is generated in any one of several possible formats.

5. *Approve the requisition.* Business rules are applied against the employee's requisition to determine whether the purchase can be made on his or her own authority, or if it requires a higher-level approval. If approval is required, the requisition goes through a work flow process, potentially passing through multiple levels of approval. Managers can approve or reject requisitions on the Web using the browser interface.

6. *Create a purchase order (PO).* The e-procurement application interfaces with the ERP server to create and record the PO. Upon approval of the requisition, the e-procurement system either generates the PO, combines the requisition with other requisitions for similar products from the same vendor, or splits the requisition into multiple POs to different vendors. The PO is then recorded in the company's ERP database or accounting system.

7. *Transmit the PO.* A PO may be transmitted to a vendor in one of many alternative ways, as EDI over a proprietary value-added network (VAN), via fax, or over the Internet as e-mail or eXtensible markup language (XML) formatted messages.

8. *Vendor receives the PO.* If the PO is received via EDI/VAN or XML, the vendor's ERP database or other order-entry system receives and automatically records the document. If the PO is received via fax or e-mail, human intervention is required.

9. *Query requisition status.* Using a browser, the employee can ask about the status of the PO. The employee enters a PO number and receives the status of his PO based on updates provided by the vendor or shipping agent through a real-time link to the e-procurement application.

10. *Goods shipped.* The vendor ships the goods and may generate a message (known as an advanced shipping notice) to the company. Once the company receives the goods, it may generate an evaluated receipt settlement (ERS) and provide immediate payment on delivery.

11. *Receive invoice.* If payment is not via ERS, the vendor sends an invoice to the company's network. The invoice enters the company's network either through the proprietary VAN or through its Web server via the Internet. Once in the company's network, the invoice is sent to the ERP application server where the transaction server processes it and updates the database.

12. *Pay invoice.* Through electronic funds transmission (EFT), the company pays the vendor once the invoice is received and processed. Other methods of payment include procurement card, where the company provides a credit card number at the time of requisition. This precludes creating a purchase order/invoice paper chase.

Not Just Indirect

Although the business case for moving into e-procurement is usually made in terms of bringing indirect procurement under management, most companies moving in this direction understand that significant elements of their direct spending can also be managed in a similar way—especially the more commoditized elements. As the number and range of electronic catalogues increase and the number of industry procurement portals escalate, the ease of e-procuring even the most obscure and industry-specific items will grow.

Advantages to Both Parties

At first, this process may look like buyers simply putting the squeeze on sellers. But there are advantages to the seller as well. Approximately 20 percent of paper-and-pen purchase orders on which sellers act are incorrect in some way. Resolving these errors requires human intervention and thus drives up transaction overhead costs. E-procurement purchase orders are correct because of the checks built into the system. The seller can reduce its sales and sales administration workforce, since it knows that it has a blanket contract with a company and is guaranteed payments for authorized orders that come through the e-procurement channel. Even with a reduced margin, increased volume and a more efficient process can actually increase seller profit.

Savings through Compliance, Reduced Costs, and Process Efficiencies

Contracts can be written with national or regional suppliers, whose catalogue information is vetted by the corporate buyer or third-party provider, aggregated with other suppliers' catalogues, and then put on the company's intranet. Employees who use the intranet buying system will find it much easier to buy from the sellers who have been precertified and whose materials are on the corporate intranet.

In the paper-and-pencil world of indirect procurement, compliance with prenegotiated contracts is as low as 30 percent in some companies. If such a company can increase compliance to even 50 percent, the savings can be enormous and the technology will pay for itself very quickly. Some companies have much higher compliance.

We believe that the e-procurement systems most companies will build first are those impacting the "requisition to purchase order" stage of the procurement cycle. By increasing compliance from 30 percent to 75 percent with the internal e-catalogue, the company could save 7 or 8 percent of managed indirect cost. As process refinements occur during the first year, the equivalent of another 1 percent of indirect cost can be saved.

From this position of better information, better compliance, and streamlined processes, the company can possibly leverage the size of its total cash outlay in order to negotiate price reductions of another 3-to-5 percent. Further automation of the indirect procurement process, encompassing the entire "req to check" sequence (requisition, purchase order, three-way match, payment) can possibly slice off the equivalent of another 1-to-2 percent of indirect costs.

The key to the level of savings possible is the amount of indirect spending that is e-procurable. Not all goods and services can be easily catalogued. We estimate that for a typical high-tech manufacturing company today, taking on board perhaps 50 percent of total indirect spending is relatively straightforward. Beyond that amount, it becomes progressively more difficult. Services, in particular, are difficult to

A MAJOR BUILDING PRODUCTS MANUFACTURER

A major building products manufacturer has recently completed the integration of its SAP R/3 software with its Web-based purchasing and supplier catalogue software. The company is rolling out its system to 23 facilities in the United States, Canada, Mexico, and the Dominican Republic. The project will, when completed, put on-line the company's 16 major indirect suppliers, who account for more than 80 percent of its indirect procurement.

This multimillion dollar company expects to save between 20 and 30 percent on indirect procurement through greater compliance, lower price, and reduced processing costs.

ONE OF THE LARGEST COUNTIES IN THE U.S.

In addition to companies, not-for-profit agencies and governments can also benefit from e-procurement.

This county, one of the largest in the United States, had processes and procedures that had grown unwieldy, based on available resources and technology. The county's procurement processes and inventory management systems were affected. The county purchases millions of dollars in goods and services every year, and until 1998 had no unifying purchasing system.

Paper forms and manual processes were used. The county sought to automate and e-nable its procurement in order to:

○ Reduce inventories through integration between county warehouses and suppliers, giving real-time availability and price

○ Expand the local supply base and comply with procurement objectives for small and minority-owned businesses by making it easier for them to do business with the county

○ Streamline the procurement process to achieve more control over purchasing

○ Achieve higher automation and delegation through a business-rules-based procurement system that allows distributed desktop requisitioning and procurement.

The results included a simplified and streamlined process through higher automation, delegation, and rules-based procurement. Employees spend less time in unproductive paper-pushing

---

ONE OF THE LARGEST COMPANIES IN THE U.S. *(Continued)*

activities and more time in value-added purchasing activities, such as contract negotiation and supplier management. The process was improved significantly.

The county expects to save about 9 percent in its cost of goods through better comparison shopping, amounting to millions of dollars annually. In addition, the county expects to save $29 million over the first five years of the new buying arrangement by closing warehouses.

---

standardize for cataloging purposes. The use of XML and supplier-side configuration and estimation tools to extend the range of what can be transacted through a self-service catalogue model offers a ray of hope.

Other Kinds of E-Purchasing

In addition to e-procurement, other forms of e-purchasing include:

E-Sourcing. E-sourcing allows individuals working in R&D or procurement organizations to find parts, components, and subassemblies for prototypes and subsequent production models. The difference between e-sourcing and nonproduction commodity e-buying is that in e-sourcing, decisions are made on the basis of functionality and characteristics, not purely on the basis of product classification and price. The e-sourced products form part of the finished product. Therefore, e-sourcing is a way to determine which direct goods to buy.

While e-procurement is available to a large number of people making frequent low-value purchases, e-sourcing is only really used by a small number of specialists. E-sourcing allows engineers to go out and look for things in a different way than they do now; with the search engine, people base their product searches on their performance attributes. Pioneered in the electronics industry by companies such as Aspect Development, these tools are being used in other industries for other products.

Once the sourcing decision has been made, a framework agreement is struck for the supply of these direct materials, which are then typically ordered on a machine-to-machine (ERP to ERP) basis as part of the production process.

E-Auctions: The Buy-Sell Channel and the Efficient Market. Electronic auctions can be used to establish supply contracts (that is, as sourcing mechanisms) or to immediately acquire or dispose of goods on a spot-price basis.

As a sourcing strategy, the reverse auction is a particularly effective mechanism (the lowest bidder wins the right to supply the required goods or services). Depending on the strategy, sellers' competing bids may or may not be visible within the auction time window. Typically such an electronic invitation to tender would be issued only to a pre-qualified list of bidders. Companies will either make the short-list selection from their own preferred vendor list or, in the case of a new supplier, from supplier performance information available from a procurement portal. Such supplier performance information will be collected and disseminated in much the same way as Amazon.com collects and disseminates reader book reviews. This would allow a company to issue an invitation to tender to companies with, say, four-star or better customer reports.

For spot-buying, electronic auctions are useful for buying commodity items (of which the company does not need a steady supply) at a guaranteed price, presuming that the company has some flexibility on timing (to take advantage of seasonal or other market movements) and that it is capable of warehousing or storing the goods.

From the sell side, electronic auctions are useful for selling commodities to a wider market or for disposing of surplus products that the company does not want cluttering up its usual sell channels.

Goods bought or sold in B2B transactions through electronic auctions are not differentiated in any way. Because of this, there may be little value to an individual company's setting up its own auction on its electronic sell channel; selling through a third-party auction site might be just as effective. However, because the technology to set up an auction is not very expensive, some companies may want to run the auction themselves—perhaps just for disposals.

Knowledge Is the Key

Because transaction processing technology is becoming ever more sophisticated, conflict concerning the value of the information that passes through this channel is inevitable.

Three types of transactional technology exist: e-mail (between people and unstructured); EDI (between machines and tightly formatted); and process-formatted (between people and machines). The latter (human-to-machine communication) embodies the highest e-business value.

The buyer uses the technology to open a window into the seller's business by e-browsing, and to try to make the purchasing process more efficient and more pleasant (for those who find human-to-computer communication to be pleasant). At the same time, the seller is trying to capture as much information about the buyer as possible.

If today, a seller company sets up a Web site to sell B2B, it can only really target small- to medium-sized businesses; these companies purchase the same way that individual consumers do, by giving up information about how they make choices.

Big businesses are increasingly saying, "Send us your electronic catalogue, and we will approve portions of it for our intranet. You will not know how our decisions are being made; you will only know when we have made a decision to purchase from you."

Ninety percent of what a buying company saves using e-procurement results from the way it organizes the knowledge it has. Perhaps 10 percent is saved through process enhancement. Spreading knowledge internally about contract terms helps increase contract compliance. Knowledge of what the company is buying helps to leverage that buying into better terms and conditions.

Figure 1.7 and Figure 1.8 illustrate the variations on the sell/buy channel and where the knowledge sits. These are adversarial models, where each company wants the knowledge to sit on its side of the technology firewall.

Figure 1.7   Sell/Buy Channel: First Variation

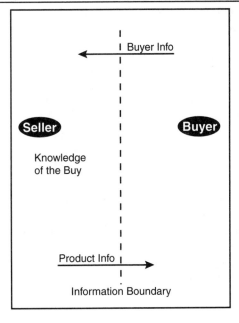

Figure 1.8   Sell/Buy Channel: Second Variation

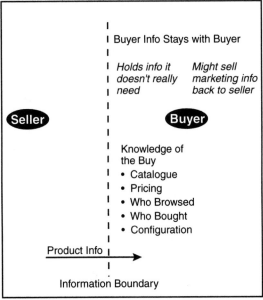

Catalogues and Configurators: Using XML, the Best of Both Worlds

Figure 1.9 illustrates the improved semicollaborative model of e-procurement that is now becoming available because of XML, a recent but rapidly developing and important breakthrough. With XML, business information is exchanged in highly flexible ways and sellers can create a collaborative sell site that includes, say, a product configurator. The buyer exits his or her company's intranet and enters the sell site, browses, tinkers with product configuration, and so forth. Then the individual's work is brought back into the buying company's intranet, where a requisition is placed. The requisition, which now contains all the detailed order configuration information that was developed on the sell site, is still processed through the buyer's system. In this way, the necessary internal work flow and information collection is maintained before the PO is issued back to the supplier.

This technology affords buying companies continual control over purchases, while allowing selling companies to gain some information about buyers' behavior in terms of their browsing habits, the product-build

Figure 1.9   XML-Enhanced E-Procurement Model

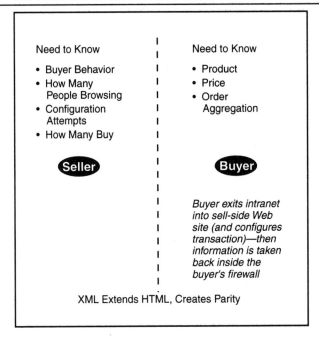

options they investigate, and their general shopping patterns. Even more important, it helps extend the range of products and services that can be made e-procureable by making available the seller's own (previously internal) configuration or estimating tools to the buyer on a self-service basis. As a result, we expect to see ever more complex products and services available for on-line purchase.

2

Snapshot One: Effects of Channel Enhancement on Organizations, People, Processes, and Technology

Moving into the e-nabled world affects a company across five business dynamics: customers and markets, products and services, people and organization, business processes, and information systems/technology.

Changes that occur to customers and markets and those to products and services are discussed in detail in Chapters 1, 3, 5, and 7. In this chapter, as well as in Chapters 4, 6, and 8, we discuss, where appropriate, the effects on people and organizations, business processes, and information systems/technology that occur in each of the four snapshots of the panorama.

Figure 2.1   Effects of E-Business: Channel Enhancement

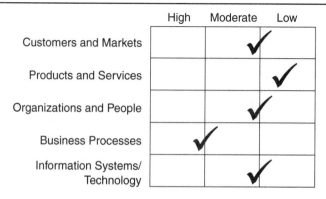

The effects on these five business dynamics in the channel enhancement snapshot of the e-business panorama are illustrated in Figure 2.1.

GENERAL EFFECTS ON ORGANIZATIONS AND PEOPLE

How different is the change that must be achieved in moving to an e-business environment compared to the change involved in other major business efforts, such as implementation of an ERP system or process reengineering?

When asked this question, we respond with several important observations:

○ Transforming from a traditional business into an e-business is harder than starting as an e-business.

An e-business organization can develop in one of three ways: started as an e-business; created (or acquired) as an e-business unit within a traditional company; or transformed from traditional business. In new e-business ventures, workers can be hired with the understanding that change will be constant, and this organizational factor can be built into the informal contract between the employer and employees. However, in traditional organizations that must be transformed, traditional business behaviors have been recognized and rewarded over the years; both the message of the e-business model and the corresponding behaviors and norms will have to be "sold" to the work force.

○ E-business causes movement from "transparency of information" to "transparency of context."

Over the past 10 years, technologies such as e-mail, voice mail, and ERP systems have broadened and deepened access to, and availability of, information. This increased transparency of information throughout the organization has eliminated the need for layers of managers and has flattened the organizational structure. Today, e-businesses must harness information transparency to provide a business context that focuses and sustains accelerated action and results. Organizations must now promote the transparency of context, or, in other words, visibility of the business model.

○ E-business causes movement from "empowerment" to "responsibility for results."

Many traditional companies can operate successfully with many managers and employees not truly understanding the organization's strategic direction or business model or the linkage of individual-to-organizational performance. However, e-business managers and employees at all levels must understand the organization's context for action—and the shifts in this context—to fully, rapidly, effectively, and measurably contribute.

○ Communications must be focused and continuous.

The e-business vision and strategy is very important and demands continuous leadership focus; it cannot be based on a discrete initiative segmented across time or projects.

○ The entire organization must be integrated as early as possible into the climate for change.

Through active involvement in change, employees participate in determining new ways of doing business as the organization moves into the e-business world. Employees see and feel the new reality. Moreover, they can see how they may or may not fit into this new world.

Such integration is especially important as interactivity among employees—and in later stages of e-business among entities within the value chain—drives internal and external organizational changes. By establishing the foundation for change in the initial stages of its e-business activities, a company can more rapidly move up the e-business curve.

SPECIFIC EFFECTS ON ORGANIZATIONS AND PEOPLE

In its most rudimentary form, the e-nabled buy/sell channel need not have a large impact on an organization. However, it is a "cool" idea that, if approached in the right way, can energize many businesses. If e-commerce is successful, it can literally take over the business and have a huge organizational impact. Increased volume through the e-channel can fragment a company by putting great pressure first on the sales force and then on the company's back-end processes and those who carry out the activities there.

Even if a company doesn't mean to disintermediate its distribution network—either internal sales people or outside distributors—an e-sales channel that ties directly to the customer can do just that, undermining all of the relationships that have been built throughout the existing sales and distribution system. The company ends up needing to mediate channel conflicts within its own organization and within its network of business partners.

At the back end, the company needs to begin integrating its supply chain more tightly. Also, the company's leaders must be thinking that if their organization can create such a successful direct link to customers, so can competitors. This realization mandates the need to begin working on adding services to products to build tighter relationships with customers, increase the cost to customers of switching to a competitor, and negate any commoditization of the product. These issues all add to the pressure on the organization.

Enhancing the buy channel has organizational effects on both buying and selling companies.

For the selling company, this change means a new selling process required for working with high-volume buyer-controlled channels operated by its highest revenue-generating customers. A series of midlevel sales relationships is supplanted by a single high-level executive relationship. Such a change generally precedes a reduction in the size of the sales force. In effect the buying company is forcing the selling company to disintermediate its own sales force, whether the selling company wants to or not.

For the buying company, e-procurement will probably be the first big corporate Internet/intranet application that touches everyone in the company. The technological change is small, but the cultural change is huge. E-procurement is a terrific way to introduce the technology to individuals within the buying company; there is only a small potential for any large problems to occur, and problems that do occur do not have an impact on the company's customers. The potential for cultural gains is enormous.

In complying with the new buying regime, individuals will use not the phone or fax to order, but the intranet, accessed through their desktop computer. For individuals, there is some loss of choice in the buy; that control shifts to the corporate entity.

Local buying relationships also go away, as do the quid pro quo arrangements that historically cemented many of these relationships. Buying decisions become less political, more directly based on price, and increasingly based on service level and delight with the business relationship.

Effects on the Organization

Making the business case for change of behaviors around processes or culture is key. Notwithstanding the organizational origins of the e-business, leadership must identify and communicate behaviors consistent with targeted cultural and process models. Moreover, leadership must ensure that the message is disseminated throughout the organization accurately, in a timely fashion, and with sufficient detail.

Accuracy reduces misunderstandings and misalignments. Timeliness imparts urgency and currency. Detail provides the proper context for employee evaluation of business and skills requirements. This is all especially critical for businesses shifting to e-business rather than those that begin as an e-business.

Establishing the Business Model.   The initial business model should establish the key behaviors for e-business, such as sharing information across the work force and internal responsiveness. From the start, one of the most important actions at the organizational level involves developing the right behaviors and overcoming the cultural roadblocks.

Depending on the competitive landscape and opportunity window, an organization may need to rely on forced compliance to change behaviors that were successful in the past. However, the e-business environment requires active, organic, accelerated change.

Overcoming Resistance.   Organizations undergoing change may face several types of resistance:

○ Resistance based on the need for additional information
○ Resistance based on lack of understanding and uncertainty (fight or flight)
○ Resistance based on deep mistrust.

The need for more information is by far the most common form of resistance. This must be mitigated through use of active communication by leadership, as well as employee involvement in the change effort.

Over the past several years, the key cultural hurdles for Web transaction processing have included determining a return on investment, end-user education, and project management. While these factors are critical to successful transformation to an e-business organization, they are secondary to the lack of shared vision hurdles such as cross-department conflicts and getting business and technical management approval.

Effects on People

Key characteristics of individuals who will thrive in an e-business organization include a high risk tolerance; flexibility; teaming skills; and the ability to appreciate and thrive in ambiguity, build relationships to achieve business goals, admit mistakes, and move forward. In this early e-business effort—channel enhancement—there is an emphasis on the roles, skills, and fit of individuals in the current and future e-business organization.

The cultural business model should identify and map specific roles, the integration of roles, the links between the organization and the individual, and the skill sets of individuals to the organization's strategy and business model. Mapping identifies the focus for transforming the organization and moving it along the evolutionary curve.

Planning and Maintaining Employee Skills.   Planning for required future skill sets must be performed early in the process to identify initial gaps, support smoother transitions in later stages, and instill into the evolutionary process the ability to seamlessly create and discard skills as necessary without significant retooling or downtime. Maintaining employee skills is the third most frequently cited challenge, according to e-business executives surveyed by PricewaterhouseCoopers.

At the outset, a company must work to communicate the correct message; by demonstrating an openness to individuals willing to undertake the changes and challenges of the e-business environment, a company begins the process of change by integrating the individuals.

Creating the Interactive Workplace.   In e-business, companies must connect the right individuals to each other at the right time and create an interaction. In its research on differently structured e-businesses, Forrester Research argues that the challenge lies in meshing 20-year veteran employees with telecommuting Web employees who define loyalty as sticking with one job for at least the time required before they can cash in their stock options.

Shift in Communication Behaviors.   Tacit and explicit, as well as formal and informal forms of communication should be managed in order to support the organizational change strategies and new business environment. New communication patterns will likely be enabled through technologies. Active management of such communications can be traumatic at the individual level.

An explicit communications and knowledge-management program should be an integrated component of the e-business transition. Moreover, individuals should be encouraged to provide key content for these organization-wide programs.

EFFECTS ON BUSINESS PROCESSES

E-business is a disruptive technology. The use of e-business technology has serious implications for the way that companies manage their day-to-day operations. For example, channel enhancement requires fundamental changes in the way existing processes are executed. These new processes are not totally different from previous ones, but they do represent a new way of doing things. In addition, some processes may be eliminated through channel enhancement, freeing up resources to focus on more value-added activities.

Channel enhancement also requires businesses to develop processes in new areas. Specifically, management of e-business-related content is critical for successful marketing, buying, and selling over the Internet. Not only must businesses create processes in this area, but they must assign ownership of these processes and train their employees to execute activities within them.

Need to Reengineer Existing Processes

The following sell-side and buy-side processes must be reengineered as part of channel enhancement: marketing, customer management, sales (including order management), and procurement of indirect materials. To implement these process changes, the processes themselves must be clearly defined during the design of the new information systems. Employees should represent their respective areas during the design, construction, and implementation of the new processes, facilitating the buy-in necessary for the processes to be successful.

However, the employees themselves will not know all of the e-business technology capabilities. Therefore, e-business process experts are required to lead the development and roll out of the new processes.

During design, employees should be assigned ownership of the processes. As part of their responsibilities, process owners must educate members of their team on the new processes. In addition, process owners must work closely with system implementation managers during design and construction to ensure that the system functionality and processes are aligned.

During implementation, process owners are required to train their team members on the new system's use, in accordance with process procedures. After implementation, process owners should look for opportunities to improve processes and solicit process improvement suggestions from team members.

Processes That Must Be Modified.   As part of channel enhancement, the following processes must be modified:

1. *Marketing.* The Internet is an entirely new channel for marketing. Marketing must develop a strategy to get customers to the company's site, such as links from other sites or relationships with portals. At the same time, it should not forget the power of established media and the possible synergies between the old and the new.

Companies must also decide which marketing materials to post on their Web sites and determine the site's aesthetics. Web technology allows customers to directly access information on products and services, place orders, and get answers to specific questions. Because all of these interactions can now be captured with e-business technologies, companies are able to analyze trends in purchasing, identify geographic/cultural differences in buying habits, and in general determine what's hot and what's not.

As a result, marketing groups must figure out the appropriate promotion and advertising campaigns for their target segments. Web technology allows these marketing campaigns to be delivered, analyzed, and modified in real time. For example, marketing organizations must analyze buyer data to determine the correct point-of-sale promotions, including cross-selling and up-selling offers.

All of these considerations have a significant impact on the new processes that must be developed in the marketing area.

2. *Sales and Order Management.* Channel enhancement provides a drastic change to the way companies perform sales and order management activities. Order management employees who formerly took sales orders over the telephone are now free to perform troubleshooting on orders or to perform other value-added activities, including maintaining sales data on the Web site, such as pricing and product descriptions.

Effects of price changes can be assessed by quickly measuring the change in sales volume that results from a temporary change in price. In addition, sales representatives are now able to obtain up-to-date information in real time on products, markets, customers, and competitors. This capability allows the reps to concentrate on increasing revenues and sales.

3. *Customer Service.* E-business technology eliminates the need for a CSR to be available by phone every time a customer has a simple question or requests a simple answer. In some situations, CSRs may respond to e-mails for customers who could not be serviced directly from the Web site. It is crucial that customer e-mails are acknowledged at least as promptly and efficiently as fax or physical mail: Failure to do so results in dissatisfied customers and poor perception in the marketplace. Several early major corporate Web sites with customer response e-mail capability found they were swamped with messages and were completely unprepared to deal with the flood of inquiries—a potentially great opportunity became a marketing disaster.

Internet technology also allows CSRs to have interactive chat sessions with customers. In addition, CTI allows customers to click a button on the Web site to contact a CSR for assistance. When the CSR is engaged in the call, he or she has received all of the information detailing what has been communicated via the Web. The CSR can then see what the user is seeing on his or her screen, bring up the customer's information automatically, and reduce the time it takes to solve the problem.

4. *Procurement.* Using e-business technology, the procurement process for indirect material is radically changed. Because all indirect

material purchasing information exists in an electronic catalogue, requisitioners do not any more have to waste time searching for materials and services. Procurement staffs are relieved of an administration burden and, as a result, buyers have more time to focus on more value-added activities, such as negotiating long-term contracts with preferred suppliers.

Using an extranet e-procurement solution, requisitioners can check product availability, pricing, and order status on-line. Procurement processes are streamlined even further as a result of the requisition approval work flow provided by e-procurement solutions.

Using e-procurement solutions results in reduced requisition-to-delivery times. This results in lower reorder points and less inventory. All of the cost savings associated with e-procurement, including streamlined process flow, lower inventories, and better contracts with suppliers revert right to the company's bottom line.

Need to Engineer New Processes

Channel enhancement strategies challenge companies to manage their Web site's content by creating processes to generate, organize, store, retrieve, and distribute that content. This applies to both external Web sites and internal intranet sites, such as procurement catalogues.

Content management is the combination of processes and systems architecture that allows a company to contribute to, collaborate on, and control text, graphics, and multimedia, and even the programmable applets that appear on a Web page.

Content management is important to all areas of a company that have presence on the company's Web site. For example, a company that markets and sells on-line must manage marketing content (promotions and advertisements), sales content (pictures and descriptions of items for sale), and order management content (prices). A company that collaborates with business partners on design efforts must manage the creation, organization, storage, and distribution of design drawings and other design information.

A company must dedicate a team to manage content across all of the Web sites on which the company appears. This team should include members from all areas that have a stake in the Web site. Centralized team management helps ensure consistent content management processes across all areas of the company. Team members should work together to develop the process and agree on standards for technology and formats.

Content management processes generally fall into three categories: those that contribute site assets, those that collaborate across organizations, and those that control delivery. Content management processes should be simple enough so employees from across the company can contribute easily.

The process for submitting content should be simple. Using standard content templates makes contributing easier for authors and does not require knowledge of hypertext markup language (HTML), the basic Web document description language. All Web content should be organized logically and stored centrally, so all can easily locate what they need.

The content management team should define work flow procedures for approving submitted content. This provides the control necessary to prevent inadequate or erroneous content from reaching the Web. It must also establish mechanisms that prevent content from being overwritten.

Finally, the content management team must agree on how content will be presented to users. The team needs to write rules for dynamic population of Web pages. Dynamic pages free the content management team members from having to create each page themselves, allowing them to focus on business issues. Dynamic Web pages can also be used to personalize content for users.

EFFECTS ON INFORMATION SYSTEMS AND TECHNOLOGY

Moving to an e-business environment impacts a company's technology strategy and how it uses technology in a multitude of ways. Most of these technology changes, and concomitant changes in technology strategy, occur regardless of the e-business snapshot in which a company is operating.

Global and 24×7 availability of the Web makes a company's internal workings and shortcomings somewhat, if not totally, transparent to business partners and customers. Because of this, e-business forces a company to do the right things and magnifies the situation when a company does the wrong things.

E-business is an outgrowth of available advanced technology. Hardware and software advances have made e-business a reality. The combination of affordable computing power, simple and standard telecommunications protocols, and enhanced security allow e-business to flourish.

As a result of today's technology, desktop and server computers have computing power rivaling that of yesterday's mainframes. This, combined with advanced programming languages, databases, and a common telecommunications protocol, has enabled the business community to develop and implement e-business solutions.

The consumer market is fostering more technology-dependent business relationships. And consumers have higher expectations of software applications. This is truly the first time the consumer market has driven the business use of technology. Business users see how technology is making their personal lives easier to manage, with applications such as on-line banking and bill paying. In turn, consumers are applying these same principles and expectations in their business lives.

E-business relies on the standardization of technology. Users require a single technical infrastructure that can communicate with all of their trading partners. In the past, various telecommunications models existed, with no single standard in place. Internet standardization allows developers to focus on applications and not on infrastructure issues. Technology complexity is becoming more and more transparent to both users and developers, enabling them to focus more on business relationships and less on technical architecture.

The big question for businesses regarding technology is, Which executive "owns" e-business? Is the business owner of the Web-enabled supply chain the chief information officer (CIO) or the chief operating officer (COO)? Is the business owner of the Web-enabled distribution chain the CIO or the Vice President of Marketing? Is the Web "owned" by the corporate head office, or by the business units?

However businesses answer these questions, the CIO must closely manage the expectations of clients throughout the corporation. Having entered the twenty-first century, we find a situation akin to the one that faced corporate leaders in the early 1980s, when desktop computers were being brought into companies by so-called processing guerrillas.

Figure 2.2 illustrates how information systems advance over time. Advances in hardware and software occur as step functions, while advances in user applications occur in a linear fashion.

Sometimes smart users get ahead of the available, formally developed software, and the hardware that runs it. Garage-programmers build systems that work, but they are undocumented and often unmaintainable. That was the case with e-business during the early 1990s. Now, at the dawn

Figure 2.2   How Information Systems Advance Over Time

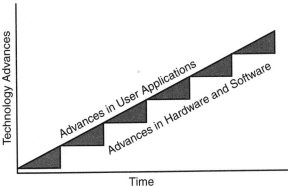

of the twenty-first century, it appears that the technology—both hardware and software (and more importantly, security)—has caught up with the early adopters of e-business solutions.

As businesses move forward, effective systems for e-business need to be developed following the basic principles of structured systems development methodologies. Development time frames can not be reduced and short cuts can not be taken just because Internet technologies are available to develop the system. Building an effective system requires careful and thorough analysis of business requirements and systems design.

While developers need to delve into the technological guts of their company's e-business operations, most others in the organization do not. However, it is important that everyone have a basic understanding of the terminology and operations.

GLOSSARY OF E-BUSINESS TECHNOLOGY

As a precursor to developing an understanding of the technology components of an e-business system, one must be familiar with the client/server system architecture in wide use today.

Client/server architectures consist of a number of client computers (desktop or laptop computers) used to display information to a user. These are linked to a server computer that runs applications (programs) and/or stores data in a database.

Servers function in business environments that require high-volume, intensive programming. The server receives requests from a client to process or retrieve information. After performing the requested function(s), the server sends the result to the client for display to the user. Clients may host applications that perform relatively simple functions such as work processes, graphic design, or small database management.

Application Programming Interface (API): API is a set of calling conventions that defines how a service is invoked through software. API allows programs written by users or third parties to communicate with certain vendor-supplied programs, and allows users and third parties to add functions to vendor-supplied software.

Applet: Applets are highly portable, machine independent, application components that can be executed either on a Web server or locally within a client browser. Applets are installed, maintained, and upgraded on the server, and are transparently downloaded on demand from the server to the client whenever needed. They are stored on the client machine and "refreshed" from the server the next time the client connects to that particular server.

Component Object Model (COM): COM is a Microsoft protocol originally designed to provide interoperability between Windows applications.

Common Object Request Broker Architecture (CORBA): CORBA is the interoperability standard for object-oriented applications communicating over heterogeneous networks.

Distributed Component Object Model (DCOM): The COM model is extended by DCOM, allowing clients to access components across a network and supporting client-to-server and server-to-server connections between Windows 95 and Windows NT systems.

Firewall: A firewall protects a company's internal computing environment from infiltration. Firewalls consist of dedicated hardware and software systems that provide security by screening network traffic and validating information flow between networks.

Hypertext Markup Language (HTML): HTML is the page description language used to create a hypertext document. Hypertext documents are commonly the underlying formatting for the World Wide Web. They provide a way to display documents on different browsers and machines.

Hypertext Transport Protocol (HTTP): HTTP is the protocol for moving hypertext files across the Internet. It requires an HTTP client program on one end and an HTTP server program on the other end.

Internet Inter-Object Request Broker (ORB) Protocol (IIOP): When a client machine uses an applet, the applet in the browser interacts with the applet server—the server that stores business logic—via different protocols, one of which is the IIOP. An applet server runs Java or other object-oriented applets, extending the applet concept from graphical user interface (GUI) client-side components to the enterprise-wide server side.

Java: The Java programming language developed by Sun Microsystems is an object-oriented language. It can be used either to develop Internet applets or as a general-purpose application development language. Java programs are written to run on hypothetical computers known as Java Virtual Machines (JVMs). Any operating system or application that mimics a JVM can run a Java program.

Transmission Control Protocol/Internet Protocol (TCP/IP): This suite of protocols defines the Internet and allows communication between different types of computers and networks that are connected to the Internet.

Virtual Private Network (VPN): A VPN is a communication network operated by a common carrier that provides what appears to the user to be dedicated lines but that actually consists of a public network backbone. Essentially, a VPN configures a private network within a public network.

Web Browser: A Web browser is a client application that allows a user to view and interact with content on the World Wide Web or on a company's intranet or extranet. The browser processes text, graphics, and in some cases sound and video. It also downloads and processes files as required. The browser's most basic responsibilities are requesting data from a server, interpreting the data it receives, and presenting the data to the user.

Web Server: A Web server combines hardware and software that retrieves Internet Web information and transfers Web pages to a Web browser. The Web server also provides messaging, data, interaction management, and secure communications.

Web Server Application Programming Interface (API): Web server APIs address interaction between Web servers and corporate data. A Web server API enables the information flow between the browser, Web server, and corporate data store. For example, an API allows authorized users to view on a browser financial reports generated directly from a back-office accounting system database.

eXtensible Markup Language (XML): Like HTML, XML is a meta language for describing data. However, XML enables the interpretation and manipulation of data in more intelligent ways than are possible with HTML. For example, with XML, data can be processed by applications resident on desktops or servers; HTML merely enables data to be displayed by a browser. XML documents resemble HTML documents, but the similarity ends there. XML documents contain field tags that describe the structure of their content (data). HTML only describes how a document should be displayed.

Overview of E-Business System Architecture

Web computing provides the platform for a new style of application architecture and deployment. Web-based e-business systems consist of numerous components operating reliably and securely.

Figure 2.3 illustrates how a simple e-business site might be assembled. The primary element is a Web server, which runs a program that implements the HTTP protocol to exchange messages between the server and a Web browser. The server typically hosts the seller's Web home page, interactive session management procedures, and catalogue and order methods.

Another element may include a payment gateway or an external service to validate and authorize credit card transactions or other payment methods. A third element may be integration between the Web storefront and back office systems and applications. Integration allows traditional

Figure 2.3   Assembling a Simple E-Business Site

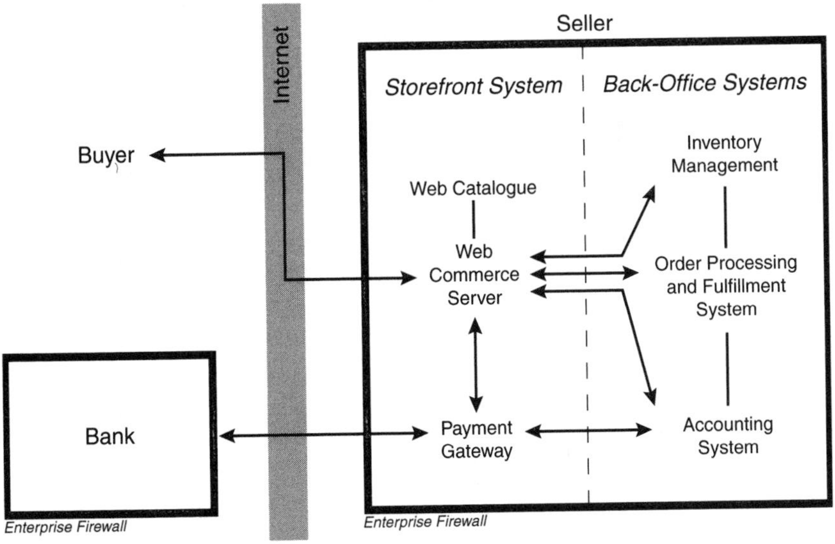

retailers and catalogue merchants to leverage their existing systems and infrastructures.

As e-business sites have become more functionally complex and feature-rich, and as traffic to these sites has increased, the simple Web server architecture has expanded rapidly into tiers of application and database servers. This expanded architecture allows high-performance e-business sites to achieve greater scalability and flexibility.

Figure 2.4 illustrates a typical architecture in which the Web server acts as the initial entry point into the site and dispatches appropriate requests, such as a catalogue search, to the commerce servers.

For sites with many hundreds or thousands of simultaneous users, load-balancing procedures may route requests to various commerce servers that, in turn, respond directly back to the Web browser. These commerce servers typically assume responsibility for conducting the transaction and maintaining sessions with the Web browser.

E-Business Platform Application Programming

E-business is moving toward a more interactive and customer-oriented exchange. This requires extensive programming on network servers and clients. Applications can produce unique Web pages in real time, based on a combination of information from the user and information stored

Figure 2.4   Typical Commercial Web Site Architecture

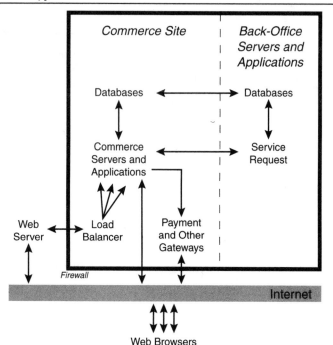

on the server side; they can also allow users to interact with applications running on a Web server or other enterprise server.

A server can do more than send static content. It can also cause a browser or other client to execute a "plug-in" or helper application. Another option is to send a program in some scripting language directly to the browser.

These programs, sometimes called applets or active content, are interpreted by code in the client machine. Applets can range in complexity from simple animation add-ons and sophisticated graphical user interface (GUI) functionality, to handling business logic in the client.

Various development languages are used for writing e-business platform applications. Although previously some have been dedicated "client" or "server" languages, the trend today is to use the same language in both environments. The three most common script languages for the Internet are Java, Java-Script, and VBScript.

Applet languages are platform independent and can be read by any recent Web browser on any operating system, as long as the browser understands the language.

Physical Networks

E-business is linked inextricably with the Internet and Web-related technologies. However, the Internet is a chaotic place, and companies may wish to stay with an established network service provider to manage their critical connections. In addition to maintaining the physical network, a service provider may also play a key role in hosting Web sites, acting as a firewall, or operating electronic commerce servers. Reliability of connection, scalability of architecture, and overall capacity are areas where service providers can offer the assurance that an e-business requires.

The network infrastructure that underlies the e-commerce operation requires careful consideration. If a company has established a Web presence, it will have already addressed some of the issues regarding Internet service provider (ISP) selection, network security, and server availability.

However, the e-commerce requirement is often significantly more stringent, both in terms of reliability and security, than a company has previously encountered. Many companies are not content to entrust to the Internet their business-critical connections with supply-chain and demand-chain partners and customers, and seek to establish an extranet using a VAN, a virtual private network (VPN), a public data network, or a private line.

Enterprise Integration

New systems need to work together. Enterprise integration links entire sales, production, and delivery processes and systems electronically into one seamless flow of information among a company, its customers, and its supply chain and demand chain partners.

Integration between new and "legacy" systems allows an organization most effectively to use its available information and helps it serve customers better. For example, a company may want to integrate a new Web-enabled sales application with its existing manufacturing systems to allow for seamless order-to-ship.

The key technology issue for application integration involves how an e-business configures applications that are based on different technologies and with different business processes and data models to work together in a common way on a network. The challenge is for a company to understand how best to accomplish the appropriate degree of integration.

Integration can occur in forms that vary along multiple attributes. In its simplest form, integration can mean the ability to export data files from one application and import them into another, possibly after undergoing some translation between different data formats.

More sophisticated forms of integration can differ in several ways. For instance, rather than exporting files from the source application and importing them into the target, the source system may be able to invoke actions in the target system.

Data integrity and consistency are important to e-business. In order for a company's internal operations to run smoothly, employees must be able to trust the accuracy of company data. A great deal of caution must be taken when transferring data between two systems. It is essential that data not be altered or destroyed during integration.

As the number of systems that need to be integrated increases, so does the risk of encountering data integrity problems. Data integrity can be achieved through careful planning and system integration. Testing cross-system links to validate data integrity often takes significantly longer than building the actual interfaces.

Applications

A number of packaged applications have been developed to support sell-side and buy-side channel enhancement. However, many transaction-oriented Web sites still are custom built to meet unique needs and to provide functionality that can not be purchased off the shelf. Vendor offerings vary widely in the extent to which they provide a ready-made solution.

Some products offer a tools-oriented platform approach, which provides a programming, transaction, and database management environment. Others are out-of-the-box solutions, which simplify creation of a storefront or e-catalogue, using "wizards" that guide users through the process or design templates.

The general trend in software solutions is toward packaged applications. As time passes, more out-of-the-box applications will be developed that enable a company to quickly add new capability to its e-business solutions portfolio. Thus, the need for custom-developed applications will decrease. The explosion in e-business is very much driven by the availability of packaged solutions for a variety of business needs, e-procurement being, perhaps, the best current example.

Security Requirements for E-Business

With the expansion of e-business, security issues concerning electronic transactions have come to the forefront. While most companies have implemented security models within their own businesses, more concern is being placed on protecting the company, its data, and its key systems from outside attack. In addition, companies that are promoting e-business as a primary means of commerce are facing strict security demands from customers. Those companies that cannot demonstrably mitigate the security risks of e-business run the real possibility of being left out of the game.

Firewalls protect internal networks from unauthorized outside access. Firewalls consist of dedicated hardware and software systems that provide security by screening network traffic and validating information flow between networks. Firewalls are used to enforce a Web site's security policy by mediating traffic between the site and the Internet or other external network.

But even keeping unauthorized users off the network does not always result in a secure environment. Computer viruses, which can be transported over networks through files and other means, present a real threat. Many companies have desktop virus scanning, virus scanning at the firewall, and other methods of checking for these potentially damaging programs.

In addition to viruses, security can also be breached by rogue applets downloaded onto a local machine and executed, resulting in system havoc.

Many companies are implementing private networks, either through extranets or VPNs, to increase security. Extranets are accessible by business partners and their customers, but not by the outside world. VPNs create private connections that guarantee some measure of security and bandwidth availability.

Security technology is called upon to perform several functions in e-business transactions: authentication, confidentiality, secure delivery, privacy, and nonrepudiation.

Authentication.   Parties to a transaction need to establish that their counterparts are who they say they are, at least in the sense that they are authorized to approve the purchase. For example, if a customer uses a credit card number, the merchant needs to establish that the customer is the authorized card user.

Confidentiality and Secure Delivery.   The main confidentiality concerns in e-business, as in other business interactions, focus on what the vendor or merchant does with customer information once it is provided and on how the system protects confidential information.

Proper use of confidential information is more important (and more difficult) than simply encrypting information as it crosses networks. Each party needs to ensure that private information, such as merchant prices and customer credit card numbers, can be transferred securely from one to the other.

Mutual Privacy.   The parties in a transaction need to ensure that private information will remain private once it arrives at its destination. Credit card numbers and other customer information need to be stored securely at the merchant's site, and the customer and merchant need to agree on how merchant information, such as prices and availability, will be used by the customer. Security technology offers an electronic means, via the digital signature, to verify that each party agrees to whatever arrangements are adopted.

Nonrepudiation.   The parties in a transaction need to be certain neither can repudiate an agreement once it is agreed to. Security technology can prevent parties from claiming they were not the ones who signed the agreement.

Secure Payment Technology: SSL or SET.   The most popular process in use today to protect sensitive information such as payment data uses the SSL protocol, which was developed by Netscape and is now a de facto standard. SSL encrypts data sent between two parties by constructing a communication connection in which all data is encrypted before being transmitted over the Internet.

Handshake routines at the onset of an SSL session share identifying information between the two parties, select one of several encryption algorithms to be used, and create the necessary session-specific encryption keys.

SET is a standard describing a complex authentication mechanism that makes it extremely difficult to commit fraud. SET includes a method for authenticating all parties with third-party certification.

SET offers authentication services currently lacking in SSL transactions. SSL has only a weak built-in feature for authenticating customers and merchants. Adopting SET, however, requires significant investment by all e-business players.

3

Snapshot Two: Value Chain Integration

Today, individual companies compete against one another to deliver value to customers. But tomorrow, e-nabled companies will join together to deliver value to customers as part of e-nabled value networks. To move to e-nabled value networks, companies must learn to get beyond simply working with business partners; they must also fully integrate with them. We call this *value chain integration* (Figure 3.1).*

Figure 3.1   Snapshot Two: Value Chain Integration

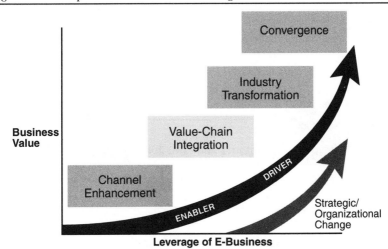

* See the Appendix for a detailed view of the e-nabled value chain.

WHAT IS VALUE CHAIN INTEGRATION?

Value chain integration is the joining of business processes and information systems among customers, companies, and suppliers and other business partners to seamlessly transact business. This requires the ability to electronically communicate through the entire relationship, from helping customers design or buy product, to communicating requirements to suppliers through production and delivery. For the first time in the history of business, a cost-effective technology—the Internet—is available to facilitate value chain integration. Figure 3.2 is a schematic view of value chain integration.

Imagine a customer placing an order and having it travel electronically to the offering company, as well as to all of its suppliers. The customer can request order status at any time, day or night, and has confidence that the information he or she receives will be correct.

Companies that have fully integrated value chains can provide customers a higher level of service, which confers on them a true competitive advantage. Companies are using the Internet to sell products, receive orders, and seamlessly flow order information directly to their manufacturing systems. Enabling the supply chain with e-business technology has helped companies achieve 20 percent or better reduction in supply chain costs.

Visibility of key information throughout the production process allows companies to move from a reactive to a proactive supply chain. According to Forrester Research, by 2001, more than 70 percent of

Figure 3.2   Schematic View of Value Chain Integration

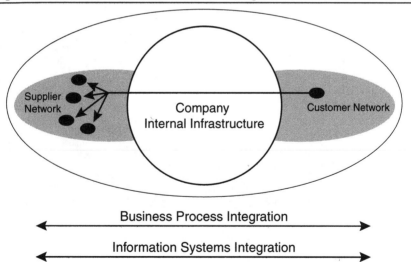

companies will share demand, inventory, and order status with supply chain partners. In the mid-to-late 1980s, using EDI, leading companies began working with suppliers and customers. Internet technology allows these companies, and all others, to share information more cost effectively, while maintaining more control over the physical product flow.

An E-Business Example: Checking a Customer Order

A customer order status check with a company that does not utilize e-business technology involves the following steps:

1. The customer calls the company for status information.
2. A customer service representative looks for the order status on the internal management system, which says the order is in process at a subcontractor facility.
3. The rep telephones the subcontractor facility.
4. The subcontractor records the information and says she will check it out and get back to the rep shortly.
5. After several hours, the subcontractor calls the rep and says the order was shipped via a third-party carrier two days earlier.
6. The rep asks the subcontractor to call the shipping company to inquire about the order delivery date.
7. The next day the subcontractor calls the rep with the shipping company information.
8. A day and a half after the original inquiry, the customer calls to complain.
9. Meanwhile, the shipping company delivers the order at the company's shipping dock.

Customers make these requests hundreds of thousands of times each day in manufacturing businesses around the world, explaining the reason for the thousands of expediters companies have engaged. With customers and business partners connected in an e-nabled value chain, resolving such a request takes only seconds. The e-nabled process eliminates all of the phone calls, running down the order, and dealing with inaccurate data in the system.

To optimize the value chain, business partners will integrate processes and systems to allow quick response to customer orders and unplanned changes. Order management must be able to integrate tightly with manufacturing and planning to share availability with customers. Manufacturing must be synchronized with procurement of key components to ensure schedule adherence. Product development must work

Figure 3.3   Impact of E-Business on Information and Physical Flows

E-Nabled Information Flow	Improved Physical Flow
• Real Time • Accurate • Built-in Controls • Link to Value Network Partner Planning Information	• Reduced Cycle Time • Quick Problem Resolution • Reduced Material-Related Delays • Reduced Change-Order Delays

closely with order management to offer customers "designed for 'E'" products that permit easy ordering over the Web. To simplify ordering, highly complex products may have to be redesigned to allow customers to use an on-line configurator as a means of selecting options and/or functionality, thereby eliminating the involvement of a customer service representative.

Retail, distribution, manufacturing, and key component suppliers need to work to a common forecast to avoid stockouts or excess inventory. Actively sharing critical information is the key for tightening these relationships across companies.

The underlying primary benefit of value chain integration is speed. Speed drives cost—cost of inventory, cost of labor, cost of planning, and cost of dissatisfied customers who have to wait for answers to their most basic questions.

E-business speeds information flow. Information flow speeds physical flow (Figure 3.3). In this way, e-business reduces physical flow queues, the delays associated with decision points and approvals, and design configuration errors. At the same time, it expedites order processing and status accuracy, component part and material ordering, project planning, and delivery and installation.

E-NABLED EXTRAPRISE

Historically, each company has formulated its business strategy around its internal value chain. Individual companies compete against one another to deliver value to customers. Many larger companies have ERP systems that serve as the underpinning of their operations.

But tomorrow, e-nabled companies will join together to deliver value to customers as part of an extraprise. An extraprise is an entity comprised of the company's customers, the company, and its suppliers. Business transacted through the extraprise will link business processes and information systems using a new business model. We call it the extraprise value network (EVN) (Figure 3.4).

Working within the extraprise, companies will develop business strategies with their business partners in mind. And a whole new breed of information systems will be created that integrate the processes and information flow among partners. In the not-too-distant future, we believe, third-party software suppliers will begin to bring to market modularized software solutions for extraprise operations, what we call extraprise resource planning (ERP II) systems.

At first, ERP II systems may look more like a patchwork of Web-enabled point solutions. But eventually, they will become packaged, integrated, and marketed by global business application companies like SAP, Oracle, and Microsoft. The real question is whether one of today's unknown e-business players will become one of tomorrow's ERP II leaders. The race is on.

The Internet provides the glue that makes all this happen. It provides a low-cost, user-friendly, and nonstructured format for efficient and effective intercompany communications. Now, with the technology in place to create extraprises, each company can formulate its business strategy with its business partners to optimize the EVN.

Companies must learn to share their business intelligence about customers and processes. In the extraprise world, a company may only keep secret the technologies and processes within its area of core competence. And, since the cost of moving digital data around is cheap, many EVN companies will outsource nonstrategic business processes. Additionally, working closely with suppliers in the extraprise, EVN companies will explore new ways of conducting business, such as negotiating the portion of

Figure 3.4   Extraprise Value Network (EVN)

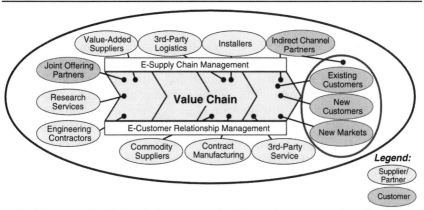

Real-time two-way flow of information from customers through companies to partners and suppliers.

total profit each participant in the value network will receive from the delivery of goods and services to customers.

The company at the center of the extraprise (the extraprise network master) is responsible for managing a network in which information is substituted for inventory at every step of the process of delivering value to customers. Today the network master is, in many instances, the large, powerful producing company that possesses the resources necessary to pull together suppliers and business partners and to instill the standards required to construct a value network. However, in the future, e-business technologies and applications and customer data mining and analysis may shift the role of the network master outward to the organization closest to the customer—the one that understands how the customer eats, drinks, and sleeps. The company that owns customer knowledge and loyalty will be in a position to place significant demands on companies that want to optimize their customer relationships. This fundamental power shift in traditional business models may dramatically change the way providing companies work and negotiate with distributors, resellers, and retailers in the chain. The challenge for the powerful producing companies is to implement strategies that employ e-business technologies to capture customer knowledge and loyalty before downstream intermediaries build a significant presence.

Barriers to Developing the E-nabled Extraprise

Although the benefits are clear, stumbling blocks to creating e-nabled value networks and extraprises also exist. For example, perfect information squeezes margins for all members of the network; information technology allows for nimble entrants to cannibalize the value chain through disintermediation of current players and/or creation of new intermediation opportunities; and a large information technology (IT) investment across the entire supply and demand chain is needed to create a seamless, tightly integrated network.

Moving from value chains to value networks requires that companies focus on communications, relationships, and knowledge. Executives need to recognize that they are living with a new set of realities. E-partners throughout the value network must at all times be completely honest with each other. Business is no longer about a set of bilateral relationships; rather it is about an integrated set of relationships. Finally, what a company knows creates leverage; it needs to know not only what it knows, but more importantly what it does not know—and how to acquire that knowledge.

Getting your customer to become a part of the extraprise value network requires a solid value proposition. Customers want on-time delivery, good price and quality, and overall value. Increasingly, they are also seeking personalized service offerings, ease of doing business with the seller, and a cost-versus-service proposition optimized in the customer's favor.

Selling companies are interested in reducing cycle time, finding least-cost methods, building product/service differentiation, growing shareholder value, and optimizing the cost-versus-service proposition in favor of the company.

The traditional value chain puts each binary relationship of customers and sellers in an adversarial situation, as each tries to optimize the cost-versus-service proposition in their own favor. A successful extraprise value network, however, requires a change in paradigm. All players in the network must work in a collaborative environment, based on a win-win-win strategy among customers, the company offering products and services, and the offering company's partners and suppliers.

Until the mid-1990s, this was only a dream. Corporate leaders and management consultants realized that to make this vision a reality, two major components would have to be put into place. One was a robust, realistic, technologically simple, and cost-justifiable information system. The other was trust among players in the value chain.

Several of our colleagues discussed trust issues in their 1995 book, *Beyond Business Process Reengineering: Toward the Holonic Enterprise* (John Wiley & Sons, 1995). But even where they could show examples of trusting relationships, where players in the value chain enhanced their relationships to form more tightly integrated networks of collaborators, the authors lamented the lack of appropriate IT to get the job done.

Today, that technology is available. The rush is on among software vendors to provide collaborative applications and capabilities. In this new business model, companies have to choose their business partners carefully. Technology, quality, cost, availability, and business practices are important to each business partner in the extraprise value network. Once partners enter into a business relationship, mutual success will depend on trust, information and knowledge sharing, communication, and co-owned performance measures.

Ironically, for most companies the first challenge in creating an extraprise value network is to prepare their own organizations. Most companies will have to change their processes, systems, organization, and culture to achieve rewards. Today, most companies' organizational models are built around functions that, most likely, have their own performance-based measures and reward systems. Unlike process-based organizations that value velocity, functional organizations tend to impede physical and information flows. While many companies have tried, few have succeeded in changing to a process flow orientation. To become effective components of an extraprise value network, companies will have to undergo this transformation (Figure 3.5).

Figure 3.5   Transforming from Functional to Process

Functional Organization Model

| Marketing | Development | Sales | Manufacturing | Procurement | Service |

Process Driven Value Network

Value-Added Suppliers
3rd-Party Logistics
Installers
Indirect Channel Partners
Joint Offering Partners
E-Supply Chain Management
Existing Customers
Research Services
Value Chain
New Customers
Engineering Contractors
E-Customer Relationship Management
New Markets
Commodity Suppliers
Contract Manufacturing
3rd-Party Service

A process-oriented operating model will align processes, information systems, and performance measures to seamlessly communicate customer order information throughout the value network.

Building an Extraprise Value Network

The EVN has two component pieces (Figure 3.6): the extraprise supply network, which encompasses the providing company and its suppliers and business partners in the supply chain, and the extraprise customer network, which encompasses the providing company, its business partners in the demand chain, and the customer/consumer.

Figure 3.6   Components of the EVN

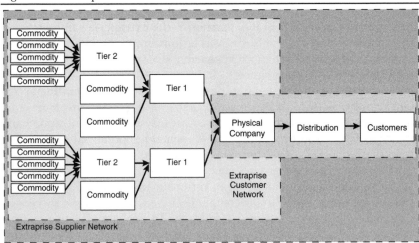

In the EVN, information flows from the collection of marketing research about a new product, through product development and the sales-order process to production and procurement, and on to business partners and suppliers, all within minutes.

The network master is the gateway for all partnering and information sharing. E-business tools enable collaborative planning, forecasting, and contractual transactions. Performance is measured based on value contributed to the network's relationship with the customer. And rewards are structured to maximize the performance of the entire extraprise value network.

The value proposition to the company establishing the extraprise value network is that the EVN provides the company ultimate agility and flexibility to adapt to changing market conditions. Through the EVN, the company possesses the processes and systems necessary to be able to shift activities to or from business partners (capacity-based outsourcing). Decisions to use partners can be made in real time, based on demand, capacity, cost, and responsiveness.

In moving to an EVN, a company can streamline product realization by focusing development efforts on collaborative design and by leveraging its marketing research and customer feedback, engineering, and business strategy in order to create leading-edge products and services.

For example, an engineered products company can recast itself as a service-based organization by e-nabling site engineers, project managers, installers, capacity planners, and others, thereby providing access to information and tools to provide fast, cost-effective, quality service, either directly or through business partners. Such a company will release designs and ship, deliver, and install parts on time. It will also enhance cash flow by performing project/order management and invoicing in an accurate and timely manner.

Additional benefits of an EVN include reduced inventories (since information serves as a substitute for inventory); reduced order-to-cash cycles (value network velocity); increased responsiveness and flexibility; more effective customer-focused business processes leading to reduced costs; and new markets and sales channels enabled by each value network's unique performance characteristics.

EXTRAPRISE SUPPLY NETWORK

Over the past 30 years, information systems have helped to rationalize the information in the production functions of a single business. Over time, these single business systems ultimately evolved into one integrated business information system.

In the 1970s, production companies implemented materials requirements planning (MRP) systems to rationalize and streamline production.

In the 1980s, these information systems matured into manufacturing resource planning (MRPII) systems. The early 1990s saw the growth of ERP systems.

ERP, the cornerstone of the supply network, focuses on managing an organization's internal resources, that is, its human, financial, and physical assets. Managing these enterprise assets not only includes tracking and recording them but also optimizing them across the enterprise. For example, ERP software can record the financial impact of a sale as well as the physical movement of product. Furthermore, it can optimize the movement of goods by sourcing from the appropriate warehouse and/or choosing the right method of transport.

Today's ERP software is mature and complex. It offers a large range of functions that an organization can apply and customize to support the business. ERP software's primary focus today is to support an organization's internal processes: It provides the "plumbing" that keeps most organizations functioning. Companies can purchase ERP software from such vendors as Oracle, SAP, Baan, JD Edwards, i2, and PeopleSoft among others, or build it internally. Most large companies use a mix of vendor-supplied and internally developed systems. Companies that implement ERP software expect their business processes to become more efficient and flexible and less expensive.

Because ERP systems are a key component of the value chain, they are well positioned to work in coordination with e-business technologies. In fact, the two technologies can supercharge each other. ERP software can accelerate e-business implementations by supplying the base data and underlying information needed by e-business applications. For example, e-business technology may be used to personalize a customer's experience as it relates to order tracking, while the ERP system works in the background supplying data about expected delivery dates, status of the manufacturing process, price, and other details of the customer's order.

Organizations implementing e-business technology must understand the role that ERP plays in the overall value chain and be confident in their ability to implement and maintain both technologies.* Companies that place too much emphasis on e-business run the risk of incurring high costs (to coordinate with ERP systems) and of not meeting customer needs (because of inaccurate data). Those that overemphasize ERP in today's market could disappoint customers (who now expect every business to be a dot.com company) and limit their future options.

Although a number of large ERP software companies have been slow to keep up with e-business technology, most are now getting up

---

* See Grant Norris, James R. Hurley, Kenneth M. Hartley, John R. Dunleavy, and John D. Balls, *E-Business and ERP: Transforming the Enterprise* (New York: John Wiley & Sons, 2000, forthcoming).

to speed quickly. They have deep pockets for investment, a history of successful innovation, and a huge installed base of customers looking for answers. The challenge for ERP vendors in the future will be to leverage e-business technologies that link companies with their business partners.

Now that we have entered the twenty-first century, corporate information systems are being extended to link upstream to suppliers' information systems and downstream into distributors' and customers' information systems using an electronic supply chain, often called an *e-supply chain*.

What Is an E-Supply Chain?

Members of an e-supply chain (Figure 3.7) use technology collaboratively to improve B2B processes in terms of speed, agility, real-time control, or customer satisfaction. The e-supply chain is the communications and operations backbone of the extraprise supply network that links suppliers and business partners together as one cohesive, producing entity.

E-supply chains span multiple enterprise boundaries, requiring companies to develop cooperative business processes. Unlike an EDI implementation, e-supply chains exhibit true collaborations among supply chain partners.

However, the biggest obstacle to attaining this state is not technology. It is the cultural, organizational, and people barriers at work in a collaborative environment. According to a leading industry research

Figure 3.7   Extraprise Supply Network

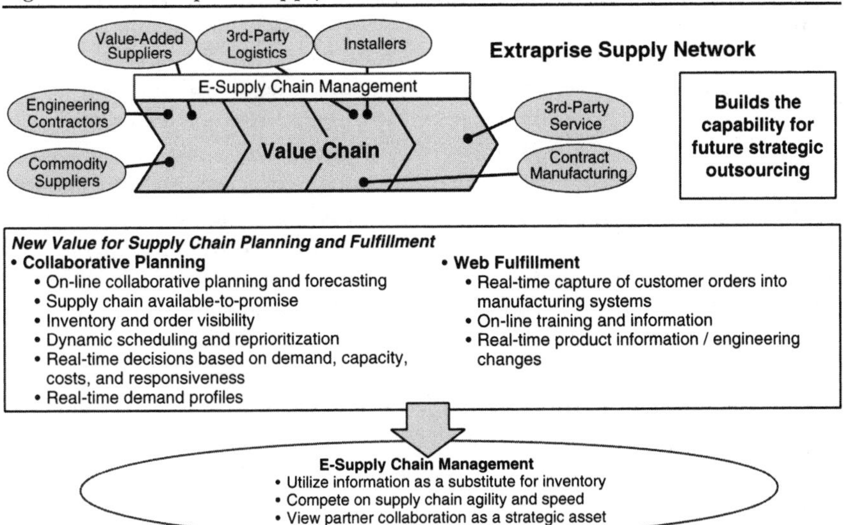

firm, 68 percent of Fortune 500 companies believe cultural resistance of staff and management is the biggest hurdle to implementing technology.

The e-supply chain has two key success factors. First, companies must view partner collaboration as a strategic asset. Tight integration and trust among partners generate supply and production speed and reduce inventory costs. Second, since information visibility across the partnership serves as a substitute for inventory, it must be managed as inventory is managed today, with strict policies and daily monitoring. Speed, cost, quality, and service are the measures of the success of an extraprise value chain. Consequently, companies must clearly define their value and demonstrate to partners their willingness to learn in this environment.

The e-supply chain consists of five components:

1. Supply chain replenishment
2. Collaborative planning
3. Collaborative product development
4. E-procurement
5. E-logistics.

Supply chain replenishment is an integration and distribution strategy to align real-time demand with suppliers and partners to improve customer responsiveness. In the future, customers will be able to order complex products and services on-line using configurators, thereby encouraging companies to design products, where possible, in standard models with limited customization. This, in turn, will drive companies to reevaluate their production operations to increase efficiencies and to implement streamlined processes.

Much as on-line orders eliminate intermediary steps in the traditional ordering process, production for many traditional companies can be optimized by their adopting e-nabled assembly-to-order or make-to-order strategies.

A traditional assembly-to-order strategy forecasts and builds subcomponents or subassemblies up to a point of customization. Then, when a customer order is received, the parent company only performs a final assembly operation using inventoried subassemblies designed to customer specifications and unique functionality requirements. With an e-nabled assembly-to-order strategy operating in an extraprise supply network, companies no longer need to store component and subassembly inventories on site. Rather, they utilize their relationships with network suppliers and partners to provide these items as needed. As an order is received for an assembly-to-order product, an immediate electronic notice is sent to all subcomponent and subassembly providers down the chain. Parts are then delivered directly to the assembly company production line at a predetermined point-of-use physical location in a time-phased fashion. Quality controls established in the extraprise value network relationship allow for parts to be received without inspection. Incoming parts are identified by the assembly company's numbering schema and, in many instances, by brand. Behind the scenes, data mining tracks customers' historical preferences, time and delivery statistics, and the performance of suppliers and partners. The latter is not to alienate partners but to provide information that enables the value network to plan and operate more effectively in the future.

A make-to-order production environment may have many of the same operating mechanics as the assembly-to-order strategy with one exception: Supplier and partner companies must react to an ever-changing real-time demand passed through the parent company from the customer. With assembly to order, production planning is engineered to hedge lead times. This is accomplished by building inventory of common subassemblies. Companies operating in a make-to-order environment, however, must design processes and systems that tightly integrate suppliers with the parent company to eliminate or streamline nonvalue, time-consuming activities.

E-business can also redefine how companies manage production and demand. As many companies expand operations to meet the demands of having a global presence, managing components, assemblies, and production requires a Herculean effort. Many company order management and production systems do not track global inventories. With the e-supply chain, companies will have total global visibility of inventories, production planning, and scheduling. (Optimization software is currently being developed and deployed in leading global companies.) With these e-business applications, companies will use the Internet to communicate in seconds to production facilities and warehouses around the world. Some of these newly developed applications integrate with existing ERP systems; monitor production, demand, and inventories; and make recommendations on sourcing, scheduling, and inventory management. This new level of readily available information will have a dramatic impact on decision making. The benefits for these organizations will be lower inventories, less duplication, streamlined processes, reduced operating costs, and, above all, a greater control of the business.

Collaborative planning focuses on operations, production, inventory, and distribution planning processes across multiple enterprises using e-business technology. The result is synchronized product flow, the ability to optimize resources at all locations over a larger capacity base, and drastic reduction in inventory. However, the key to success is in the trust and delivery reliability among the collaborative partners in the chain.

Key component, manufacturing, and distribution partners have real-time access to customer order information. The extraprise network master creates initial forecasts and all other partners provide changes to these forecasts. Forecasts are shared, so all parties are working to a schedule aligned to that common view.

Order and forecast performance is made globally visible through electronic links. As schedule, order, or product changes occur, immediate adjustments are made to all parties' schedules to account for the change. The resulting process allows the parties to work together to define the manufacturing and inventory policy most responsive to customer service requirements, changing customer needs, and supply chain costs.

The greatest value of e-business in a supply chain production environment is that it enables the complete integration of suppliers and partners, thereby improving the speed of shared information and optimizing throughput. The backbone driving this value is effective communication through a low cost medium—the Internet.

Collaborative product development involves the design and implementation of product development processes both internal and across multiple companies, and their impact on the organization as a whole. When properly implemented, e-nabling technologies can provide speed, accuracy, and real-time control to improve product launch success and time to market. The value of this component is in greater speed-to-market resulting in increased revenues or margins for new products. Also, reduced development costs can result from tight integration and streamlined communication channels.

From the perspective of internal product development, many large companies face the challenge of learning how to work in an integrated manner with staffs in multiple, dispersed locations. Seamlessly linking designers and engineers to share information and build on each other's ideas results in productivity rewards greater than any that could ever have been achieved in the past. For the design community, knowledge is critical to success. Transfer of that knowledge to other designers keeps a company creative and innovative. Imagine the benefits of managing product designs from one central location while carving up and distributing pieces of the design to coworkers around the world and knowing that the design, when completed, will be fully integrated. E-business processes and systems allow companies to achieve this capability today, and the Internet provides the low-cost medium for information transport. In fact, the challenge of implementing this type of solution is not technical. Rather, it involves the complexity of getting coworkers quickly and accurately to comprehend and complete their allocated work assignments.

Within large organizations communication is often limited to that which takes place between and among work groups. For years organization design specialists have tried to solve the problem of how to get different organizations within a large company to work together more effectively. The marketing, product development, and production organizational chain has been central to this issue. In most companies these organizations have different reporting structures, different goals and objectives, and different performance-based reward systems. Yet they depend on each other for success.

Ironically, in the e-business world the case for integrating these organizations is even more compelling. Take product design, for example. Product design receives input on customer needs and desires from the marketing organization and turns it into physical product. Product design then releases the drawings to production.

However, before a company migrates to an e-business sales channel, all three organizations must be perfectly aligned. Marketing and sales organizations must understand the limitations of product configurators and Web-selling capability and not offer more than Web service can practically and economically deliver. They must weigh the benefits of limiting orders to set models and structures against the potential loss of customers who feel their unique needs are not being met. Product development must collaborate with marketing to communicate about what can be realistically sold using product configurators. Together, marketing and product development must understand the impact their decisions have on production. Unlimited options with associated bills of materials will cause mayhem in production. With most companies, a linear relationship exists between the number of complex options offered to customers and the costs and delays associated with inventory and production.

Traditional products companies entertaining the idea of moving to a Web-selling channel should fully understand the organizational impacts of such a move. They need to ensure product development organizations collaborate with marketing, sales, and production. Optimally, marketing, sales, product development, and production should all be members of the team that redesigns end-to-end processes that measure success against one set of performance metrics.

E-business provides companies the opportunity to link electronically with their customers, business partners, and key value-added suppliers. The product development process of the future will be less dependent on internal designers for knowledge and innovation. Rather, it will leverage the benefits of the collective thought and expertise that exists in the extraprise value network. Relying on organizations outside the company will require new processes and systems, and, most important, changes in organizational culture.

Customers will require that providing companies be able to electronically interface with their product development and design systems. Requirements and specifications will be sent electronically to providing companies. In response, proposals will be sent to customers electronically. In requests for proposals (RFPs), customers will require that providing companies demonstrate their ability to conduct business electronically.

Collaborative product development processes will be structured to share information among customers, value-added suppliers, and providing companies on a daily basis. Scheduled formal design reviews will give way to interactive, real-time product development with built-in controls and links to project management configuration and reporting. On-line prototyping will be used to gather quick and high-quality customer feedback. Visible testing results and product design changes will accelerate resolution of the issues that drive up product development costs and extend development times.

The lines defining the collaborative design process will also change. Electronic information sharing will support all activities, from creating operating manuals to electronic imaging for advertising and promotional campaigns. Specifically, in the future, electronic designs will be imbedded into company Web sites so customers can not only see a picture of the product, but also be able to turn it to any angle, lift it up, and analyze it in their own physical environments.

E-procurement is the redesign and implementation of procurement processes among multiple enterprises using e-business technology. E-procurement applications significantly improve the procurement of production-related items. In years past, designers and engineers would slave over thick parts catalogues looking for the right functionality to incorporate into their designs. Even when they selected a part, the paper catalogue offered little help in determining whether it would fit or interface well with sister parts. With today's direct e-procurement applications, parts can be quickly identified with electronic search tools. In many cases, fit and interface capability is automated and software internal controls tell the inquirer about cautions and problems that may occur. The result is a better purchase price, lower processing costs, and higher product quality.

On-line catalogues can be used to eliminate redesign of components in product development. Visibility of available parts and their attributes enables quick decision processes. On-line purchase orders expedite the agreement; advanced shipping notifications and acknowledgments streamline the delivery processes.

E-logistics is the redesign and implementation of warehouse and transportation management processes using e-business. E-logistics will allow distribution to couple routing optimization with track-and-trace capability.

Distribution resource planning can be extended to retail units through vendor-managed inventory. Inventory levels can be woven into overall collaborative planning efforts by focusing supply chain efforts around customer service levels. Final assembly or packaging can be performed at the distribution center to reduce finished good inventory levels.

E-logistics can also provide electronic links to government agencies for import or export documentation, expediting the travel time and allowing companies to participate in a global supply chain. Other examples of on-line regulatory filings include hazardous materials and new drug applications.

In the future, companies will be able to outsource many of their e-logistics activities to traditional service companies such as FedEx, UPS, and a host of others using e-business technology to expand backward through the value chain. These companies will play an integral role in serving customers, providing companies, and suppliers in the extraprise supply network.

Information and physical product will flow seamlessly from node to node as all network members focus collectively on satisfying individual customer needs.

In one example of how the e-supply chain works, a customer logs onto a personalized Web page and customizes a product to his or her specific needs, based on on-line product information. The on-line product configurator provides a quoted price and availability for a variety of "what-if" product configurations.

Upon accepting the quote, the customer initiates the order with the push of a button. The configured order is directly linked into the manufacturing system. Real time availability to promise results from visibility of inventory based on collaborative forecasts and dynamic scheduling.

Strategic supply partners jointly agree to the order, based on predetermined rules. Once the order is received into the system, suppliers, distributors, and third-party logistics providers are notified of the order. Supplier replenishment policies are adjusted accordingly. Distribution and transportation are also scheduled.

Auctions, aggregators, or exchanges capture nonstrategic supplies. Inventory and order status can be accessed immediately by customers or partners across the Web through collaborative planning capability. E-logistics flows the order with track-and-trace capability, performs hazardous materials reporting, and handles import/export documentation through linkages to government agencies.

Extraprise Supply Network Partner Relationships

Communication with suppliers and business partners is a critical component of any company's ability to develop, produce, and deliver products or services. The e-nabled company communicates more effectively, and in real time, with its suppliers and business partners.

The first way this helps a company is simply by taking cost and time out of its purchasing activities. Effective communication also allows a company and its suppliers to jointly design products, collaborate on forecasts, and transmit production schedule changes in real time.

An open, fast communication mechanism is essential for companies entering into joint business activities. For example, a company with intensive shipping volumes must remain in constant communication with its logistics provider in order to make adjustments for shipping load requirements, as well as changes in pickup and deliver times.

Not all suppliers and business partners are alike. Some suppliers provide materials that are used in production; others provide indirect goods such as desks, computers, paper, and pens. One business partner may perform an outsourcing function. Another may provide a complementary product or service that the two companies package as a joint offering.

Because companies operate in different ways with different suppliers and partners, relationships with suppliers and partners need to be managed differently. E-business can play a role by providing different advantages, depending on the nature of the relationship.

Relationships with supply chain partners take three forms: commodity-based, strategic, and go-to-market.

Commodity-based relationships are those in which a supplier provides a commodity product. Commodity products can be either production (direct) or nonproduction (indirect) materials. An example of a commodity-based relationship is that between a supplier of office suppliers (indirect material) and a semiconductor manufacturer. Another is that between a supplier of silicon (direct material) and the same manufacturer. Decisions on purchasing commodity materials are usually made on the basis of cost and service, although availability and transport distance are sometimes also factors.

Strategic relationships involve the supply of noncommodity inputs to the production process. These relationships are critical to the company's day-to-day operations. An example is a supplier of circuit boards to a computer manufacturer. Another variation of the strategic relationship is one in which a company outsources a business process within the value chain, such as logistics or distribution operations. Decisions on purchasing strategic goods or services are made on the basis of five variables: fit to the need, quality, service, time (delivery reliability), and cost (price).

Go-to-market relationships involve an even higher level of intimacy. In these relationships, companies either jointly offer a product/service, or, with one another as part of a consortium, deliver a combination of products and services. For example, a business application outsourcer may partner with a telecommunications provider to empower e-nabled customers to access applications remotely. Another example would be a consortium of hospital suppliers jointly sponsoring a Web site where hospital purchasing agents can browse and purchase hospital supplies from one or more of the participating companies.

Commodity-Based Supplier Relationships

Relationships with suppliers of commodity products are often overlooked and ignored. All companies purchase indirect goods, which by definition are commodities. Many manufacturing companies also purchase commodity direct materials.

While cost is the primary determinant of where a company purchases commodities, other facts sometimes come into play. These include product availability, physical proximity, ease of the transaction, and customer service. Because of the number of substitutes for any given commodity, relationships with commodity suppliers have been treated with little respect. In such cases, short-term buying decisions historically have precedence over long-term relationships. Local sourcing is common and fast delivery is a given.

When analyzing historical and future relationships with suppliers of commodity products, it is helpful to differentiate between indirect procurement and the purchase of direct materials. There are differences in the way business is conducted with these two suppliers. Companies can also e-nable their purchasing of these categories in different ways to reduce costs.

Traditional Direct Good Commodity Relationship. Purchasing departments frequently give more attention to direct commodity products than to indirect materials. In addition to cost, purchasing decisions are largely made on the basis of delivery lead times; suppliers of commodity materials add value by providing product on time with minimal disruption to the production schedule.

Suppliers often ship material to manufacturers on consignment, allowing them to pay only for what they actually use. However, as with indirect material, if a commodity supplier raises price, customers are likely to look to another supplier for the same product.

Today, inefficient communication between a customer and its suppliers results in missed delivery windows and excess inventory. Forecasts and production schedule changes may not be transmitted to these suppliers with enough time for them to respond, resulting in delivery of the wrong quantity at the wrong time. Due to the "nervousness" in this scenario, suppliers and manufacturers both have a tendency to build inventory in anticipation of poor planning and communication breakdowns.

E-nabled Direct Good Commodity Relationship. E-business can make a tremendous difference to the scheduling and purchase of direct commodity materials. A company can use e-business technology to share forecasts, inventory information, and production schedules electronically with suppliers. In these collaborative relationships, information is substituted for inventory, while high-frequency preplanning maintains synchronization in response to variations in supply and demand.

Effective and efficient material management is achieved by close collaboration with key preferred suppliers. E-nabled vendor-managed inventory (VMI) is based on sharing demand forecasts, current inventory levels, and logistics information with suppliers. Using VMI, the preferred supplier can automatically determine inventory requirements, self-manage replenishment activities, and communicate shipment notices. Effective VMI results in the following benefits:

- ○ Cycle-time reduction. Sharing information e-nables the supplier to better plan and deliver to forecast demand.

- ○ Head count and cost reduction. Eliminating manual steps and reducing the cost of inventory offers significant savings.

- ○ Improved accuracy. Sharing timely and accurate information reduces the possibility of inaccurate and/or incomplete deliveries.

Strategic Supplier Relationships

Companies place a higher value on their relationships with suppliers that provide key components of the manufacturing process. For example, an automobile manufacturer must maintain a close relationship with the company that provides seating for its cars. Such suppliers are critical to the end product's success. Communication with strategic suppliers takes place at a number of points along the manufacturer's value chain.

Business partners that provide a critical product or service on an outsourcing basis are also important. Typically, an outsourcer is responsible for managing the operations within one or more areas of a company's value chain. An outsourcer may perform this function for several companies. For example, a personal computer manufacturer may outsource its logistics to a company that specializes in it; that company may also provide logistics for many other engineered-products manufacturers.

Traditional Strategic Component Supplier Relationship. Suppliers of strategic components require frequent interaction throughout the value chain. These suppliers are often involved in product development, as their components are key to the success of the overall product. A manufacturer and a supplier must agree on design specifications, delivery mechanisms, and component prices, before beginning production. Inefficiencies in communication between supplier and producer design teams can result in delayed product release dates.

The producer and supplier must also establish a mechanism for communicating forecasts and production schedules. Both parties must agree on schedules that are feasible for each company. In addition, changes to forecasts and schedules must be communicated in as close to real time as possible.

Often, inefficiencies in forecasting and scheduling result from lack of collaboration between manufacturers and suppliers. In addition, suppliers may not communicate schedule changes with enough lead time for suppliers to respond. As a result, suppliers build up inventory in anticipation of changes to the schedule. Obviously, this is wasteful.

E-nabled Strategic Component Supplier Relationship. With e-business, companies can revolutionize how they procure goods and how they interact with strategic-component supply partners. In order to achieve competitive advantage, products need to be brought to market as quickly as possible. In addition, product cost must be driven as low as possible. During the product development period, suppliers and manufacturers can use extranets or the Internet to perform concurrent engineering—the continuous, iterative process of design, matching materials and component capabilities with the original product brief.

This allows for faster turnaround times with suppliers during design. E-business communication with suppliers also lowers cost by coordinating and simplifying procedures to determine product specifications, develop designs, and execute design changes. Because strategic materials are integral to the success of the end product, much more time and effort are spent working with strategic-component suppliers than with commodity-good suppliers.

In addition, suppliers of strategic components are often specialized, making it difficult to locate another supplier in the event of a part shortage. Therefore, communication of inventory, pricing, forecasts, and production schedules occurs more frequently. The critical nature of these components requires companies to focus heavily on developing collaborative, long-term relationships.

E-business serves as a key to bridging gaps in communication in order to create a near real-time link with suppliers. E-nabled programs such as VMI and collaborative planning, forecasting, and replenishment (CPFR) help achieve success. In addition, long-term pricing agreements and blanket purchase orders may be communicated electronically between companies.

For example, Adaptec is a $1 billion global manufacturer that designs and builds hardware and software to speed up data transfer between computers, peripherals, and networks. The company sells its host adapters, network interface cards, storage controllers, and other systems to Dell, IBM, and other makers of computers and peripherals.

Adaptec is a semiconductor company that coordinates production of its integrated circuit products with several contract-manufacturing partners in Asia. This manufacturing approach eliminated the company's need to invest over $1 billion in fabrication facilities, but increased its need for seamless communication.

With operations in the United States, Asia, and Europe, and with key suppliers worldwide, Adaptec sought to increase procurement and decrease cycle times with the supply chain, reduce inventory supplies, improve end-of-quarter shipments, and increase customer satisfaction. After analyzing opportunities for cycle-time reduction in the supply chain, Adaptec identified areas where it could e-nable the supply chain to achieve these results.

The company designed an e-business solution using Extricity's Alliance software to interface with three key suppliers, TSMC in Taiwan, Seiko in Japan, and ASAT in Hong Kong.

Through this e-nabled link to its strategic-component suppliers, Adaptec reduced supply-chain cycle time by 50 percent and inventory by 25 percent and saved $10 million annually in inventory costs while, at the same time, increasing customer satisfaction. Adaptec predicts that its efforts will return 15 times the project cost over the first three years of operation.

Process Outsourcing Relationships

Outsourcing relationships are nothing new. For years, companies have worked with business partners to off-load noncore business processes within the supply chain. Traditional areas for outsourcing have included logistics/distribution, subassembly manufacture, and employee benefits. Companies have also established reseller relationships with business partners to eliminate the costs of selling directly to end customers.

Outsourcing relationships allow a company to achieve significant cost savings while focusing on the most value-added areas of its business. However, lags in communication and a paucity of information have made outsourcing difficult to manage. In some areas—certain ERP applications, for example—outsourcing has been significantly hindered by the lack of a reliable communication mechanism.

E-nabling the outsourcer relationship has radically changed the outsourcing landscape. The essential difference in the e-business era is that these activities have been greatly streamlined and can be offered at low cost and with better service.

In the past, parties to outsourcing relationships relied on paper communications or dedicated private networks to communicate information. Private lines were very costly.

In fact, many company proposals for process outsourcing were rejected because of the cost and complexity of moving enormous amounts of information to and from the outsourcer site. Because of this, outsourcing was hindered from growing to its full potential.

However, with the Internet as a means of communicating, outsourcing will become a way of business for many companies seeking to focus on their core competencies or in search of additional capacity. Companies are beginning to define new business models, using process and application outsourcing as a key.

Outsourcing has seven benefits:

1. Improved business performance and profitability, gains in competitive advantage in the market place, reduction in operating and administrative costs, and, therefore, increased shareholder value

2. Ability to concentrate on core, value-adding activities

3. Reduction in system/technology investment

4. Organizational flexibility; faster, cheaper competition- or opportunity-driven changes in organizational design

5. Reduced infrastructure investment (both people and equipment)

6. Reduced head count

7. Aggregation benefits not obtainable by the company in its own right, such as volume discounts for indirect procurement or larger content libraries for media companies.

EXTRAPRISE CUSTOMER NETWORK

The company that owns the customer relationship influences the extraprise value network. The company that owns the customer relationship positions the network's strategies, processes, and systems to support customer needs. The extraprise customer network includes the customer, indirect channel partners such as distributors and resellers/retailers, and the providing company (Figure 3.8).

Figure 3.8 Exraprise Customer Network

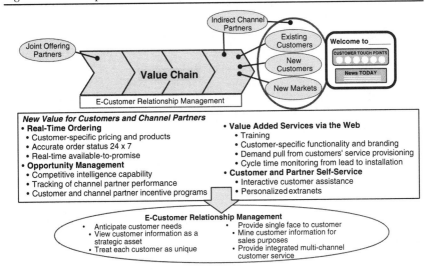

Managing the E-Customer Relationship

Customers are increasingly waking up to the fact that they can create wealth (new value) by working creatively with business partners to drive new forms of revenue, or by working with partners to reduce costs and the cycle times of products.

Customer delight is the key. Research has shown that only delighted customers are truly loyal customers. Customer delight provides a level of customer satisfaction that keeps customers coming back.

Providing a relationship that is merely "satisfying" as opposed to "delightful" leaves a company vulnerable to others seeking to take customers away because they are easier for the customer to do business with. Information technologies enable nimble players to create new value for customers. Creating new value for the customer is accomplished through strengthening customer relationships by integrating sales, configuration, planning, and design processes with customers through new and existing channels.

Most companies today are designed around processing transactions and getting product out the door. Depending on the industry, a customer's allegiance to a company is mostly based on the product or service itself, the price, or the level and quality of the customer service provided.

Typically, most companies have a set of preferred customers, but welcome orders from any qualified inquirer. Since the industrial revolution, companies have viewed orders as nothing more than demands for their products or services. As the source of revenue, customers are treated with respect to encourage repeat business.

Over the past several years, the advent of customer-information systems has allowed a company to capture data about customers in hopes of identifying unique buying attributes or trends. However, not until the application of the Web have businesses operating in a mass production world been able truly to personalize relationships with customers. This ability is launching new competition for businesses to achieve lifetime value (LTV) from current customers and to put strategic plans in place to go after LTV for new customers and in new markets.

In the world of e-business, companies have the opportunity to replicate the personal customer relationship that existed prior to mass markets. Companies are able to use knowledge of the customer to personalize customer service while continuing to sell standard products.

At the same time, ease of interface, fast fulfillment, reduced order-processing costs, and enhanced customer service are increasingly attracting new e-business-minded customers. These customers have the ability to change allegiances rapidly, and at little or no cost, and to search in real time for the greatest customer service possible. Customers determine for themselves the level of customer service required.

In the Web-enabled world, order-processing cost is greatly reduced, not only for the customer but especially for the seller. The customer uses the seller's information network and self-service technology to search for information, conduct the mechanics of the transaction, and check order status. This gives the customer much more control over the transaction and reduces the time necessary to make requests to a customer service representative over the telephone.

Real-Time Information: Key to the Relationship

The customer is now able to acquire a myriad of information 24 hours a day, 7 days a week, including in-process order status, real-time available-to-promise (whether the item is in stock), customer-specific pricing and products, and time-definite delivery dates. That same customer can also access integrated systems that share information, interactive customer assistance, and personalized customer systems that know about the individual customer's particular needs and desires.

Although at this time only cutting-edge companies have gone this far, the technology is available, and in the near future if a company does not have this capability, customers will find another company that does. A wise man once said, "Customers are funny, they don't always tell you they are dissatisfied with your service, they just go elsewhere." For survival, companies will implement customer relationship management (CRM) as a competitive differentiator.

Customer relationship management approaches use e-business technology to build stronger bonds with customers by anticipating customer needs, treating each customer as unique, and providing a single electronic face to customers across business silos. Internally, processes that do not support customer requirements and do not encourage a tight customer relationship need to be reengineered or eliminated. Companies have to examine their business processes to prepare for providing information to customers and others in the external world.

E-business profoundly accelerates the potential for customers to move and for companies to try to keep them. E-business decisions across the entire company need to be imbued with the customer perspective. Companies are beginning to view customer information as a strategic asset, utilizing data-warehousing and data-mining techniques to their advantage.

Customer relationship management means providing new value for customers by allowing customer-specific pricing and products, 24×7 availability of accurate order status, and real-time available-to-promise information. But it goes further than that.

As members of an EVN, customers receive via the Web such value-added services as product training, customer-specific functionality and branding, demand-pull of products from customer's service provisioning, and cycle-time monitoring from lead to installation. Customers are also eligible for special incentive programs.

This may mean, for instance, that smaller companies can join in indirect procurement plans at the network master's negotiated discounts through the network master's indirect procurement Web system. It may mean that customers that are small companies can tie into the larger network master's third-party benefits administration program, travel program, or other corporate value-added programs.

Customer relationship management means anticipating customers' needs, viewing customer information as a strategic asset for both parties, and treating each customer as a unique entity with unique needs and desires. It also means providing a single corporate face to the customer, wherever the customer may touch it, through different business units, regional offices, or operational organizations within the company. Customers expect integrated, seamless, multichannel customer service. Such service should be transparent to the customer whether the service is being provided by the network master or by a third-party provider.

Customers who leverage e-business dramatically change their view of the business. Today, most customers have to talk to an account representative or navigate a seemingly endless spiral of voice recognition systems to get product or service information or status regarding an order. In the e-nabled company, information systems are customer-centric—engineered around customer information touch points.

Customers using such systems see a whole new face of business. In an effort to delight customers and build loyalty, companies must provide customers with simplified, effortless ordering and equally effortless customer service. Personalized Web pages, loaded with information-based value and targeted to enhancing the business-to-business customer's experience, will soon become commonplace.

With these new technologies in hand, companies are beginning to fight for customer relationships by providing a higher level of information-based services. In the future, business customers with a problem or inquiry will have access to a Web-based customer service system unlike anything available today.

Features of Web-Based Customer Relationship Management

Web-based customer relationship management is in its infancy today. Current systems provide capability for one-to-one marketing and rudimentary streamed video and sound but are still mostly push marketing with transaction processing.

Tomorrow's business-to-business customer experience will be far more exciting, providing more personalized value-added information than the customer would normally think to ask for, and providing links to other related sites that compliment the customer's interest and buying experience. To facilitate this experience, over the next few years, significant advances in streamed video and digital audio will appear.

With one click on a company's extranet, customers will be able to access all information pertinent to their dealings with that company. In the future, once a customer accesses a company's customer management home page and enters an identification number, the individual will see a series of buttons. These buttons act as a conduit for touch points between the customer and the business.

Touch points between the customer and the extraprise network master may include any or all of the following:

○ General product information

○ Product marketing information

○ Ordering, placement, price quote, configuration, and track status

○ Customer care/service, including technical support, general inquiries, frequently asked questions (FAQs), and problem solvers

○ Project/order administration, including invoicing and billing history, account summary, and unresolved issues

○ Communications, including events, planned training, and promotions/incentive programs

○ Collaborative design workroom, including product simulation, product specification, and joint-design work space

○ Collaborative demand planning workroom, including demand forecasts.

On the front end, these buttons provide the customer an easy-to-use gateway to business information through a personalized channel that is easy to navigate and enjoyable to operate. On the back end, once the customer's identification is matched, data will be pulled from various information systems and set up against the customer's unique set of buttons. The system will immediately identify unique attributes about the customer and/or the customer's business, such as previous purchases, buying thresholds, and what problems the customer has encountered in the past.

Many of the larger utilities have moved to this level of customer service already, albeit as part of their customer service call center rather than as a self-service Web feature. If a customer calls one particular natural gas utility in the Mid-Atlantic region of the United States inquiring about usage or service, the customer service representative's system

ONE OF THE WORLD'S LARGEST HIGH-TECH COMPANIES

A leading high-tech company wished to surpass a competitor that was already selling more than $1 billion per year via the Internet. They designed and built a comprehensive global Internet program, launching several core applications within months, and implemented an Internet-based network of business partners. The company established distribution channels in 27 countries, achieving savings of $3 million per year on knowledge management and $10 million per year on improved forecasts. Customers were offered direct access to consumer data, and the company created 175 custom Internet sites for major accounts. Retail kiosks were installed in 5,000 locations at 10 major retailers, achieving $20 million per month in configure-to-order purchases. And an early run-up in stock performance against the company's major competitor resulted from e-business supply chain improvements.

reads the caller ID and pulls up the customer's account history within seconds of the call. Additionally, the system has a record of all gas appliances and a usage history.

For a customer wanting to know why his or her gas bill is so high in the summer when the gas furnace is not in use, the customer service representative can say that the customer also has a gas water heater that is used all year round. In the past, this inquiry would have triggered costly and time-consuming research. It may have even led to a service call to check the pipeline or customer equipment.

This business-to-consumer example provides a simple illustration of the potential of a company's use of customer information and the Web to provide information-based value that attracts and retains customers and lowers costs. Companies are only beginning to realize the power of information-based value for customers.

4

Snapshot Two: Effects of Value Chain Integration on Organizations, People, Processes, and Technology

As a company works to integrate its business operations with those of its supply chain and demand chain partners, a host of effects occur regarding organizations and people, business processes, and information systems and technology. Figure 4.1 illustrates the intensity of those effects across five business variables.

Figure 4.1   Effects of E-Business: Value Chain Integration

	High	Moderate	Low
Customers and Markets			✓
Products and Services			✓
Organizations and People		✓	
Business Processes		✓	
Information Systems/ Technology		✓	

EFFECTS ON ORGANIZATIONS

In this second snapshot of the e-business panorama, the impact on the company's organization is extended to include its customers and demand chain partners on the front end and its supply chain partners on the back end. Customers and suppliers become integrated into the company's change process.

Where there may have been a history of mistrust of suppliers, the integration of supply chain partners forces creation of a trusting relationship. Where there may have been an inclination to guess about customer demand or dictate how needs would be met, the integration of demand chain partners forces creation of a relationship where the company truly listens to the marketplace.

The win-win-win outcome associated with successful value chain integration requires the consensus of value chain partners. This is a key concept. Value chain partners must understand that the guiding principle behind optimizing an extraprise network involves targeting improvements that provide a win for suppliers, a win for producers, and a win for the customer.

Integration of customers and suppliers into the company's e-business environment changes measures of success. For example, selling a particular quantity may no longer be the yardstick. Instead, increasing a share of business with key customers or signing liaison agreements or exclusive contracts may be a better focus.

An effective chief executive officer (CEO) must be able to envision the multiple future states that are possible given the options with which he or she has to work within the extraprise. He or she must be convinced that value chain optimization will result in the best mix of future sales for the company. Each CEO must then set in motion a set of common goals and measurements of personal activity that will ensure attainment of long-term benefits. Rewards and compensation should be linked to performance of key individuals and organizations that embrace working in the kind of open culture required for an effective enterprise value network.

EFFECTS ON PEOPLE

Individual behaviors must shift to accommodate supply chain and demand chain partners, especially if, in the past, these new players have been perceived as incidental or peripheral to the company's business. Metrics linked to new behaviors at each level, including the job level, must support the cultural shift. True collaboration will come only when the win-win-win concept is transmitted down to the individual worker and his or her incentive structure.

Establishing appropriate metrics within this snapshot for how people and work groups must deal with business partners lays the groundwork for the more aggressive and increasingly externally focused behaviors that take place in the third and fourth snapshots.

Managing the communication efforts and keeping individuals focused on their roles is critical. In their eagerness to carve out a niche in e-business, some employees may be unable to focus on maintaining the parallel systems that must support non-e-nabled business. Employees who continue this work are important and should not be treated like outsiders. The company has an obligation to assist them in developing a skill set that will keep them working when the entire business becomes e-nabled.

Integration with supply chain and demand chain partners includes opening communications among and sharing previously unshared information with new players. Individuals can quickly be overwhelmed by a high volume of data and information, some of which requires rapid analysis and decisions. They require new tools and skills to cope effectively with this influx of information.

In addition, new processes for collecting information, creating priorities, sharing information, and giving feedback require new cultural norms and skills at the individual level and across the value chain. Successful execution in this snapshot requires an understanding that people are a critical element in the value chain. As such, they must be involved in efforts to optimize extraprise network performance and must share tangibly in the benefits.

EFFECTS ON PROCESSES

A value chain has two distinct flows: the physical flow of material and the information flow. E-business directly improves the information flow and the creation of networked communication.

Historically, information flows have been physical, that is, paper based. Telephones, fax machines, and computers enabled combined physical and electronic information flows. Traditionally, each value chain participant has managed its own processes and the computer applications that supported those processes.

Within such a structure, a disconnected value chain environment is the result, where inefficient data transport mechanisms bridge the gap between value chain participants. Sometimes intermediaries bridge this gap, adding cost, time, and complexity.

In the value chain integration snapshot, e-business begins to play a primary role in determining the nature of a company's relations with other value chain participants. Here, the opportunity exists for a network of companies to more rapidly exchange information and for previously segmented processes to come together in a seamless information flow.

However, being at the center of such a value network—being the network master—necessitates a dramatic change in a company's business model—specifically, in the way a company thinks about its business processes.

A value network master no longer thinks of its processes as internal. Such companies must shift their focus and think of their business processes as spanning supply chain and demand chain partners all the way to the customer. In other words, such companies must take a holistic view of the business processes that stretch beyond their organizations and individual business processes and make up the core business of the newly created extraprise.

In the extraprise value network, well-defined processes are necessary to efficient operations. Each of the companies within the network must accurately execute its part of any business process in order for the process to work well. In a collaborative way, partners must ensure that their own processes do not deoptimize the extraprise for self-benefit at the expense of extraprise partners.

This collaboration requires rethinking processes in a way that provides a win-win-win outcome among suppliers, companies, and customers, an outcome where customer focus takes priority for strategic reasons. Value chain integration requires companies to reengineer their current working relationships. Often these relationships are based on the use of old technology. Full value, even from reengineered relationships can not be derived until the technology is also upgraded.

In other instances, companies must look to interact with new business partners to create value. Such practices require companies to engineer new processes in conjunction with their business partners. These changes are significant, and, to be successful, require strong leadership and careful planning and cooperation among companies.

Companies that can successfully move to integrated processes within the value chain stand to gain significant presence in the marketplace. Other companies will look to them for leadership because of their outstanding relationships with business partners and efficient operating models.

Deciding which current supply chain and demand chain partners should be targeted for inclusion in the extraprise and which should be excluded will involve tough decisions. However, in the long run, companies that partner fairly and take the win-win-win idea as their guiding principle, will attain e-business leadership.

Reengineering Existing Processes

Companies are waking up to the fact that the Web is an ideal platform for building integrated, highly efficient relationships with customers, as well as with supply-side and demand-side partners. While there are obstacles to replacing traditional supply chains with new, intercompany processes and Web-based systems, the potential benefits are huge. They include lower overhead costs, quicker time to market, lower cost of goods, and ultimately improved customer satisfaction.

Existing company processes have rarely been engineered or reengineered. Most often, they have evolved. Even those companies that have made great strides in reengineering their processes have come up against organizational and technological walls that prevent their reaching optimal process performance. E-business standards are breaking down the technological walls with a fervor.

Accepting the strategic necessity of integrating value chain activities results in extraprise-wide reengineering initiatives that will no doubt uncover company-specific processes that have suboptimized the value chain. A fundamental commitment to the principle of win-win-win as a means for gaining long-term strategic advantage will be required to convince partners to discard process steps designed for short-term, self-serving personal advantage.

Each individual process in the value chain contains within it e-business opportunities. Streamlining the intercompany exchanges among value chain participants ensures optimum performance in these key processes. Indeed, the competitive model is shifting from competing companies to competing value chains. It is becoming increasingly urgent for companies to build or join the extraprise that will effectively compete in the evolving e-business world.

In many cases, companies already work closely with their business partners. For example, many manufacturers seek supplier input in joint product development initiatives. These same companies also exchange sales forecasts and product schedules with suppliers to promote on-time delivery of component parts, thereby increasing efficiency in the supply chain.

In the past, the linkages among companies were disconnected. They were managed using technology like EDI batches and e-mail. Companies would think of a process as internal. When a process was completed, the company would pass the results "over the wall" to the next entity in the value chain. With e-business, companies have the ability to reorganize these relationships and focus on reducing the friction in communication and data transfer.

Because communication in the e-business world is faster and more flexible, companies have the opportunity to sit down with their business partners and redesign business processes across companies to realize joint gains. However, this opportunity is not easy to seize.

One way to capture it is to form process teams comprised of members from the value network master and its value network partners. Team members should include individuals who have a stake in the overall process. The teams should discuss how communication among the entities is currently performed, and how it could be performed differently using e-business.

Ideas for process redesign should come from all team members and focus on the benefits to be gained from streamlining. Whether the goal is cost savings or revenue generation, a compelling incentive to participate should be provided. The process steps must be clearly defined and all should agree on the types of information to be shared.

Implementation of the improved processes should be managed jointly, with deadlines set for milestones. After implementation, the team should continue meeting to discuss process improvements. By using a structured (modular) approach, companies will be able to implement interenterprise process improvements in other areas. The great speed at which this enables the development of digital value networks confers a key competitive advantage, allowing companies to attain positions as value network master.

Many companies are using e-business to streamline different elements of the value chain. For example, some manufacturers give supply chain and demand chain partners direct access to their manufacturing systems so that they can track inventory, engineering changes, shipment status, and other critical factors in near-real time. Others have gone to supplier-managed inventory and invoiceless payment upon electronic receipt.

In addition, major opportunities exist to apply e-business to supply chain activities such as planning, purchasing, and logistics. By sharing up-to-the-minute demand forecasts via extranets, supply chain partners can dramatically cut inventories and improve in-stock performance. In theory, a company (an airline, for example) can extend its capability to dynamically plan for capacity and evolve into an entire extraprise through use of real-time collaborative optimization models that increase value chain returns.

On the purchasing side, many buyers and sellers are able to cut administrative costs by implementing on-line catalogues and order management systems. Especially in the area of indirect procurement, e-business technology can be leveraged to attack costs that in many organizations equal 30 percent of company revenues. Often, these functions are tailored for the company's business partners, but the capability to extend purchasing to all extraprise members is an opportunity ready and waiting to happen.

Engineering New Processes

E-business affords a company the opportunity to execute new strategies that create value. A progressive e-business-based strategy must be accompanied by new business processes that reach out to business partners. Examples of this can already be found in companies that have pursued e-business-enabled disintermediation, reintermediation, and outsourcing strategies because they have dramatically changed existing business processes.

The aggregate effect of individual company efforts to execute these strategies is an improvement in value chain efficiency. A coordinated effort that spans extraprise membership has the potential to optimize the benefits for those who disintermediate, reintermediate, and outsource, as well as for value chain customers.

Companies that have cut out the intermediaries in their demand chains by selling directly to consumers have had to develop processes to manage their new relationships with end customers. These include new approaches to sales, distribution, logistics, and customer service. The total cost of these moves must be considered and collaboration with partners will help companies to avoid false starts.

Companies that have found success through reintermediation have created innovative processes to support their strategies. For example, content and information aggregators such as eBay and other e-auctions have created business models around bringing together buyers and sellers who may not have previously known one another to efficiently conduct business. These new, creative models require new, engineered business processes that go beyond a company's walls. The successful reintermediator recognizes the value proposition to targeted value chain participants and is a true driver of e-business evolution in specific markets.

Companies that outsource have determined that they can deliver more value by focusing on core competencies and leveraging outsourcers to achieve efficiencies in noncore parts of the value chain. By outsourcing such functions as logistics/distribution and information systems, these companies have improved performance in key areas, while reducing operating and administrative costs.

The fundamental decision to outsource is based on recognition of a company's lack of ability to extract value efficiently from a process. Would-be outsourcers need to understand how to leverage e-business technology across several clients. The goal is to extract value efficiently from aggregated operations where independent executions have been unsuccessful.

However, the decision to outsource is not easily made. To ensure that outsourced processes are performed accurately, a company must develop strong communication protocols and a reliable network infrastructure with its outsourcer. In addition, employees who previously performed outsourced activities must be reassigned to other areas, allowed to manage the outsourcing relationships, or released. A solid collaborative network will provide opportunities for the transfer of human resources to support outsourced functions and the reassignment of others to new areas of value-added activity.

The method for building and executing value chain integration processes is not much different than that described for reengineering channel enhancement business processes. The major difference involves relationships. Often relationships with new business partners must be established to ensure cooperation among all of the companies involved. As with any new business relationship, each company must earn the trust of its new business partners and provide a strong strategy for creating value. A company's business partners should all share in the value network's success and possess a sincere commitment to the win-win-win proposition.

EFFECTS ON INFORMATION SYSTEMS AND TECHNOLOGY

With value chain integration, companies must project their thinking about technology issues beyond the enterprise. Within this snapshot, the company's linkage to its supply and demand chain partners cannot be successful without a careful consideration of the information systems and technology components that enable these linkages.

This is not to say that the information systems and technology discussed in Chapter 1 are no longer relevant. On the contrary, a company in this snapshot must have successfully met the pertinent technology challenges of the channel enhancement snapshot in order to compete successfully.

Enterprise Value Network Integration

With e-business, more applications touch customers and supply chain and demand chain partners directly than ever before. As a result, the need to adjust the supply chain rapidly, plan collaboratively, schedule across companies, and personalize customer treatment, all drive tighter linkages among various applications used by each company in the enterprise value network. The challenge, therefore, is for companies to understand how best to accomplish the appropriate degree of integration.

For example, a company must use applications from another company's work over a network, even though the other company's application may be based on a different technology and work with different processes and different data models. Applications that are standards compatible and scalable will win out in most instances, but where there are custom or nonstandard applications, a whole suite of facilitating applications is developing.

One approach to this dilemma is to use vendor-supplied tool kits known as enterprise application integration (EAI) middleware to provide the business logic, as well as the data transfer aspects of application integration. Middleware connects two applications and passes information between them.

EAI middleware vendors supply prebuilt adapters or connectors that can be used to link the functionality of leading ERP package applications from such vendors as SAP or PeopleSoft. The middleware vendors also supply tools to build connectors for custom-developed software.

Some EAI middleware packages emphasize integration among business processes rather than just among information systems. These packages provide business process interfaces for typical functions such as order entry so that a new order placed via an e-commerce Web site can contact and update all the applications from various companies involved in the order entry process.

Middleware provides a big benefit to a company by allowing it to connect its e-business systems to other companies' applications. This allows the company to establish business processes that extend beyond the enterprise to supply chain and demand chain partners and to customers in order to create a fully functional extraprise.

To make these external linkages work successfully, communication and trust among partners is essential. In addition, the companies involved must ensure data integrity and consistency in order that employees have faith in intercompany processes.

eXtensible Markup Language

Another emerging facilitator for intercompany communications is the meta language XML, which is designed to provide structure to semi-structured or unstructured data. Thus XML can be used to exchange data between different application systems, both inside and outside a company's information system boundaries. The advantage for e-business is that XML allows companies to exchange information in a more free-form manner.

For e-business, this means many more possibilities than before for organizations to partner and exchange data. If information systems are XML-compliant, data can be exchanged directly, even between heterogeneous information systems. Even so, XML describes the structure of the data rather than its semantics. Partners must agree on the meaning of the data they are exchanging, and a number of initiatives are underway to create internationally accepted standard definition sets. In any event, XML will play a crucial role in business-to-business communication and collaboration.

By reaching out to customers, supply chain partners, and demand chain partners, a company can position itself as a true network master that controls the flow of information among entities. In addition, a company can achieve significant cost savings and drive revenue growth.

Network Security and Reliability Issues in Value Chain Integration

The great volumes and high value of data crossing enterprise boundaries necessitates heightened security measures. The importance of firewalls and virus protection is magnified. Secure extranets that include virtual private networks (VPNs) and private lines are commonplace in companies that engage in value chain integration.

With so much information flowing between companies, there is a great need for high bandwidth and network reliability. (Bandwidth refers to the volume of data that can be transferred over a network connection within a certain time period.) High bandwidth allows a company to exchange large volumes of information in a relatively short period of time.

To share large volumes of information in near real time, a company must have a dependable network. Network disruptions can mean missed opportunities for business partners and can cause customers to lose faith in the company. Active, reliable networks allow a company to conduct business efficiently and to react immediately to sudden changes in the business environment.

5

Snapshot Three:
Industry Transformation

Companies can use e-business to enhance performance by creating new sales and customer service channels or by making indirect procurement more efficient. These channel enhancement strategies characterize the first snapshot of the e-business landscape. Companies may also employ value chain integration strategies (snapshot two) to harness this new technology in building an enterprise value network that links customers and suppliers together.

But, as indicated by the third snapshot of the e-business panorama—industry transformation (Figure 5.1)—e-business has the capacity to change both company and industry business models. Unfortunately, most bricks-and-mortar company executives have little or no idea of the size of the threat facing them or of the potential for their companies to create new wealth. Should they be worried? Yes! Should the impact of e-business be on the boardroom agendas of most companies today? Absolutely!

E-business has the potential to change everything about business in the future. As companies find new ways to use the Internet for strategic decision making, they will erase the lines between industries, face tough competition from new types of intermediaries, and uncover enormous opportunities to penetrate new markets.

To be sure, some of the recent Internet-only entrants (the so-called pure plays) are basing their entire existence on one or more of the strategies undertaken in the industry transformation snapshot. Many of these start-ups are betting everything on the presumption that in the future, customers will use the Internet as a channel to buy everything from groceries to big-ticket items. And in the business world, start-ups are creating community relationships by aggregating offerings from multiple companies to provide one-stop shops for business customers and consumers alike. The theory is based on the premise that if one

Figure 5.1   Snapshot Three: Industry Transformation

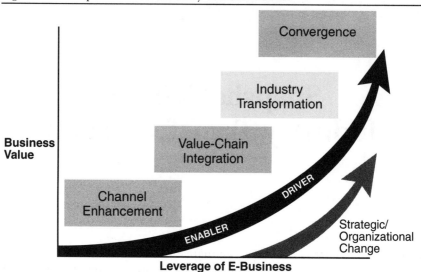

source can provide all customer needs through an easy-to-use Web site, customers will have no reason to go elsewhere.

But what about the traditional organizations that built their wealth through means other than the Internet? How should they react to the momentum of pure-play Internet providers? Do they risk losing their customer base? What will the digital age mean to these companies? Among traditional companies, e-business has the potential to change everything including strategy, process, structures, systems, people, and culture.

For the first time in recent history, a new technology provides the potential for some companies to leapfrog others by reinventing themselves for the future. The key word is "potential." The truly creative and fast-moving companies will prosper at the expense of complacency and indecision in boardrooms of others. These new business strategies and models will fully leverage e-business to transform industries and create and expand markets.

WHAT IS INDUSTRY TRANSFORMATION?

In an industry transformation, business models are reconfigured to take advantage of the full power of new technology—in this case the Internet. Imagine how most executives would feel waking up tomorrow and reading in the *Wall Street Journal* that a new, direct competitor with a positive, hip brand was offering similar products more quickly and at less cost. Or imagine one of the same executives watching television one evening, seeing a commercial for a new company, and noticing the word Internet appearing among bright colors and fast-moving images. Intrigued, she reaches for the remote to turn up the volume and discovers that this ad is for a new company offering new services bundled with her company's products and targeted at her company's customers. And then, the grim realization: This new player is disintermediating her company by positioning itself between the company and its customers.

The Internet can be an executive's best friend or, as in the foregoing scenario, worst enemy. Executives who take control of this new technology can lead their organizations into an era of incredible growth and wealth. However, those who become complacent risk rapidly losing the competitive edge in this brave new world.

The Internet is a technology-based communication mechanism that, through speed, collaboration, and personalization, allows people and businesses to communicate more effectively. Its most powerful effect is to transform relationships within and between companies. In the future, this capability will be the heart of frame-breaking business models.

Working with partners that a company relies on to provide a product or service has always caused executives headaches. They fear that which they cannot control. Many companies shy away from outsourcing or developing long-term relationships with suppliers and other business partners. The Internet provides the technology to enhance communication and collaboration with suppliers, distribution partners, and even customers in a way that makes them an extension of the company.

Customers are on most executives' minds. Without customers, a business cannot exist. Traditionally, customers have been grouped into buckets of like attributes called *market segments*. The Internet provides a mechanism for going well beyond market segments to personalized customer requirements. With properly structured data warehouses and data mining capability, companies can target customers and their buying needs with a new level of detail.

The proper strategic alignment and planning of speed, collaboration, and personalization distinguish the e-business leaders from the followers. Industry transformation is determined by how companies and industries change once the leaders fully grasp and assertively take advantage of the opportunities provided by the new business models.

In order to be competitive in the e-business world, companies will have to make key decisions about selling their products and services through an e-business channel; creating an extraprise by linking their internal organization with supply- and demand-side partners and customers; defining how to position themselves in light of new infomediaries such as facilitators and aggregators; and utilizing customer information as a strategic asset.

In the next five years, executives will be forced to understand this new technology and its potential. In the new business landscape, executives will orient their business models to either end of the e-business spectrum. Companies must decide if they want their businesses to remain companies that provide physical goods and services or to become companies that push this technology to the edge and evolve into e-business-based knowledge companies.

WILL A COMPANY BE A PHYSCO OR A KNOWCO?

Much of twentieth-century business was predicated on adding value to component parts in order to develop marketplace offers. The foundation for these offers usually requires the movement of physical parts around the factory floor, purchasing capital equipment, and managing sizable inventories of raw materials, work-in-process, and finished goods.

Today, not much has changed, although many companies have made significant strides in taking time and non-value-adding steps out of their manufacturing process through techniques such as just-in-time. We call companies operating in this traditional business model physical companies, or "physcos" for short.

A physco has a well-established base in physical assets, for example, a printed circuit board facility, machine shop, or food processing plant. Indeed, the best physcos have mastered value at the process level. They are able to offer the marketplace a product that they can produce better than, or as good as, any other company in their industry.

Over the past few years, a new breed of companies that focus their core competencies on knowledge of a product or service has emerged. We call these companies "knowcos." By using information as a strategic weapon, knowcos break the traditional business mold. Typically, a knowco designs its strategic assets around a very specific capability and works with business partners to fill in the gaps.

Probably the best example of a knowco is Cisco Systems. Riding the Internet, Cisco created an organization focused on data networking products and services. The company keeps close control over its unique properties—product design, product management, and marketing. These core competencies are knowledge based. Cisco outsources much of its production. The company realizes that manufacturing its product, albeit important, does not differentiate it in the marketplace and that others can perform this activity with a high level of quality and efficiency.

In order for a knowco to be successful, it must have one other core competency: the designed-in capability to operate in an extraprise that leverages strategic relationships to build and distribute its products. We call this capability *value network management.*

To optimize the value network, knowcos and physcos have to adapt working standards for software applications, technologies, and communications. Figure 5.2 provides examples of the many applications and

Figure 5.2   Applications and E-nabling Technologies Available to Knowcos
and Physcos in an EVN

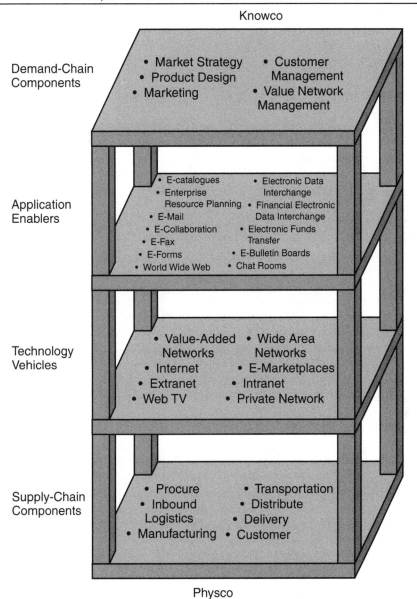

e-nabling technologies available for knowcos and physcos operating in an extraprise value network.

The future business landscape will include both physcos and know-cos. Whether there will be many physcos providing goods for each knowco, or only a few mega-physcos providing goods for myriad tiny knowcos is an open question. What is known is that while physcos will focus on building best-in-class processes in order to serve as value-network partners, knowcos will build and manage brands, establish a strong value network team, and own customer/consumer relationships.

In this new business model, the company that owns the customer/consumer relationship will control the value network. Knowcos are positioned to do just that.

FROM E-SUPPLY CHAIN TO VALUE NETWORK MANAGEMENT

The e-supply chain links supply- and demand-side partners and customers with a company to give that company the ability to flow transaction processes from customers through to suppliers. Knowcos tend to outsource most of the noncore components of their business and focus on core competencies that provide them strategic advantage. Value network management is the process of effectively deciding what to outsource, when to outsource, and for how long to outsource in a constraint-based, real-time environment based on fluctuating demand. For example, a knowco may become a virtual company by managing the brand and leveraging strategic partners to operate business processes. Knowcos that transform this capability into a core competency will create a strategic differentiator in the marketplace of the future.

Successful companies will be able quickly to adapt to changing demand and market conditions. In essence, a company that succeeds at value network management will have infinite capacity to produce highest quality, lowest cost products. In short, value network management lays the foundation for making the transition from physco to knowco.

Theoretically, companies that master value network management will also be able to raise all of their business processes to best-in-class. These companies will invest in *their* core competencies to strengthen their market differentiation and will buy noncore competency processes from external partners (Figure 5.3).

From the point of view of strategic analysis, most businesses' core competencies carve out their niche in the marketplace and define what they do. If one looks at the steps in a value chain for a typical product-oriented company, one finds that most have only a few core competencies. However, in order for a company to produce a product for the

Figure 5.3   Value Network Management

	Perform Marketing	Develop Products	Perform Sales	Manage Orders	Procure Materials	Produce Products: Circuit Board Assembly	Sub Assembly & Test	Cable Mfg.	Final Assembly & Test	Manage Logistics/ Distribution	Manage Customer Service
Core Competency	●	●									●
Best-in-Class Process	●	●	●	●	●	●	●	●	●	●	●
Knowledge-Based	●	●	●	●	●						●
Physical						●	●	●	●	●	
In-House	●	●	●	●							●
Outsource	●	●	●	●	●	●	●	●	●	●	●

marketplace, it needs to have access to a physical presence in areas outside its core competence.

For instance, a company specializing in state-of-the-art electronics may have a core competency in product marketing, design, and development. But because it must also produce the product itself, the company invests millions of dollars to construct a manufacturing and distribution facility.

There are four reasons why such companies tend not to use external providers to manage noncore processes and reinvest capital to strengthen core competencies—those that differentiate these companies in the marketplace:

1. A company may view its noncore processes as strategic and proprietary because of embedded technology not found elsewhere. These companies can investigate alternative approaches such as stripping out the part of the process that is proprietary and outsourcing the rest, or possibly selling or licensing the process capability to a third party.

2. Many companies are concerned about losing control of schedule, quality, and flexibility of such noncore processes as production, for example. Schedule, quality, and flexibility are functions of how well a company manages its value network. If a company determines that value network management is a core competency, then it should invest to build a network with business partners that includes the controls and relationships

that will eliminate this concern. For example, many companies place staff in strategic partner facilities to coordinate daily schedules and quality issues.

3. Many companies have invested heavily in plant, equipment, and resources to build production capability. Walking away from these investments is very difficult. As e-business becomes pervasive, many companies with large investments in plant and equipment used to produce commodity-type products will find it more cost-effective to sell these assets and outsource production. As an option, companies may:

   ○ Go to a shared service model with manufacturing as a separate profit center

   ○ Begin providing contract manufacturing services to other companies

   ○ Spin out the manufacturing facility as a management buy

   ○ Contract to the new, third-party contract manufacturer, using the Internet to conduct transactions processing.

4. Finally, companies are timid about entering into relationships with other companies because of the risk and complexity of working in an environment with multiple processes and systems. Companies must develop the capability to partner with external providers to compete in the new business world. Behind the scenes, consortia of software, technology, and telecommunications companies are building the infrastructure and standards companies will use to tap into secure, high-speed networks to conduct business on a plug-and-play basis.

   This new model is characterized by the renting of tailored applications (SAP, Oracle, or some other software) rather than investment in hardware, thereby considerably reducing the capital investment required to establish or run a business. The model is almost like a return to time-share computing, with one major difference: In the world of e-business, the customer will never be beholden to the supplier. The customer will retain the knowledge, and the relationship will be based on a service-level agreement between the supplier and the customer.

   Once this is in place to simplify the process and remove the risk, most companies will conduct business in this manner.

BUILDING THE E-INFRASTRUCTURE

Before the Internet, companies wanting to conduct electronic business with business partners would have to establish expensive dedicated or dial-up lines. Often the transactions processed over these lines were heavily structured and initial costs limited the capability to only large companies with high transaction volumes. Today, many businesses have adopted the Internet as a way to transact the same sort of business.

Imagine a world of businesses linked together via a backbone in which each company focuses on its core competencies and uses that link to buy all other supporting capabilities, processes, and services. Imagine a company free to focus on building its brand and customer relationships, while everything else—from strategic service partners, value-added suppliers, and human resource services—is only a click away. Imagine a company with a fraction of the resources and infrastructure of its physical counterpart, but with far greater revenues.

On the technology horizon, a few companies and consortia are building a secure, high-speed network that will make many current business models obsolete. One such consortium, led by Qwest, is leveraging its Internet communication capabilities to become an application service provider.

Qwest is partnering with application software providers and with a hardware provider to deliver business applications over an Internet-based global network. Qwest is establishing CyberCenters to host the services provided over the network. This strategy allows Qwest to expand its market offering of Internet-based services.

The goal is to build a capability whereby companies will use an advanced, standardized network to connect their business partners and to offer on-demand business applications sometimes referred to as "apps on tap." These methods of operation allow middle-market companies to access functionality once restricted to multimillion dollar implementations. And for large companies, this approach offers creative alternatives to the huge annual investment for developing applications and operating systems centers.

Other consortia are working on similar constructs. The result will be opportunities for companies and their competitors to choose new business models in the future.

OPERATING IN THE VALUE NETWORK MANAGEMENT WORLD

Executives leading companies into the twenty-first century will face unheard of challenges. With the creation of business model-transforming tools such as the high-speed backbone, many new things are possible.

New threats face established businesses with loyal customers; new opportunities await suppliers; and for customers there are new options.

In the value network world, companies will have to build businesses that focus on three key principles:

1. Owning the customer relationship
2. Focusing on differentiating core competencies
3. Building the best value network to provide other competencies.

Value network management is the art of optimizing relationships among customers, internal operations, and business partners and suppliers. The value network manager continuously monitors work load, forecasts, changing market conditions, capacities, bottlenecks, network partner operations, and threats to company throughput, such as potential labor strikes.

Working with optimization software, value network managers direct demand placed on the company for its products or services either to internal capacities or to fulfillment from business partners in the network. Advanced planning and optimization (APO) software synchronizes production schedules throughout the network.

Customer inquiries for order status are immediately provided through the customer-centric Web site, which is fully integrated with shared value network information systems.

With value network management, companies can quickly adapt to market shifts. A knowco will have the agility to take on threats from competitors and respond with new products and services more quickly because it does not need to factor in costs and utilization of physical assets, such as updating capital equipment, when making strategic decisions.

Let us look at a typical product-oriented company with core competencies in product design, marketing, and customer service. The company has significant investments in manufacturing, warehousing, and logistics, and other noncore areas, and has an information infrastructure.

This company is a good e-business because it has already determined that its differentiating core competencies are knowledge-based assets aligned with the customer (product development, marketing, and customer service.). The company should assess its capabilities in these areas and identify how it can build best-in-class processes and capabilities using e-business technology to improve performance and electronically connect with other companies and customers. If the company decides to pursue a knowco strategy, it can build a value network management core competency and eventually divest noncore physical assets. Such a move, if executed effectively, would free up capital to reinvest into building stronger differentiating core competencies.

Electronic business applications for product development, marketing, and customer service are advancing at a rapid rate. (A detailed description of these processes and how they can be e-nabled appears in the appendix.) Over the next few years, leading companies will want to evaluate their capability in these areas.

Most will find that the Internet, data warehousing, and data mining provide many opportunities to speed design and development, offer new techniques for collaborative working relationships, and create new methods for strengthening relationships with customers. Additionally, in the value network model, customer service will become customer satisfaction, with a strong emphasis placed on answering the question, "Did we do everything to make this customer want to do business with us again?"

From an investment standpoint, payback for properly applying e-business for improving customer-facing processes and systems will generate revenue and enhanced customer loyalty, improve cost efficiency, and position a company to take on new threats as the competition begins to develop similar capabilities.

Operationally, a company needs to understand the types of business partners they work with on a daily basis. For a typical products-oriented company, there are six types of business partners (Figure 5.4):

1. Strategic service partners

2. Value-added suppliers

3. Commodity suppliers

4. Nonstrategic service partners

5. Network operations partners

6. Application service providers.

Figure 5.4   Operating in a Value Network Management World

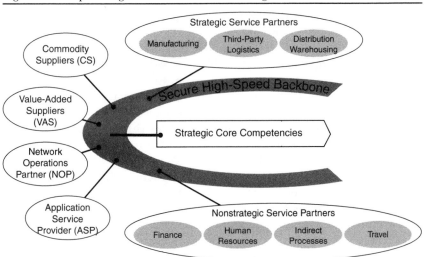

These in turn fall into one of three types of relationships: strategic, nonstrategic, or infrastructure.

Strategic service partners and value-added suppliers have a strategic relationship with a company; they are almost an extension of the core business. Commodity suppliers and nonstrategic service providers differentiate by low cost, premium service delivery, and convenience. Network operations partners and applications service providers are all about meeting a company's objectives by providing a cost-effective alternative to building internal infrastructure.

Operating in the value network model, a company will go "on the backbone" (a term we use to connect externally with these partners). Executives making strategic e-business decisions must understand that the availability of so many services over the Internet in the future will dramatically change the way they must interact, align, and develop contractual relationships with partners. Furthermore, managing partners based on their value to a company's success will be an operating imperative. For example, a company may choose to build and invest in a partnering relationship with a strategic service partner while it evaluates commodity suppliers for low-cost and best delivery terms.

Strategic Service Partners

A strategic service partner (SSP) provides outsourcing of pipeline business processes using a network to integrate seamlessly with its customers. For example, if a company wants to design a new product but has decided not to build the product internally, it will be able to go to a secure, high-speed backbone to procure services for manufacturing, logistics, and warehousing.

These services might be bundled together to form a turnkey capability or they might be bought as "a la carte" offerings. They might even be broken down further into more discreet offerings. For example, one company may provide final assembly and test only, while another provides sourcing components and builds subassemblies.

Each SSP will have readied its environment to accept demand from interested parties operating over a business network. In the future, most SSPs will use the high-speed backbone. Successful SSPs will have reengineered their processes and information systems to plug easily into the information systems of requesting companies.

SSPs will be prepared to handle transactions from common platforms and leading application packages. Their organizations and cultures will be fine-tuned as providers of services over business networks to extend the enterprise of their customers. They will be members of many extraprises.

Customer service will be the primary measure for SSPs. To lure would-be customers, SSPs will offer flexible payment by performance options, to ensure that they achieve certain levels of schedule, quality, and customer satisfaction. These terms will be laid out as part of a service-level agreement. One of the key success factors will be their ability to create standardized agreements—one-to-many, rather than one-to-one relationships. (Setting up individual agreements with each customer would be too cumbersome).

An SSP is a structured form of outsourcer, linked through information networks to form a community of similar providers. Outsourcing relationships are nothing new. But with the Internet, outsourcers can establish data links directly with requesting companies. And in the future, SSPs will use backbone standards to *integrate quickly* with companies searching for this type of relationship.

The value proposition for SSPs is clear. Once communications issues are resolved, SSPs provide companies with four benefits:

1. Cost displacement, by offering process simplification and execution at lower costs

2. Reduced infrastructure investment requirements, which facilitate the creation of very low infrastructure knowcos

3. Higher specialized functionality, availability, and reliability than the companies could afford to finance themselves

4. Aggregation benefits not obtainable by the company on its own, such as volume discounts for commodity parts.

Outsourcing nondifferentiating manufacturing operations will become commonplace. SSPs offering high-quality, low-cost, and high-responsiveness manufacturing-oriented services will see a significant growth spike as companies use backbones. Outsourced manufacturing for high-tech companies is projected to grow from $90 billion in 1988 to more than $200 billion in 2001. Demand for "nuts and bolts" manufacturing is escalating at an extraordinary rate. Companies are increasingly outsourcing their manufacturing operations to maintain efficiency and to contain overhead costs.

For some outsourcer manufacturers, overhead runs as low as 4 percent of sales, and utilization rates are as high as 80 percent or more. Because of their ability to purchase parts at volume discounts and to manufacture globally, these companies can integrate additional functions such as purchasing, logistics, and warehousing, with their operations.

In the personal computer (PC) industry, Solectron is teaming with the industry's largest distributor, Ingram Micro, to handle PC manufacture inexpensively for companies such as HP and Compaq Computer. Using Web-to-hand orders, Solectron and Ingram Micro have launched a new way of building custom-made PC-based systems that speeds communication and reduces assembly time. As a result, PC companies can focus on their core competencies such as marketing, brand management, and quality assurance.

Solectron has tightly integrated itself with its customers and suppliers. The company's new-product introduction process is characterized by a physically and electronically linked value chain. It is customer focused and identifies supplier input early on as a key component in product development. Information technology binds suppliers, customers, and Solectron via an extraprise-wide computing system that facilitates the exchange of engineering and other relevant data.

In this virtual factory, a customer places an order with a reseller for a brand name, customized PC, which is built to the customer's specifications and then shipped directly to the customer. Communication from the reseller to Ingram Micro and to Solectron's assembly facility occurs electronically in real time. After the order is placed, Ingram Micro routes the information to the appropriate Solectron site. Upon receiving the information, Solectron performs an inventory check for available parts and, based on the response to the query, either procures parts from suppliers or uses inventory.

Based on the location of where the parts are being procured and on the capacity of the assembly line, Solectron then sends Ingram Micro an expected ship date. If this date is different from that promised to the customer, a real-time alert is sent to the sales representative.

Once the parts are in place and the product assembled, it is shipped to the reseller or directly to the consumer. The distribution and shipping logistics are also included in the process. Ingram Micro and Solectron have established a goal of two days from when all materials are available to when the item is shipped.

With seamless e-business networks providing the framework for external communication, companies will explore opportunities to change the feel and shape of supply chains. With this capability, they can receive and fill orders by shipping from third-party production facilities to customers without ever touching the product, thus coming closer to being a knowco.

Companies contemplating using SSPs should determine how they want to manage the relationship. Using an SSP for pipeline production processes requires sharing proprietary design information. An SSP must have procedures in place to guarantee confidentiality and security of knowledge-based assets. Given that most companies will try to partner with the highest-rated SSPs, they should make sure that the SSP has constructed "Chinese walls" between requesting companies to eliminate the concern that product designs will be compromised.

Value-Added Suppliers

Value-added suppliers (VASs) provide engineered or configured parts or subassemblies, unique to client-specific requirements. Three examples of VASs are:

○ A metalworking company fabricating a large custom cabinet for a computer system

○ A supplier building an aircraft subassembly

○ An electronics company providing software for game simulation.

In the past, communicating client-specific requirements would consume reams of paper and involve countless personal trips from the requesting company program managers. Additionally, both the requesting company and the VAS had to manage the communication of engineering changes and problems that arose in production. E-business provides these companies with a solution that significantly improves communication, speed, and cost. By linking the two parties' information systems through a network, information can flow freely between the parties. Furthermore, as the backbone is implemented, VASs will find they can offer more than engineered production value to their customers.

By being tightly integrated, VASs will be able to position themselves to provide consultation earlier in the design and requirement development process. The VAS will be able to design in "produceability" prior to finalizing requirements. This should improve the relationship.

At some point in the relationship, a customer company may want to outsource some of the design process to the VAS. This could result in even faster delivery intervals and lower contracted cost for parts.

Companies integrating with VASs over networks need to address the same concerns about proprietary designs and confidentiality as when dealing with SSPs.

Commodity Suppliers

Commodity suppliers (CSs) provide business component parts and subassemblies commonly available on the market. The Internet worries many CSs. Customers are no more than a click away from searching for and finding an alternative supplier. The backbone will breed third-party commodity-part aggregators who will do a customer's comparative analysis and recommend from where to purchase. Third-party aggregators are those who match buyers to sellers of goods but may not produce goods of their own. Their core competency is understanding markets for specific types of goods, aggregating goods, and maintaining and utilizing customer buying habit data.

Third-party commodity aggregators build their service costs into the quoted price to make them transparent to the transaction. Still, a purchasing manager in need of a long list of parts will gladly hand the job off to a third-party aggregator.

Where does this leave direct CSs? Some will bundle services to their products to attempt to reintermediate themselves by providing differentiated value through information-based services. Other CSs will try to hold on to their long-standing relationships with companies by providing them with other value-added, information-based services, such as statistical procurement and inventory analysis.

Third-party aggregators will also provide value-added services to product designers. Within networks, they will develop and sell standard part catalogues on line, which include part specifications, recommendations to use or not use, operating reliability and history, and comparative prices. Additionally, some third-party commodity aggregators will create a "part generator" program that allows designers to document specifications and operating requirements and then recommend a part.

Regardless of the future of individual CSs, companies that need commodity parts will benefit from this advanced technology through improvements in cost, speed of delivery, and customer service.

Nonstrategic Service Partners

Nonstrategic service partners (NSPs) deliver outsourcing capabilities for commodity-type administrative and other business processes, including accounting and finance, human resources, indirect procurement, and travel—all processes integral to a company's ability to operate. However, most companies do not gain competitive advantage by being the best in class for these processes, which are considered a cost of doing business.

Every one of these services can be outsourced today. Companies like ADP, which provides payroll processing, already have well-established processes and systems. So why do companies not outsource these portions of their business? Some companies believe they can perform the processes themselves less expensively. Others view establishing outsourcing relationships as too difficult when they consider the complexity of trying to align their processes and information systems.

In some instances, e-business has already begun to transform these kinds of processes. E-procurement of individual materials was the hottest e-business activity in 1999. In the future, companies will source most of their nonstrategic services from NSPs using the backbone. Companies should begin to realize that many current business models have been in place for so long that the value proposition is no longer valid. Administrative processes burn significant investment capital that can be used to strengthen differentiating core competencies, and conducting business over the Internet to outsourcing providers is safe and will eventually become a way of life.

A word of caution, however. There is a fine line between outsourcing transaction processing for administrative processes and protecting a company's confidential knowledge. Companies, as they move to outsourcing these processes, need to separate and protect knowledge about strategic financial decisions, personnel, and any other knowledge set that may put the company at risk if it falls into the hands of an unscrupulous third party.

Network Operations Partners

Network operations partners (NOPs) use a secure, high-speed backbone to connect companies with SSPs, CSs, VASs, and NSPs. Today, most companies rely on existing ISPs such as America Online, Microsoft, or a host of smaller, often local ISPs to connect their businesses with the Internet and the outside world.

In the future, NOPs will replace these links. Selecting an NOP will be a key decision for companies building a value network management capability. NOPs will provide companies the gateway to the backbone and the standards and interfaces integrating with partners. This is called plug-and-play capability. They will build, maintain, and service the secure, high-speed backbone. Specifically, NOPs will:

○ Provide the use of the required computing and network hardware

○ Provide secure network connectivity to authorized users

○ Assume total responsibility for ongoing operation of IT systems

○ Provide assistance in scaling and upgrading the system

○ Provide integration templates to link extraprise value network partners.

Companies will turn to NOPs for full-service and application-based information systems outsourcing. They will integrate business applications software and hardware, networks, and other third-party capabilities such as nonstrategic partner services. In the future, NOPs will most likely market their services jointly with, or even as, an application service provider.

Application Service Providers

Application service providers (ASPs) deploy, manage, and lease packaged application software to customers from centrally managed data facilities.

Application service providers will offer these services for either a flat monthly fee or on a transactional basis. Initially, ASPs will target middle-market companies of approximately $50 million to $1 billion in annual revenue, of which there are about 40,000 in the United States alone.

These companies are candidates for initial rollout of services because they do not have the investment power to take on multiyear, multimillion dollar implementations of ERP systems but still want the competitive power that these applications provide. As the middle market proves to be successful, ASPs will begin to penetrate large companies of $1 billion and more.

Forrester Research predicts that the worldwide market for software applications outsourcing will be $21 billion by 2001, and application rentals will reach $6 billion. IDC estimates the ASP market will grow to $2 billion by 2003.

Figure 5.5   The "World" Before and After ASPs

Before ASPs	After ASPs
Large Business Focused	Small and Medium Business Focused
Costly One-to-One Solutions	Cost-Effective One-to-Many Solutions
Difficult to Implement (months/years)	Easy to Implement (weeks/months)
Heavy Up-Front Investment Including Hardware and Software Purchase	Minimal Start-up Costs due to Sharing of Hardware Costs with Other ASP Clients
High-Technology Risk Including Upgrades and Obsolete Technology	Reduced Technology Risk to the Client as the ASP Provides Total Technology Solution
Unpredictable IT Costs	Fixed-Fee Model for IT Costs
Large, Lump-Sum Payments	Monthly Per-User Payments
Managed In-House	Managed Off-Site
Unpredictable Time Frames	Set Time Frames and Service Level Agreements Covering Performance and Availability

Figure 5.6   Varying Levels of Value

Factors	Little Customer Pain			Serious Customer Pain
Application-Specific Expertise	E-mail	Intranet	Data Mart	Enterprise Resource Planning
Ongoing Maintenance				Sales Force Automation
Integration	Spreadsheet	Groupware	Product Data Management	
Implementation				Customer Relationship Management
	Word Processing	Web Hosting	Basic E-Commerce	

ASP Adds Convenience			ASP Adds Significant Value
Low Value	Depth of requirement		High Value

Figure 5.5 compares the world before and after ASPs. The value of the ASP relationship depends on the complexity of the applications leased. Figure 5.6 illustrates how the level of value varies. Figure 5.7 illustrates how quickly this concept took hold in early 1999.

E-PARTNERING

E-partnering is a relationship among companies that use e-business to share business improvements, mutual benefits, and joint rewards. As companies shift their business models to work in value networks, the form of the relationships becomes critical to success.

Traditionally, companies strove to be Number One in what they do by squeezing every last penny out of suppliers and service providers. They operated as if they were the only player in the game. A good example of this is the relationship between management and unions during much of the twentieth century. However, in the value network world, the opposite is true. A company's success will strongly depend on its relationships with its business partners. Companies need to adopt a mentality and organizational culture that promotes working with other companies and measure their success by how well they collaborate.

In structuring business and contractual relationships with strategic partners, companies should seek mutually beneficial relationships by carefully considering what both parties have to gain. E-partnering takes the extraprise concept a step further by affecting the core of company

Figure 5.7   The ASP Concept Takes Hold

"Investors and major software developers are pouring money into an emerging market to provide corporations with business programs that are available as services on the Internet, instead of owned outright by the companies."

- Inter@ctive Week Online

"The market for software rentals is about to explode. For users, that could mean dramatically lower and more predictable costs, much faster access to new applications and far fewer administrative headaches."

- Computerworld

"Most of the growth will come from hosting applications, such as electronic commerce and other functions. Among the competitors: IBM Global Services, US West, USinternetworking, and ZLand."

- Internet World Daily

"No need to buy software . . . a simple word processor, a browser and an Internet connection are all that is needed . . . Serving Web applications off the Web is the new technology trend. Complex software is moving away from the desktop and the corporate central server to the Internet. The trend is the single most important inflection point in the technology industry during the next year."

- Forbes Digital Tool

". . . the utilities of the next century, providing an essential service with all the reliability and security of the electricity or telephone company."

- Forrester

relationships. Companies that decide to build e-partner relationships have to accomplish 10 critical goals:

1. Set guidelines for pro-actively working together for the benefit of both parties.

2. Integrate processes and systems to seamlessly link the companies.

3. Jointly develop performance objectives and measures to guide their relationship.

4. Share customer and market knowledge.

5. Collaborate on forecasting, production planning, and inventory management.

6. Jointly invest in improvement efforts, addressing cross-company processes and systems.

7. Promote a culture that values each other's contributions.

8. Jointly develop products and services.

9. Share risks.

10. Share rewards.

The glue that holds e-partnerships together is the ability to communicate faster and cheaper utilizing the Internet. For companies operating on the backbone, e-partnering will become a way of life.

INDUSTRY TRANSFORMATION: OPPORTUNITIES AND THREATS

Industry transformation provides companies with enormous opportunities to grow revenue. It also opens the door to potentially devastating threats from new and existing competitors. Executives taking on the challenge of e-business leadership may face career-making or career-breaking decisions as they plot competitive strategies.

Although e-business is still in its infancy, new business models promise to dramatically change the competitive landscape. Following are a few rules that govern this new world.

Customer Relationships: Knowledge Is King

In the e-business world, two things are certain: owning the customer relationship and customer knowledge is paramount. Companies must not let other companies or intermediaries get between them and the customer. E-business makes getting access to customer, product, and market information easier than ever. Competitive threats may come from anywhere.

In a world where much business is done electronically, traditional intermediaries such as distributors and retailers may eventually disappear or be forced to transform their role. In the e-business world, the role of intermediaries—either start-ups or transformed companies—is to broker information and transactions.

Facilitators and Aggregators. Information intermediaries come in two varieties: facilitators and aggregators. Facilitators merely move information around, matching buyers with sellers, and take a modest transaction commission for their processing time. Aggregators know what has happened in the transaction and leverage this knowledge for their own good. They are aggregators of knowledge, not merely of transactional data.

The e-business world creates abundant opportunities for facilitator intermediaries. New entrants will pop up, getting between companies and their customers. They even exist today. For example, some telecommunications companies use facilitator intermediaries to capture new customers and increase revenue share. The facilitators use large databases of names, addresses, and telephone numbers to sell aggressively telecom products and services to a market that is, in many cases, untapped by traditional telecommunications selling practices.

These facilitator intermediaries even package company products and services differently, promising, for example, a "special deal" if a customer buys through them. Often the "special deal" attracts customers with added convenience and personalized service, even though in most cases, they can get the same service from the company directly.

The facilitator then sells the new customer to the providing company. Providing companies use facilitators to expand their reach at a low cost and to supplement their existing sales forces. Facilitator intermediaries often work in environments of low overhead and administrative cost.

With the Internet, technology facilitator intermediaries will grow. The Internet opens the door to facilitator intermediaries to collect information more easily and quickly, and at lower cost than through traditional database marketing.

Aggregator intermediaries are on the other end of the spectrum. Aggregators act more like traditional businesses in that their value is not only to bring customers to providing companies, but to use the knowledge of the transaction as an asset to grow their own businesses. Aggregators are more like today's resellers and distributors. They often have brand recognition, and in some cases, they actually add value to the physical product by, for example, tailoring final assembly to the customer's unique needs.

Aggregators will flourish in the e-business world. The Internet allows aggregators to identify and pursue customers through a new channel and to electronically connect their operations with their suppliers to adapt quickly to changing customer needs, to lower processing costs, to build brand equity through personalized service, and to create new forms of information-based revenue.

While providing companies will view facilitator intermediaries as an additional channel for revenue, they have mixed feelings regarding aggregator intermediaries. Aggregators are a blessing and a threat. They are a blessing because they own market relationships that may not be attainable through existing sales approaches and so provide a means for selling the provider's product. They are a threat, however, because with the Internet, aggregators can grow their business rapidly and expand far beyond their existing role to eventually compete head-to-head for new markets with the providing company.

Additionally, using the ubiquity of the Internet as a means to conduct business, aggregators can and will cross-compete, providing companies' products and services for their own benefit.

Both facilitators and aggregators are already beginning to create downward pressure on prices, causing formerly product-push companies to apply their customer information and understanding to improve customer service and to become true consumer-centric organizations.

Third-Party Aggregators and Own-Product Aggregators. Companies can, possibly, battle independent or third-party aggregators by becoming aggregators themselves, using their product lines and brands as baselines from which to add products and services. We call this becoming an "own-product" aggregator.

The company can try to use its brand appeal to maintain premium pricing, hoping that customers will want to buy from a known, brand-name player, rather than from an unknown middleman who simply sells on the basis of finding the cheapest priced parts and packaging them. This is already occurring in the U.S. automobile market. In the past, car buyers would typically pick out the type of car they wanted to purchase, go to several dealerships to test drive and compare prices, negotiate option packages, obtain a financing plan from a bank or credit union, and then return to the dealership to complete the purchase.

With the Internet, the car-buying experience has changed dramatically. Today, a car buyer can log onto a site such as Carpoint.com or Autobytel.com, pick a car along with the desired options, compare the manufacturer's suggested retail price against the price offered by multiple dealers, determine what he or she wants to pay, place a bid on-line for a car loan, visit a dealership to test drive the car, place a bid for dealers to meet the desired price, and then decide which car to buy from which dealer and which loan to accept.

Today's Web-based car search sites are essentially facilitators, matching buyers to sellers in an open auctionlike model, and letting the parties negotiate the final deal. But they could just as easily be aggregators, closing the deals themselves and maintaining the relationship with the customer, and then searching for the best source of product and financing (and even possibly insurance and warranty service/maintenance facilities).

While these sites would probably have to buy through various manufacturers' dealerships in the short run, chances are that over time, if they build enough of a consumer base, they could disintermediate the dealers and buy directly from manufacturers, in effect becoming a Web-only virtual dealer.

A major automotive manufacturer is trying to stop this from happening by building a Web-based customer connection. A virtual dealership gives car buyers access to multiple data sources in real time with information on availability, features, financing options, and test drive calendars. The site attempts to sell directly to customers by allowing them to configure and order cars on-line. The site not only offers many preconfigured vehicles, but it also allows buyers to custom order other configurations, to compare products with those of other companies, to peek into dealer inventories, to apply for financing, and to trigger a negotiation process via e-mail.

The company is deliberately not disintermediating its dealers. The Web site is an alternative to, not a substitute for, the traditional manufacturer-dealer-consumer relationship. Users have access to thousands of dealerships. In order to reach its goal of closing all Web sales within 48 hours of an order, the company is building a regional distribution center system that gives customers car options dealers may not carry.

The company has a possible advantage in its efforts to be an own-product aggregator and fend off any incipient third-party aggregators. It already has an established and highly regarded financing company and might have an easier time establishing relationships with brand name auto-maintenance providers and top-line insurance companies, some of which may be leery of entering into relationships with unknown non-brand-name third-party aggregators.

Another way companies can try to freeze out third-party aggregators is by creating an industry consortia. For example, in the hospital products industry, companies sponsor a Web site where hospital purchasing agents can browse and purchase hospital supplies from one or more of the participating organizations. By combining efforts, the participating suppliers have been able to provide a common industry supply platform while creating an open, virtual network of suppliers.

In the United Kingdom, Johnson & Johnson attempted a variation on this, and proposed setting itself up as the own-product aggregator. The company wanted to run the Web site and supply logistics to all the other companies that displayed their goods on the site. This would add a level of customer service—all the goods coming at once on one truck, rather than all the time on different trucks. This plan has not yet been approved by the U.K. government, but it was highlighted in a recent government white paper on the National Health Service.

The objective for a company in danger of being disintermediated by a third-party aggregator is simple: If it owns the customer relationship, it must do everything possible to hold on to and cherish it. If the company does not own the customer relationship, it should try to get it, by becoming an own-product aggregator if necessary. If it can't get the customer relationship, it should partner to get it by making an exclusive relationship with an own-product aggregator.

Own-Product Aggregator Breakaway

As companies create strong own-product aggregator capability to defend their market positions, they may consider the value of splitting off the own-product aggregator portion of the business into a stand-alone company. This would allow the own-product aggregator to focus on providing information-based value to customers and to serve as the front end (and realistically a channel) to the once-parent company.

In a way, the own-product aggregator becomes a knowco by using information as a strategic weapon to grow its business. Many companies today are considering this strategy in light of the Internet and the incredible financial gains experienced by Internet-based initial public offerings (IPOs).

Brand: The Own-Product Aggregator Advantage.   Own-product aggregators initially built their businesses without the Internet as a channel. They have succeeded by building brand recognition. Aggregators challenging traditional companies need to establish brand recognition in order to compete.

Amazon.com and Cisco came out of nowhere to become household words. How? Each company established a campaign to build brand recognition. Fortunately for them, they were pioneers. The market responded with open arms because these two companies had developed new and creative business models using technology that intrigued customers, competitors, and investors.

Since the Internet Age was taking off, newspapers, magazines, and television flocked to hear their stories. This publicity only enhanced their image and brand. Brand recognition is critical to successful industry transformation. If customers do not know who a company is, that company has little chance of capturing and retaining the relationship.

Ironically, the same is true for aggregators. Aggregators have the same potential to grab brand recognition. But to do so requires a sustained and costly effort. With aggressive marketing, brand-building campaigns, and deep pockets, companies can turn a dream into a hot ticket on the Internet.

Notice the number of companies—both new Internet companies and companies trying to reinvent themselves as Internet companies—that advertise on television. For a company that already has name recognition, such as IBM, Charles Schwab, or Barnes & Noble, such television advertising can catapult efforts to "go 'E'." An own-product aggregator with good name recognition has a distinct advantage over a third-party aggregator for this same reason.

The Aggregator's Motto: Take My Problem Away

Customers who used to want products now want solutions to problems. In the world of physical commerce, that solution usually comes in the form of a product. In the move to a service economy, individual consumers are more frequently buying a service—in effect outsourcing such chores as lawn cutting, house cleaning, and snow clearing.

In the nineteenth century, much product assembly occurred at the point of use. People bought the pieces they needed to make household and business utensils and performed the assembly themselves. The bundling of parts, components, and subassemblies into fully assembled goods was a twentieth-century notion, created to fuel the mass production gearing up to supply a mass-consuming society.

With the arrival of the twenty-first century, e-business is poised to provide an opportunity to move back to assembly at the point of use, but with the ease of mass-produced products. This is the world of plug-and-play, where successful products are increasingly "parts" or "tasks." In this world, aggregators prosper.

Companies that offer products and services can bundle them together in infinite combinations. They can also partner with companies that provide complementary products or services. New companies, not tied to a particular line of products or services, can integrate products and services from many companies.

All of these methodologies allow companies to provide customized "dynamic bundles" of goods and services that take a customer's problem away. Dynamic bundling intermingles products and services into "fused offerings" that provide different mixes and flexibility. Usually carried out by third-party or own-product aggregators, dynamic bundling actually adds value by integrating various pieces of the offering into custom-tailored packages.

Physical components and service elements are provided by companies that provide best-in-class. Products and services can be designed to facilitate dynamic rebundling where companies will take a problem away from another company by designing and delivering a customized solution.

In the business-to-business world, the Internet also allows companies to leverage their intellectual capital about their customers and industries in order to create new service offerings that let customers outsource pipeline (but noncore competency) processes to them. In addition, modularized processes allow for easy plug-and-play product design that companies can use to link their products to those of other companies.

In this way, they can build a community of joint offering partners, or a consortia of design partners, to establish design standards. Product data management extends to suppliers and occurs via a secured extranet or secure high-speed backbone. By passing specifications to vendors, engineered products can be assembled in a collaborative process using off-the-shelf modular elements from suppliers to meet customer specifications. Additional up-front engineering expenses will be rapidly offset by not having to engineer standard components in the future, and customers are satisfied at lower overall cost.

An increase in the availability of alternatives does not change the fundamental integration requirement for deep relationships and assurances. Service discriminators shift as customized offerings to the market-of-one become commonplace. The ability to rapidly reconfigure and integrate elements beyond one's own company's product offerings—being the integrator of the network that fulfills the relationship—is the source of advantage.

In the e-nabled world, customers are more aware of alternatives and cost. But the difference between qualified and unqualified providers is imperceptible on the Web page. Therefore, the capability of providers must be assured. This will become the baseline requirement for business-to-business interactions.

An integrator—either a third-party or own-product aggregator—that wishes to maintain an advantage in the environment where service discriminators constantly shift, needs to develop expertise in partner relationship management and risk management.

There are four ways to stave off the competition, regardless of whether that competition is from an existing company or new entrant, a third-party aggregator, or an own-product aggregator.

1. *Break down the walls between industry segments.* Focus on the customer. Identify what products and services customers buy from other companies in the same industry. Think about owning the entire customer relationship, not just the piece in a given segment. Think of acting as an aggregator to provide total service to lock in customer loyalty and increase the customer's switching cost.

2. *Build the best customer service (satisfaction) capability by integrating technology.* Fully integrate the telephone, fax, Internet, and any other technology that the customer wants to use to do business.

Do not skimp on customer service. Reevaluate the power of voice on the other end.

3. *Build brand as an e-player.* Brand is even more important in the e-business world than in the physical world. On the Internet, unless a company has brand recognition, it will be lost among all of the start-ups. Brands will compete with brands. For knowcos, brand recognition will be critical. Companies need to invest in their brands.

4. *Research and synthesize customer information.* In the future, protecting customer information will be as important as protecting nuclear weapons. Everything will revolve around customer information. Data mining and trend analysis will play a key role in helping companies make product and market positioning decisions. Secure everything!

FROM PORTALS TO E-MARKETS

Like home users, companies wanting to do business on the Web must connect to the Internet through a third-party organization—an Internet Service Provider (ISP). In the B2C world, connected consumers usually seek out a "home page" as a jumping off point for their explorations. "Portals" are businesses that exist to support this need. Typically directory- or search-engine based, portals usually offer a variety of information services and derive revenues from advertising. Well known B2C examples include Yahoo, AltaVista, and Lycos. In addition to these, a huge variety of other portals have appeared, offering differentiated services and targeting various special interest groups. These aim to serve particular communities, including various business groups. Portals that target particular industry verticals (single industries) are called "vortals." The heavyweight B2B equivalent of a B2C portal is the e-market. Importantly, while portals are about information, e-markets are about transactions and business processes. B2B e-markets are in some ways analogous to B2C start-ups like eBay and priceline.com.

E-markets may be focused on single industries (vertical), or multiple industries (horizontal). They typically derive revenues from transaction-based charges, subscriptions, or both. Exchanges are the simplest type of e-market and were the first to appear. They are focused on the buying/selling process and offer a variety of simple services that support e-procurement, including electronic catalogues and search engines, transaction processing, hosted buying applications, electronic PO transmission, and a variety of auction methods. While both third parties and established industry majors can operate exchanges, those run by the majors are more likely to succeed simply because they can guarantee the crucial early volume of transactions.

Over time, in order to differentiate in a given industry or region, exchanges will need to offer additional features. They will become full e-markets offering a variety of complex professional services layered on top of basic application service provision (ASP). This transition will signal the e-nabling of entire industries. In the future, companies will interact through a web of e-markets linking product and service providers.

Value Networks and E-Markets

As companies orient themselves toward knowco or physco business strategies, they will need an infrastructure to support them. As e-business causes executives to think less about corporate value chains and more about value networks comprised of suppliers and customers, they will also begin to evaluate e-markets. E-markets will significantly transform business models. In the future, it will be possible to plan, organize, and execute many business functions—from purchasing to logistics—through e-markets. One of the strategic decisions business executives will have to make is to choose between a one-to-one relationship with a partner/supplier or an indirect connection through an e-market.

Because they provide an ideal structure for using information to significantly improve levels of processing efficiency throughout the supply chain and for creating value for all participants, e-marketplaces are flourishing. A brief look at the value of e-markets illustrates just how they are changing the way business is done.

Value of E-Markets

In most cases, the buying and selling of products today is based on one-to-one relationships between companies and their customers and companies and their suppliers. If these transactions are not automated through EDI or a similar application, they require significant human intervention. Such transactions are typically inefficient since a buyer may have to invest time in researching his or her specific business need. Point-to-point relationships between suppliers and customers do improve efficiency but require significant investment by the company wanting the product or service and by its suppliers. To further complicate matters, each supplier or customer has to solve the problem of interacting with different information management systems for each trading partner. For many companies, the effort seems daunting.

For example, one of the most compelling reasons why GM, Ford, and DaimlerChrysler decided to join forces and develop only one exchange was that their supplier community—thousands of small, medium, and large providers of parts and services—voiced opposition to a multiple exchange arrangement. They argued that they would have to invest millions of dollars to link to each auto manufacturer, not to mention other vendors in the supply chain. One automobile e-market with industry connection standards, they reasoned, would help them to do most of their business online, easily, and at less cost.

Early business-to-business e-markets consisted of two or more companies that realized they could lower overall costs and increase operating efficiencies by, in effect, outsourcing some of the nonstrategic parts of their business to a third party over the Internet. Typically these processes were associated with indirect procurement (Figure 5.8). Internet-based applications from Commerce One, Ariba, and a host of others provided the structure to make this vision a reality. Whether these companies co-owned the exchange, or whether the exchange was completely independent became an issue related to the potential for market flotation of the exchange. In the Internet-economics prevalent around the turn of the millennium, the market value of such an exchange was equal to the value of transactions flowing through it.

During 1999, variations on this model proliferated because investors realized the potential value of extrapolating this offering to all the companies in an industry. They also understood the opportunity to control and influence e-markets and the future of buying and selling in an industry vertical. GartnerGroup estimates that by the year 2002, there will be up to 10,000 e-markets.

Today, companies are using e-markets not only to procure indirect and MRO products, but also to buy and sell direct materials. E-markets

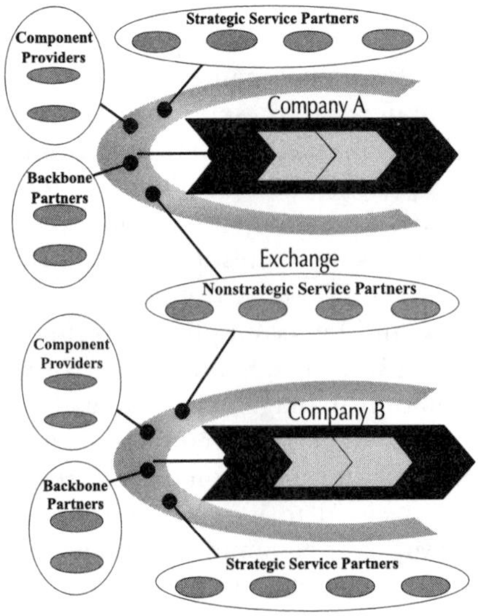

Figure 5.8   First Step in E-Markets: Focus on Nonstrategic Functions

have come of age, and many have taken on a life of their own (Figure 5.9). Some e-markets now bundle such services as finance, logistics, collaborative planning, and application outsourcing with basic e-procurement. E-markets are providing an infrastructure that enables companies that want to become knowcos to do business easily.

Like exchanges, e-markets can be vertical or horizontal. Vertical e-markets are aligned with a specific industry. Their objective is to link all of the companies in that industry so that they can conduct business over one network. In some industries, a single, powerful vertical e-market will prevail. However, in most industries multiple vertical e-markets will compete. E-Steel and Chemdex are examples of vertical e-markets. Horizontal e-markets cut across industries and support/automate such functional processes as indirect procurement or logistics. Examples include Grainger and Employease.

E-markets can originate in several ways. However, three e-market makers will tend to dominate:

1. A *company network* market maker builds and maintains the e-market for its suppliers and their suppliers. It is, in essence, a closed market focused on sharing data and providing the highest level of value to the sponsoring company while gaining processing efficiencies for supplier partners. It reduces cost across

Figure 5.9   As Exchanges Integrate with Strategic Processes, They Become E-Markets

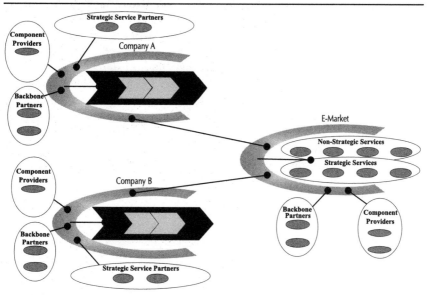

a single value chain and thus gives that chain a competitive advantage. This would be a typical physco early strategy.

2. An *industry partnership* market maker is a collective of companies that share a vested interest in providing the vertical industry a suite of products and services. Members of the industry partnership e-market benefit from significant process efficiency and reduced systems development costs. Most industry partnership market makers collectively pay for, profit from, and manage the e-market. In many examples, industry partnership market makers create independent companies to operate the e-market. These partnerships are driven by a belief that intra-industry competitive advantage is not to be had at the back-end of the value chain.

3. *Seller-led* market makers create e-markets as a forum in which to offer their and other like products and services. Seller-led market makers typically offer products and services to horizontal e-markets. Members of seller-led e-markets benefit from less costly products and services, more efficient ordering and fulfillment processing, and value-based product information. This is the B2B equivalent of the B2C mall concept and may be subject to some of the same risks.

With the growth of the e-market concept as a viable business model, new forms will develop. Once a vertical e-market is established and accepted in the marketplace, exchanges will appear that can feed off of the e-market supported by the shear volume of aggregated transactions (Figure 5.10). For example, as GM, Ford, and DaimlerChrysler build their recently announced supply market for the automobile industry, new markets will be born and attached to the parent—plastics e-markets and steel e-markets, for example—to service the automotive industry, but potentially other industries as well. Although plastics and steel are key ingredients in producing automobiles, they are also important elements in the production of many other consumer and business customer end products. Therefore, it will be interesting to see if existing third-party e-markets such as PlasticsNet and E-Steel can remain independent.

E-markets provide a unique set of value levers to the member companies. These include purchasing power, process efficiency, industry supply chain integration, aggregated content and community, and market efficiency.

Purchasing Power

- ○ Aggregate buyers into buying consortiums
- ○ Volume pricing

Figure 5.10 A Fully Evolved E-Market Will Link to Multiple Verticals and Horizontals

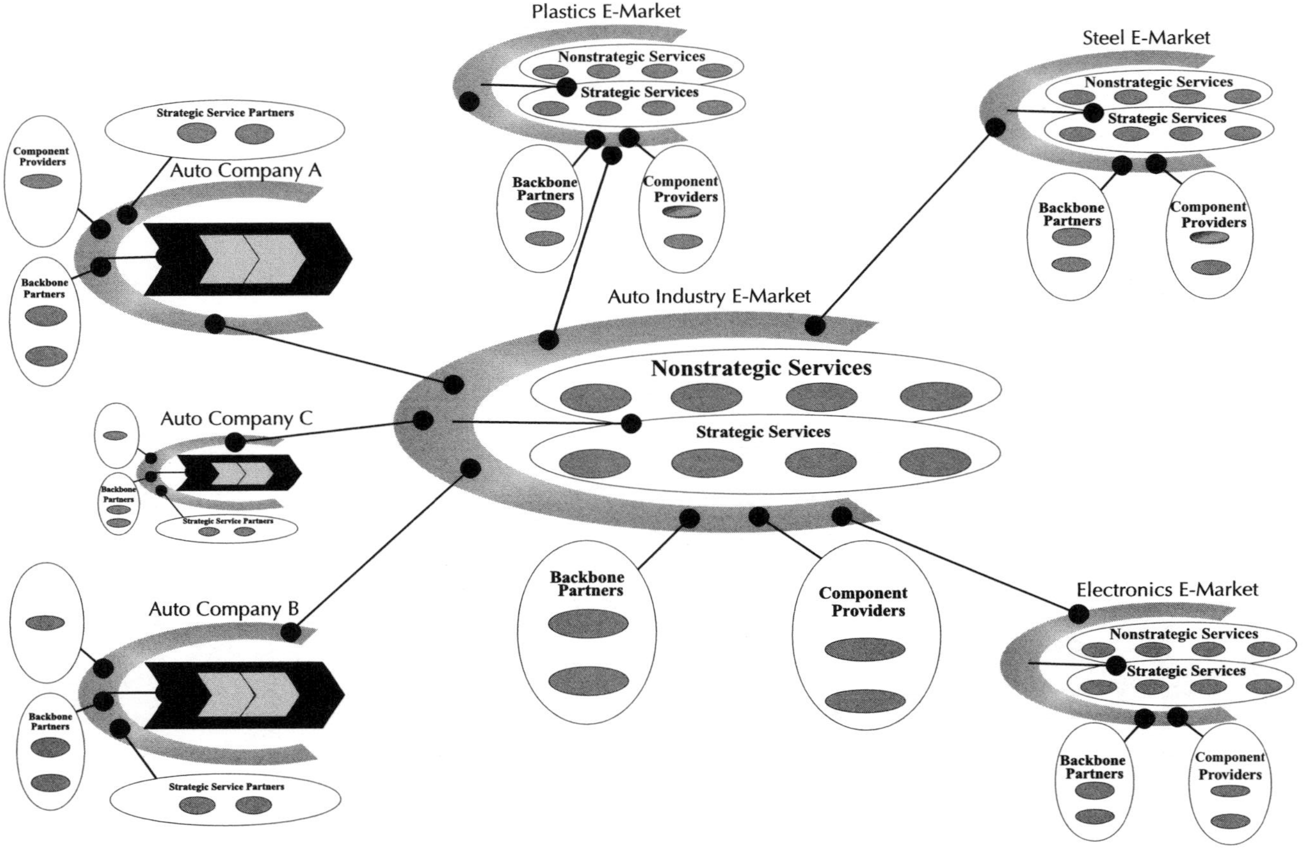

○ Better information for supplier negotiations
○ Supplier consolidation
○ Spending and control analysis and reports.

Process Efficiency

○ Electronic product searches/catalogues
○ Electronic order taking and management
○ Electronic requisition and approval (workflow)
○ Auto replenishment
○ Electronic bill presentation and payment
○ Improved information access
○ Better spending control
○ Reduced transaction costs.

Industry Supply Chain Integration

○ Disintermediation
○ Improved visibility across supply chains
○ Reduced lead time
○ Reduced inventory levels
○ Improved logistics management
○ ERP integration.

Aggregated Content and Community

○ Industry best practices
○ Knowledge management
○ Benchmarking studies
○ Monitoring/controlling reports
○ Discussion forums
○ Product information and review
○ FAQs
○ Industry collaboration
○ Newsletters
○ Network effect.

Market Efficiency

- ○ Online market making mechanisms (to connect buyers and sellers)
- ○ e-catalogues
- ○ Auctions
- ○ Exchanges
- ○ Bid processes
- ○ Access to broader range of suppliers and buyers
- ○ Improved information access.

The Evolution of Meta-Markets

Competition to create dominant e-markets will be fierce. Size and speed will matter. The largest and fastest e-markets will have the opportunity to create meta-markets that consist of a portfolio of e-market communities (Figure 5.11). Operators of meta-markets have the opportunity to extend across industry verticals and horizontal offerings and so wield significant clout in the e-business world. Assuming noninterference from government regulation, meta-markets will become the business powerhouses of the new economy. Meta-markets will be characterized by:

- ○ The ability to rapidly form and launch new e-markets (as e-market incubators)
- ○ Established customer bases from which to support new e-markets

Figure 5.11   The Evolution of Meta-Markets: The Meta-Market—A Portifolio of E-Markets

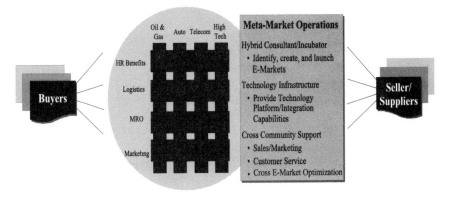

○ Broader communities in which to allocate R&D costs (for example, new online functionality)

○ Operational efficiencies via back office shared services across multiple e-markets (for example, billing, service)

○ Greater integration across supply chains

○ Expanded community and collaboration opportunities

○ Critical mass providing suppliers broader market access and buyers increased leverage with suppliers

○ Leverage of common infrastructure components (for example, servers, networks).

6

Snapshot Three: Effects of Industry Transformation on Organizations, People, Processes, and Technology

Within the industry transformation snapshot, companies use e-business to create and execute business models very different from those they used in the past. The result is a profound effect on the organization, on individuals, and on information systems and technology. Figure 6.1 illustrates the degree of change across five business dimensions. Historically, most businesses have difficulty managing major change, regardless of whether the change is driven by technology, merger, acquisition, or some other source. People are resilient and will embrace change if

Figure 6.1   Effects of E-Business: Industry Transformation

	High	Moderate	Low
Customers and Markets	✓		
Products and Services		✓	
Organizations and People		✓	
Business Processes	✓		
Information Systems/Technology	✓		

management properly prepares and educates them on its personal impact. However, most major business change is so complex that management is focused on survival of the bottom line and not necessarily on factors motivating employees. In a world of industry transformation, where current standards of major business change will be eclipsed by fast-moving decisions to ally, merge, acquire, and e-partner, executives will be required to carefully consider employee interests and well-being. After all, in industry transformation, the only stable element that a company will have—and its ultimate core competency will be—the knowledge base of its employees.

EFFECTS ON ORGANIZATIONS

Within the industry transformation snapshot, accelerated restructuring flattens the organizational hierarchy throughout the extraprise. However, for companies trying to get to this point, the potential pain factor may be high. Industry transformation requires significant change to organization structures and culture. It will force companies and their people to learn to work in an open environment with employees from other organizations as if they were part of their company.

Companies can overcome this pain by making sure the entire work force understands the change issues involved. The new business case/model and the vision for change should clearly define the organization's refocused strategy as logically moving forward from the value network master position. In so doing, the company has a better chance of maintaining an emotionally "whole" work force as it undertakes and completes its transformation.

Frequent and open communication is required to reinforce new patterns of behavior as the company changes business operations and leverages e-nabling technology throughout the organization. Such communications must clarify what has changed, what may change, and what has not changed.

Since the value network in a transforming company focuses on managing relationships at all levels rather than simply performing tasks, workers will increase their collaboration management skills. And many, at all organizational levels, will become deal makers and information brokers.

In order to accelerate change, management must drive communication and, even more importantly, walk the talk through overt actions. Within this snapshot, the company will intensify interaction with both supply chain and demand chain partners, as well as customers. Networks must be redesigned to support change and continuous improvement around process and culture and should be characterized as extended families of companies.

For example, throughout the development cycle, customers and suppliers must actively participate in establishing a collaborative environment for the development of services. Employees of one company must learn to work directly with their partner-company colleagues. To create value-added relationships, network companies must engage in an open exchange of information and ideas.

The would-be transforming organization will be responsible for managing that change, and, in fact, for developing and managing the extraprise knowledge base. The leader of the company at the heart of an extraprise—the extraprise master—must be an evangelist of change and communicate that commitment through action. He or she must also leverage personal relationships to line up support across the value network.

Ownership of that knowledge will be contested, as participants, including customers, realize the potential value of knowledge ownership. For example, a major user of travel services may choose to maintain its employee profiles and travel history behind its own firewall, as opposed to giving a third party the chance to leverage that knowledge.

EFFECTS ON PEOPLE

As a company engages in industry transformation, management should identify and target key staff as candidates for leadership roles overseeing the extraprise. These individuals will likely be those who are closest to the company's critical success path activities. They are the facilitators of activities throughout the extraprise, who have the capability to make the decisions that propel the company forward. For new companies, the challenge is to select people with the highest potential to operate effectively in these new roles and to indoctrinate them to a culture of empowerment through performance.

Management can use the opportunities arising from the accelerated change that occurs within this snapshot to move these employees into new positions. In addition to moving the best and brightest employees forward, this ensures that the company's most valuable people play critical roles in the company's interactions with its supply-chain and demand-chain partners.

Companies operating during a period of industry transformation must strive to eliminate politics from the way they do business. Partners within the extraprise will view office politics as inhibitors to success. Executives will need not only to understand how things get done (business processes) but also why things get done the way they do (organizational culture). For multiple companies to build strong, integrated relationships, culture will play an integral role. Organizations that have different business cultures may have problems working together as part of an extraprise. Industry transformation will require companies to adapt and embrace change. If one potential partner company's culture is to avoid change and risk, then that company may not be the ideal partner. Remember, operating in an extraprise requires a conscious understanding that the result of a company's actions, whether positive or negative, will directly impact the success of others.

New models of behavior are needed in this radically changed business environment. Management must ensure that the work force is aware of what new behaviors are necessary and in many cases, must literally reinvent itself as it leads by example in the face of changing roles throughout the company. Management should select individuals who model the new behaviors needed to meet the challenge of change and who can serve as mentors or instructors for others. Additionally, in order that employees see the value in the new ways of doing things as well as the pitfalls of suboptimal behavior, management should communicate examples of both.

Changes in a company's business model also bring changes in employee evaluation metrics. These must measure skills and attitudes with regard to external relationships. The external nature of the business demands proficiency in both areas.

EFFECTS ON PROCESSES

In many instances of industry transformation, a company will play an entirely facilitative role. Process will, for the most part, be fully automated. Companies that successfully engineer or reengineer processes to comply to standards that enable scalability, portability, and automated control will be able to stop implementing planned activities and start facilitating the activities of others, thereby gaining significantly better returns. In fact, processes will have to be reengineered seamlessly across partner company boundaries.

This level of process efficiency will only come when technology is being fully leveraged and substantial elements of extraprise-wide change are being successfully managed. The barriers to effecting the process changes associated with transformation heighten the advantage of new entrants over incumbents, despite size and industry complexity.

Interestingly, in the transforming industry, the focus is on core processes—those that add value in the value chain—that were once considered support processes. Management of information and knowledge throughout and among elements of the value chain will become of more value than the activities themselves.

Efficiency and effectiveness in executing support for such processes as IT and strategy management will distinguish companies once value chain activities are optimized throughout the extraprise.

EFFECTS ON INFORMATION SYSTEMS AND TECHNOLOGY

Data Warehousing

As companies struggle to cope with a growing volume of data, the focus of database management technology has shifted from data input to information output. In a highly catalogued and structured manner, a data warehouse organizes company data into a knowledge repository, ensuring that users (especially managers) have access to the right information at the right time.

As an agent of transformation, a company's ability to leverage information will supplant traditional change agents (for example, an enhanced ability to manipulate physical product in a production cycle). The data warehouse enables change, and, in the hands of a savvy company, transforms elements in an industry.

A data warehouse is the repository for a company's critical marketing and customer service decision data. (See Figure 6.2, which illustrates the inflows and outflows of data.) In this respect, data warehousing is a logical extension of the decision-support system (DSS) models that preceded it. A decision-support system facilitates management's and analysts' assimilation and analysis of information. Typical uses of a DSS include trend analysis and detection, performance measurements, problem monitoring, and "what if" scenario modeling.

A data warehouse is a special-purpose database of preprocessed (indexed, partitioned, or preaggregated) and usually many and varied

Figure 6.2   Data Warehouse: Information Inflows and Outflows

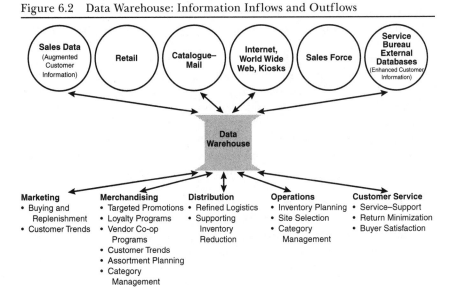

operational data extracts from a company's databases. By effectively organizing data from various databases, the data warehouse provides an orderly, accessible repository of known facts and related data that are used as the basis of inference and knowledge discovery.

Data warehouse systems enable end users to "mine" through the historical data to identify trends and opportunities. A data warehouse offers easier and more timely access to key information by making the fullest use of the data resources available inside and outside the company.

With data warehouse systems, a company can leverage the power of existing internal corporate data to improve customer marketing, streamline business operations, and better understand and forecast its financial position. The value of data warehousing is in its ability to help users make more informed and faster decisions without expending a great deal of effort to identify what data is available.

Users can make quicker and better decisions through an improved understanding of the key trends and events that affect a business. As a result, users spend less time finding data and more time analyzing it and working with other staff to make/develop collaborative decisions/solutions.

As such, a data warehouse supports a number of e-business processes, and the transaction engine that monitors the traffic from Web-based transactions is the tool that collects and accesses this data. In a company that has fully integrated its front-end Web applications with its internal process information, this transaction engine is usually an ERP system.

Data warehousing is critical within the industry transformation snapshot. With the high volume of data collected and exchanged over the Internet, a company needs a highly intelligent mechanism to collect and analyze.

Data warehousing solutions enabled companies to discover the true value of their information, and, therefore, to improve decision making, increase competitiveness, develop more focused marketing programs, and better manage customer relationships. For example, the Web and data warehousing facilitates implementation of innovative targeted marketing programs. Web-based trend analysis tools can be used to collect history on customers' interactions with a company's Web site. This information can be stored and analyzed in a data warehouse.

Using the results of data analysis, a company can "push" special information to customers that is tailored to their behavior during previous visits to the site. If a customer purchases a product during a visit, the Web site can automatically provide information about add-on or related products during the same or during future visits. Each customer encounter will be personalized.

Companies can identify and collect via the Web customer drivers and feedback about products and marketing. They can also use the information to develop advertising campaigns. All of this information can be stored and analyzed in a data warehouse. Using the results of data analysis, a company can tailor campaigns to customer demands and market standards. This process helps a company stay in tune with continually changing customer needs.

For example, in the area of CRM, companies can use information from the Web to build data warehouses that target and segment customers who purchase on-line products and services. By analyzing data warehouse information, they can also determine the drivers that help them build longer-lasting, more profitable customer relationships.

Web technology can also be used as a medium to distribute information, analyses, queries, and reports, and to periodically distribute data to a larger user community. Through data warehousing, companies share performance data and other decision-support information.

A Secure High-Speed Backbone

A secure high-speed backbone facilitates real-time communication, enabling the emergence of knowcos and improving aggregator and facilitator communication networks. The backbone enables easy, fast, and seamless communication with partners.

The rise of the secure high-speed backbone does not, however, resolve enterprise integration issues. Eventually, enterprise integration standards will evolve to support interoperable corporate infrastructures. In other words, as the sophistication of integration mechanisms between companies improves, organizations will find it increasingly easier to communicate with one another.

Integration mechanisms allow real-time communication between the applications of two organizations over a secure, high-speed backbone. Such mechanisms will be intelligent enough to transfer information among the company's systems and logically to interpret this information in the context of a single business process. This allows information that appears to have come from inside, rather than outside, the company acting as network master to be passed back and forth between companies across the extraprise.

For example, suppose a customer is on Company X's Web site, checking the status of an order, and wants to know the delivery date and time for the products she ordered. Also suppose that Company X has outsourced production and delivery of the products to one of its business partners (Company Y). The customer's status check retrieves delivery data and time from Company Y's information system and displays it to the user, who has no idea that her request for this information was sent directly to Company Y.

Through this high degree of integration, delivery data and time information from Company Y's information system can be presented instantly on Company X's Web site. Ultimately, the customer's own information systems will interrogate the company's order-status data automatically, based on the company's business rules, and the customer will deal with actual information only if she is required to take some action.

The Value Network Transformer

Industry transformation's effects on people, processes, and technology are extensive. Coordinating internal change with the change of transforming partners leveraging the entire value chain is the biggest obstacle to achieving this state.

The technology in this snapshot is not significantly different from that in previous snapshots, but, by definition, the true essence of industry transformation means accepting and implementing e-business technology. The extraprise network master may actually have to coach others to create a suite of companies that is ready to leverage technology and to manage change.

Executives of transforming companies lead the way in effecting change throughout their extraprises. Achieving a transformation may require the extraprise master company to allocate IT resources and knowledge to partner companies.

In business-to-consumer models, an extraprise must focus on change while making the relationship with the customer base a top priority. Due to the paucity of customer-specific data (market-of-one data) companies currently hold, the potential gain may be very significant for startups that lack the baggage of multiple cultural changes.

The leader of an extraprise master must also sustain an intimate familiarity with both his or her company's capabilities and with those of partner companies. The lead CEO will have to make strategy decisions for his or her company and for the extraprise.

Widespread use of the Internet as a business mechanism is still in its infancy. And even for companies playing in the industry transformation space today, technology is being pushed to the limit to support new creative business models. Executives need to keep in mind that goals and objectives designed today to become an industry transformer will be impacted over the next few years as technology matures.

Once an extraprise becomes an industry transformer, the business model may be so e-centric that the concept of e-business itself becomes obsolete.

7

Snapshot Four: Convergence

Pundits originally coined the term "industry convergence" to describe the coming together of the communications, information technology, and media industries. They anticipated convergence because, they thought, the commonality of those industries' underlying digital technology would facilitate a merging of products and services, resulting in the migration of people, processes, and business models across industry borders. A series of acquisitions and joint ventures, they surmised, would be a clear sign that these borders were, in fact, blurring.

This has happened to some extent, but not with the speed or to the degree predicted when the idea was first proposed. Although there was an underlying business reason for this convergence to occur, we believe the reason was not the most powerful of business forces. Our understanding of why this original convergence has not happened to the degree expected leads us to propose a wider definition of the term and to suggest a multiplicity of convergence strategies that transcend these original three industries.

Industry convergence is not, in and of itself, an outcome of e-business. Rather, e-business is a facilitator, or perhaps an accelerator, of convergence (Figure 7.1). Current market and industry definitions reflect history as much as optimization in customer value creation.

As many countries, and eventually the world, move toward a frictionless connected economy,* less than optimal regimes—including

---

* "Friction-free capitalism" was a term used by Bill Gates in his book *The Road Ahead* in 1995 (New York: Viking), to describe how the Internet was helping create Adam Smith's ideal marketplace.

Figure 7.1   Snapshot Four: Convergence

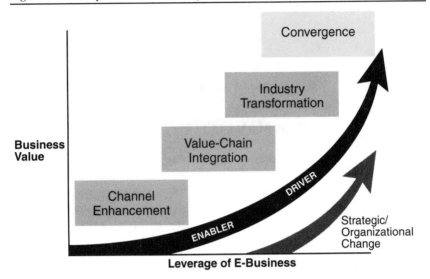

many market segments—will be swept aside. Industry convergence is about competition transcending traditional boundaries to make markets more fluidly match supply with demand.

We broadly define *convergence* as companies seeking new competitive advantage and, in doing so, changing established industry boundaries. In

Figure 7.2   Growth Platforms

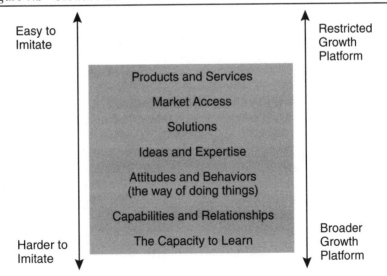

the connected economy, companies increasingly will be competing for the quality and quantity of trust-based relationships. As the basis of competition moves from products and services to relationships, the industry and market focus will move into second place, and convergence will become inevitable.

While capabilities, relationships, and the capacity to learn are harder to develop than product, services, or market access, they also present a company with a much broader platform from which to attain growth (Figure 7.2).

Knowcos, whose sole reason to exist is to leverage learning, knowledge, and relationships, will be in the vanguard of convergence.

DRIVERS OF CONVERGENCE

The key trends that interact to enable convergence are increasing customer sophistication/expectations, deregulation, competitive imperatives, and technology. Figure 7.3 illustrates these trends and a few of the specific concepts and technologies that fall within each.

Figure 7.3   Convergence: Key Trends

Technology	**Deregulation**
• Electronic Commerce • Customer Information Technology • "Death of Distance" • Digital Everything, Technology Convergence • Information Content of Products and Services Increasing Steadily	• Regulated Markets Opening Up • Fewer Regulatory Impediments in Business • Single Currency Zones • Regulators Outflanked by Changing Boundaries and Unstoppable Forces (Internet and E-Business)
Competitive Imperatives	**Customer Sophistication/ Expectations**

• Imperatives:
  - Real Growth (but in saturated markets)
  - Globalization
  - Customer Orientation
  - Knowledge and Capability as Key Assets (rather than "factory factors")
  - New Entrants
• Enablers:
  - Alliances
  - Outsourcing
	• Demand for Better and More Convenient *Solutions*
	• Increased Emphasis on Service
	• Demand for Added Value
	• Less Tolerance for Poor Standards
	• Just-in-Time Delivery
	• Global Influences
	• Brand "Savvy"

Convergence

E-business is one of the lift-off points for industry convergence. It decouples markets by breaking out the physical and information sides of a company, an industry, even an economy, and allows the information side to grow unconstrained by limitations of how the physical side can be improved.

Companies that are changing market boundaries break down traditional product and service distinctions by delivering new and different forms of value to customers. We believe the most powerful convergence strategies are those dictated by customer demand. Therefore, in and of itself, a random, technology-based convergence of the communications, media, and information technology industries would not be particularly powerful.

True convergence only occurs in the eye of the customer or consumer. (Industry designation is based on customer perception.) A company's ability or desire to offer its customers new "convergent" products or services is weighed against a number of possible barriers and inertia factors (Figure 7.4).

Success with convergent offerings will largely be driven by two factors: market credibility and ability to deliver. In the business-to-business world, beyond a basic level of credibility, sustained competency and competitiveness is the main success factor. In the consumer space, competency is sometimes simplified into the shorthand *brand*, and credibility for new products or services is known as *brand stretch*.

Some consumer brands are capable of significant stretch. Virgin is perhaps the best-known example. By making a virtue of bringing a new, "virgin," antiestablishment approach to existing areas of business, it has come to epitomize values that transcend any particular business. However, care must be taken when analyzing brand plays, as much activity is simply opportunistic brand extension that distracts from the real core of convergence: improvement in market effectiveness.

Figure 7.4   Convergence: Barriers and Inertia Factors

• Company History and Politics • Lack of Corporate Capability and Vision • Legacy Investments and Infrastructure • Lack of Electronic Commerce Penetration • Customer Inertia and Resistance to Change (even positive change)	• Logistics Practicalities • Traditional Economic Entry Barriers • Regulation • Importance of Perceived Product Specialization to the Customer • Production-Oriented Success Factors • Limited Market in Outsourcing (limiting scope for new entrants)	• Customer Dislike of Monopolies, Loss of Choice and Aspirations to World Dominance • Rejection of Non–Value-Added "Brand Imperialism" • Limit to How Much Consolidation Regulators Will Allow

Transitory ◄————————————————————————► Fundamental

CUSTOMERS DICTATE INDUSTRIES

The basis for competition is changing. Market share is being superceded by the share of customer relationships a company owns. Competitive advantage is derived more from relationship quality and less from traditionally defined assets.

Customers who find it progressively easier to deal with a company will want that company to offer even more and will be increasingly reluctant to form relationships with competitors, particularly those that are untried.*

PricewaterhouseCoopers' consumer research in 1998 found that 82 percent of people surveyed responded positively to the statement: "I don't care who supplies me with anything, providing the service is good, the quality is high, and I know where to get satisfaction if anything is wrong." Such a sentiment is both a threat to and an opportunity for companies old and new.

We can observe the symptoms of this new, customer-driven world order daily. Many of them are heightened by e-business. The following are only a few:

○ More bundling and unbundling of products and services

○ General movement from products to services (solutions), with the product viewed as a small part of the total relationship

○ More alliances to access and serve customers and to exploit technology

○ Erosion of traditional entry barriers, growth in markets predominantly driven by new entrants—Nike not Dunlop; CNN not CBS or BBC

○ Widespread investigation of brand extension and a greater focus on corporate branding, for example, British Airways entering financial services

○ Companies trying to define their businesses much more broadly

○ Conglomerates looking for synergies across business units

○ Development of hybrid value chains

○ Increasing emphasis on differentiation through service

○ Major mergers and demergers to create more focused businesses

○ "Slicing and dicing" of previously monolithic markets, for example, segmentation in telephony by customer and service

---

*See Don Peppers and Martha Rogers, *The One to One Future* (New York: Currency Doubleday, 1993), pp. 67–68.

○ Exploration and development of wider channels to market; for example, BSkyB is now "platform neutral," not a "satellite television operator"

○ Companies focusing more strongly on customer information and customer relationships

○ Wider sources and forms of competition; for example, Coca-Cola defines its main competitor as tap water rather than another brand of cola.

Markets with clear-cut boundaries are a thing of the past, and we can observe the forced intersection of many industries happening globally. As Figure 7.5 illustrates in a simplified way, companies are squeezing themselves into the intersections of industries. For example, banks now have interests in media, telecommunications, and travel services. Retailers have links to energy and telecommunications companies. Some media companies—QVC, for example—are also retail operations, and others, such as Reuters and Bloomberg, link to financial services. Energy companies, such as Shell, Mobil, and BP, are moving into retailing and others have spawned telecommunications companies, such as Energis. Fast-moving consumer goods (FMCG) and manufacturing companies such as General

Figure 7.5   Industry Converging Plays

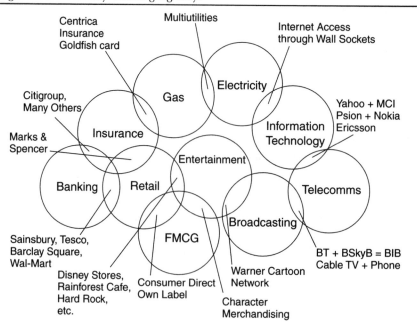

Motors and General Electric now offer financial services (GM card and GE capital).

For an established business with a customer relationship, the simplest form of convergence occurs as the business begins to leverage that customer relationship in order to provide other services or to sell other goods under the company's brand.

Grocery stores have been moving this way since the mid-1990s. They have set up relationships with banks to open branches in their stores, and some have even gone into banking under their own name. Wal-Mart, for example, sought permission from the U.S. Federal Reserve in 1999 to purchase a bank.

Supermarkets also have added gasoline stations. Some are going into Web-based grocery ordering and delivery services that are sometimes combined with Internet access provision. And once they get into billing, rather than cash- or credit-card-based transactions at the checkout, they will be discussing the possibility of aggregating bills for other service providers or for utilities. Banks are also looking to get into the bill aggregation business, hoping to leverage their ability to transact direct payment without using a third party.

The reason the grocery giants are leading the way is simply that they have saturated markets in their core industry and regard other sectors as relatively "soft targets" for increasing their share of the customer relationship.

Looking across industry sectors, we can see the extent of convergence to date. These six examples are only a small piece of the convergence pie:

1. Fourteen of the world's top 20 media companies are in information technology or Web-based services.

2. Ten of the top 20 telecommunications companies offer media services.

3. Eight of the top 10 information technology companies offer media or entertainment services.

4. Fifteen of the top 20 retailers offer financial services, and eight of the 20 sell gasoline.

5. Fourteen of the top 20 financial services companies have combined insurance and banking (and often other services).

6. Six out of the top 20 FMCG companies have media interests.

NEW ENTRANTS SPEED CONVERGENCE

If this weren't bad enough for established companies, new entrants, without pre-existing physical assets, are looking to aggregate information in order to create a new relationship with customers. These new players, essentially service companies, are attempting to become "infomediaries" and gatekeepers for product and service companies that don't have a strong customer relationship.

Precisely because customer relationship management is not product specific, those who are best at it can look to leverage their capability across a wider set of customer needs. Experts at the product end of the business will be boxed in: Actuaries cannot make cars, engineers cannot construct insurance policies.

This implies a race among aspiring customer relationship companies to secure that customer connection, achieve economies of scale, and construct the most compelling bundles and propositions. E-business accelerates the race by opening up opportunities for new entrants to come straight in at the point of customer contact.

The visibility of this race is reflected in the unrealistically high valuations of many Internet stocks—those that lose the most money seem to have the highest valuations. Such companies rationalize the huge sums they spend prior to realizing even one penny of profit as necessary attempts to gain the largest customer base. Because of their customer focus and ability to reposition rapidly, these industry-transforming aggregators are likely to be among the key instigators of convergence.

THE BATTLEGROUND

At the start of the convergence wars, one could visualize the cross-industry landscape as a game board on which the players—established companies, new entrants, physcos, and knowcos—position and reposition themselves with new products and services. Soon, though, even this will become the "old way" of looking at markets, as traditional boundaries lose their usefulness. Customer trust becomes the key.

For our purposes, the definition of trust is:

Trust = Integrity + Depth and Breadth of Perceived Capability

Trust is area specific. Businesses and brands have "zones of trust" based on their perceived integrity and experience. In the end, the battle is for customer trust that ultimately leads to customer partnership. For new entrants, however fleet of foot they may be in moving across industries, the battle is for the same customer trust that established players may have built up over decades.

Having established the scope of the battleground, and the various parties to the battle, it is possible to investigate in detail some strategies that are being brought into play.

CONVERGENCE STRATEGIES

Convergence involves multiple shifts in strategic emphasis (Figure 7.6). Many of these have appeared in the previous snapshots of the e-business panorama.

Established companies considering the convergent future are facing many deep strategic dilemmas. They ask themselves:

○ Will our lunch be eaten? If so, by whom?

○ If we stick to our knitting, do we get stuck in it?

Figure 7.6   Shifts in Strategic Emphasis

From	To
Market Research–Defined Markets	Customer Defined Spaces
Product Defined Companies and Markets (e.g., batteries)	Solution and Capability Defined Companies and Markets (e.g., power systems)
Market Share	Share of Value Created and Share of Customer
Production-Oriented Core Capabilities—Physco	Convergence Capabilities—knowco
"We have to do it ourselves"—Competing Companies	It is Better to be Part of a Winning Network—Competing Networks
Erecting Economic Entry Barriers	Creating and Managing New Customer Value through Relationships—"Customer Partnering"
Improving Corporate Effectiveness	Improving Market Effectiveness
Sales Management and Product Management	Relationship Management
Channels as Product Pipelines	Channels as Media and Information Sources
Product Excellence	Proposition and Relationship Excellence
Competing for End Customers	Competing for Relationships (of various types, including customers)
Brand Extension	Creating Unique (Corporate) Brand Platforms
Branding Products	Branding Relationships and Capabilities
Product-Centric Organizations	Customer-Centric Organizations
Value in the Product	Value in the Total Experience and Relationship

○ Is our customer relationship strong enough, or do we retreat into a niche; should we allow intermediation and become an original equipment manufacturer (OEM)?

○ Where do we find a new business and economic model—one as good as the old model?

○ What is the best balance of offense and defense?

○ Are our assets the ones that will drive future success? Do we cannibalize?

○ When do we join in? Should we be a first, second, or third mover?

Many of these dilemmas have emerged in the earlier stages of the developing e-business panorama. The complexity in the convergent world is that competition comes from within and without a given industry, and from a mix of old and new players. This is a daunting prospect or an exciting opportunity, depending on one's point of view.

To make sense of this and to suggest some answers to the dilemmas we have outlined, we have developed a framework for classifying various e-business convergence strategies. Many of these strategies—those discussed here as well as those discussed in earlier chapters—may be used in combination and carried out simultaneously.

Leveraging Relationships

Leveraging relationships is, perhaps, the simplest convergence strategy. Based on an existing relationship, a supplier sees the opportunity to extend the relationship and gain an improved share of the customer's wallet. The supplier's understanding of the customer determines the accuracy of his or her estimate of the customer's desire, or need, for new products or services. The customer's desire to buy new offers from the supplier is based on trust. A convergence play starts if the new goods or services fall outside of the supplier's traditional industry classification.

This opportunity is driven by customer choice. The new goods and services have to be meaningful to the customer, and the supplier must be a credible source. In this simplest example of convergence, there is not necessarily any direct link between the new supply and the old.

Examples of relationship leveraging include a grocery retailer, an airline, and a gasoline service station company that each offer a credit card. Depending on the supplier's market positioning (branding), the offer can be presented in different ways: convenience, quality, or assured lowest cost.

To be able to offer the new goods and services, the supplier has the choice of producing them itself or sourcing them from a third party. The latter is the more likely approach. The availability of efficient outsourcing for goods and services is essential to the convergent world's becoming a reality. For a pure knowco, of course, outsourcing is the only route to meeting customer requirements.

Bundling/Blurring

A bundling play is an adjunct to leveraging relationships. Convergence is focused on the vendor and its offer. As before, the objective is to enlarge the scope of the customer relationship—and take more of the customer's wallet—by repositioning the vendor in a wider way, typically by moving from products to services.

In this convergent offer, products and services from a number of industries are combined to offer the customer a solution. Wrapping products in a service and blurring the distinction between the two are characteristic of solution offers. The offer, in effect, redefines the industry. For instance, the auto industry becomes a mobility service when the vehicle is combined with leasing, finance, insurance, and roadside repair/recovery.

Gatekeeping

Gatekeeping is the dark side of customer relationship selling. In relationship leveraging or bundling, a customer freely chooses among vendors. Here, customer choice is proscribed by available options within a supplier-controlled environment. The concept is simple: Create a "captive" customer for whom all purchases must be funneled through the gatekeeper. To be successful in this strategy, being first mover is almost mandatory.

There are various manifestations of the capture, and in many cases the customer does not necessarily either realize or resent captive status. Ironically, the networked economy makes such capture possible. When a customer is connected to the network, depending on the nature of the connection, a variety of capture opportunities arise.

Captures may be weak or strong. A weak capture occurs through, for example, an Internet portal or buying club—where the customer can walk away at any time. A strong capture occurs where, for example, the infrastructure—a television set-top box (STB) or a last-mile network connection—physically locks the vendor in. Somewhere between the two is an access provider such as AOL or Freeserve that operates over a third-party network.

The degree to which gatekeeping can be leveraged for revenue depends on the strength of the capture. In the weak case, the opportunity is in securing the customer "eyeball," and a gain in advertising revenues rather than any direct revenues from the customer. At the strong end of the scale, not only can the vendor sell goods and services, but it can also charge third parties a tariff for access and customers for the connection, making money from both ends of the pinch-point. Such strong gatekeeping models almost inevitably attract the attention of regulators. The perceived value of the gatekeeping strategy is manifested in the valuations of the Internet portals and access providers. (Perhaps, however, they are somewhat overvalued, indicating a lack of market understanding as to the degree of real lock-in).

Some—we believe erroneously—draw a valuation analogy between a portal (weak) and a TV channel in the early days of broadcasting (strong). Weak gatekeepers, however, can become remarkably strong if they move early enough to become a de facto standard. The Sabre airline booking system and Microsoft's Windows computer operating system are archetypes of this assertion.

To create these "virtual" monopolies of customer access almost invariably requires early "seeding," such as free information, free set-top boxes, or free Internet access. The hope is to quickly make the transition to being the standard and, in so doing, create a market-entry barrier based on customer lock-in and capitalize on the customers' fear of "buying Beta rather than VHS." Metcalf's Law—the notion that the value of a network rises as the square of the number of nodes (in our example customers within the network)—works powerfully in favor of the aspiring gatekeeper with deep pockets. Exploiting this effect will be the predominant driver in a rapidly changing e-business world that lacks recognized industry standards.

Cross-Industry Competence

The extraprise and market transformation concepts extend into the convergent world. Increasingly, production-oriented competencies can be outsourced or gained through alliances. An alternative strategy for revenue growth is available for companies with limited end consumer impact that are not at the head of their industry value chains.

Some competencies are readily transferable from one industry sector to another—customer call-center operations or printed circuit board assembly, for example. Companies with transferable skills, best practices, or manufacturing efficiencies can offer these services to players in other industries. These cross-industry players, typically physcos, are sources for the services, business processes, and manufacturing required by the know-cos responsible for convergence at the front end of the value chain.

Disintermediation/Reintermediation

It is worth recalling here that disintermediation and reintermediation can be powerful convergence plays. Suppliers further down the value chain can attempt to bypass the middleman and move, for example, from manufacturing to direct retailing. New-entrant knowcos will bundle goods and services from multiple industries without a qualm, to create new customer value propositions.

Brand Acquisition

Some companies—typically service companies—will come to realize that strength in particular parts of their enterprise could offer competitive advantage in other industries.

To enter an industry remote from its core business, a company can acquire customers either through buying or allying with a strong brand or branded company. In essence this is a core competency leverage play at the front end of the value chain.

This strategy can lead to some remarkable results. Consider, for example, the Centrica acquisition of the Automobile Association in the United Kingdom, on its face, a very unpredictable convergence. It was presented to the press as a customer service offer, an unlikely rationale, perhaps, given the separation of the two companies' activities in customers' minds. (Central heating maintenance and roadside car repair?) And merging the brands would probably damage both.

But if we consider the core competencies of both companies—customer call centers coupled with fleet management and a mobile skilled repair work force—an alternative explanation (or at least a complementary strategy) becomes apparent.

Technology Convergence

The commonality of underlying digital technologies allows the creation of new, cross-industry products. Creation of the product in itself does not make for a strategy, but its exploitation to create new markets or services can have a significant impact.

Often, technology-product introductions and gatekeeper strategies are related. For example, the creation of new consumer devices—satellite TV and STBs—permitted the United Kingdom's BSkyB to make a powerful gatekeeper play. The battle to control the next generation of digital STBs, which will allow control over interactive TV, home shopping, home banking, and pay-per-view, is being vigorously fought in the United Kingdom with offers of free devices—a classic would-be gatekeeper's strategy.

One can imagine many cross-industry devices—a combination personal digital assistant (PDA)/cellphone that offers photographs of sporting events and stock quotes, for example. The trick is to devise the exploitation strategy.

Market Making

Perhaps the most exciting and challenging convergence opportunity is to create entirely new markets. Depending on new network technologies, markets (or exchanges) can be created where none before existed.

Software vendors have already created the necessary technology to operate in almost any market paradigm—auction, reverse auction, or sealed tender. Operation of these markets will further drive the efficiency of the networked economy.

Already, new entrants such as MRO.com are setting up services based on sourcing indirect goods and services. We will see the supply and demand sides of many markets being brought together more efficiently through a market-making mechanism that suppliers of vendors own independently or even jointly. These exchanges will eventually "become the industry." Smart players recognize this. (Witness the recent announcement by Ford, GM, and DaimlerChrysler of the combining of their portals.)

DIMENSIONS AND IMPERATIVES OF CONVERGENCE

In addition to the convergence strategies, we need to consider the scope of the convergence play. There are a number of "dimensions" to any convergence strategy. These are illustrated in Figure 7.7. In and of themselves, these dimensions do not necessarily indicate the success of a particular strategic move today. They will become more useful as more case studies appear and as winning or losing strategy/dimension combinations are documented.

History is not always a good predictor of the future. But convergence is challenging established companies, and a quarter century down the road, the landscape will likely be littered with corporate wreckage.

Figure 7.7   "Dimensions" of Any Convergence Strategy

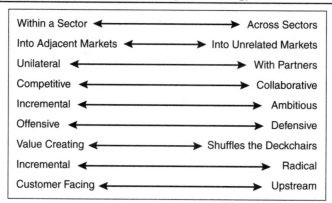

Within a Sector ◄─────────► Across Sectors
Into Adjacent Markets ◄───────► Into Unrelated Markets
Unilateral ◄─────────► With Partners
Competitive ◄─────────► Collaborative
Incremental ◄─────────► Ambitious
Offensive ◄─────────► Defensive
Value Creating ◄───────► Shuffles the Deckchairs
Incremental ◄─────────► Radical
Customer Facing ◄─────────► Upstream

In the convergent world, there are 10 imperatives for winning:

1. Take a much more multidimensional view of the competition and market definition—competing for "share of consumer trust," "share of consumer expectation," or "share of consumer expenditure," with a mantra of "follow the money." Example: Tesco competing for "share of stomach."

2. Actively seek out opportunities for market transformation and the creation of discontinuity (before someone else does it first). Example: Johnson & Johnson's leadership of the "Gateway" concept for health-care product sourcing and delivery in the United Kingdom.

3. Compete as much for the key relationships as for anything else. Example: Virgin's attractiveness to partners, resulting in such products as Virgin Vodka.

4. Build business definition and growth on distinctively strong branding capability. Example: Miniaturization for Sony.

5. Complete a shift from product orientation to customer focus. Example: Direct Line insurance.

6. Be an integral part of a "virtually" vertically integrated value chain. Example: Dell Computer's drawing on a network of partners, bucking the "we do it ourselves" industry convention.

7. Ensure the company's capabilities are delivered through simple, powerful value propositions with growth potential. Example: "The future is Orange."

8. Ensure that the organization's role in its markets is clear and defensible. Example: "Intel Inside®."

9. Recognize that the company's greatest historic strength could be its greatest future weakness. Example: Midland Bank (now HSBC) launching First Direct with no reference to its parentage.

10. Have integrity, as standards will be more transparent and anti-customer behavior harder to conceal. Example: Web sites publicizing the alleged behavior of various large oil companies.

8

Snapshot Four: Effects of Convergence on Organizations and People

Convergence will drive a number of changes within organizations. As companies cultivate their expertise at developing products and services that cross traditional industry boundaries, they will be forced to reevaluate their capabilities and operations. By thoroughly addressing the fundamental challenges in these areas, companies will be able to deliver the innovative solutions required. Figure 8.1 illustrates the effects of convergence on five key areas: customers/markets, products/services, organizations/people, processes, and information systems/technology.

Figure 8.1   Effects of E-Business: Convergence

	High	Moderate	Low
Customers and Markets	✓		
Products and Services	✓		
Organizations and People	✓		
Business Processes		✓	
Information Systems/ Technology		✓	

CAPABILITIES FOR CONVERGENCE

To achieve leadership in the convergent world, companies must nurture and cultivate a number of capabilities. The degree to which an organization is able to demonstrate these capabilities will determine its success. In a convergent world, effectively managing seven key dimensions of the business will define the winners:

1. Alliances and partnerships
2. Customer relationships
3. Customer information
4. Corporate brand
5. Facilitating technologies
6. Innovation
7. Regulatory environment.

Managing Alliances and Partnerships

Over the long term, sustained relationships are often most valuable. Successful execution of alliances and partnerships is required to gain access to the new technologies, production capacity, and channels that result in new and different product and service offerings.

Effectively managing alliances and partnerships means integrating the capabilities of other companies in a systematic and mutually worthwhile manner. Companies must maintain a strategic focus as they develop relationships with others. This includes working with solution-defined companies, as well as more narrowly focused product-defined companies.

Companies must carefully evaluate make/buy decisions. For example, it may make more sense for a company to add strength and reach by being part of a winning network than by performing all operations itself.

Finally, a win-win mindset helps create the most value in intercompany partnerships.

Managing Customer Relationships

The battle to serve the customer, or consumer, is unrelenting. In an e-nabled, convergent environment, competitors come from anywhere, at any time.

In a convergent world, the value chain focuses on customers rather than product development—a major shift. In this world, customer relationship management is the focus of the company rather than merely an activity in the value chain.

Product-based companies make money selling products. Customer-centric companies make money from the value of their relationships. However, this model is often complex. Companies need to embrace the possibility of radically changing their business models by developing profitable customer relationships that maximize value.

Managing Customer Information

Managing customer information involves effectively collecting, analyzing, and applying that information. In a convergent world, share of customer relationship, rather than market share, is the primary metric. Companies must, therefore, create value for customers, as well as for shareholders; value must flow in both directions. Effective customer information management is the key.

Although it is irrational to treat all customers in the same way, good information is necessary in order to treat customers differently. To understand the customer, one must focus on the way in which the customer interacts with the company rather than on customer characteristics and transactions alone.

Managing the Corporate Brand

Effective branding at the corporate level is increasingly important in a convergent world. Customers want to know what lies behind the company's public persona.

Product brands have often been barriers, rather than links, to customers. Brand economics work best when an umbrella or "banner" synergy is in play. Sustaining a separate portfolio of brands is less tenable in a cluttered media and business environment. Success requires integrating the efforts of all stakeholders, especially staff.

Corporate branding, which works through staff, is about managing the company's reputation across all audiences. This management is even more critical as the competitive emphasis moves from products and transactions to meeting needs through two-way relationships, where trust is the main currency. Most world-class brands are now companies or virtual companies, but many so-called brands are just companies with names.

Managing Facilitating Technologies

Facilitating (digital) technologies have far-reaching consequences. Managing them effectively means using them to solve problems and create value. For example, the prospective explosion of television channels through digital satellite and cable is well documented. But the addition of interactive capabilities to the broadcast medium will change television forever. The companies that can master the technologies associated with this medium have much to gain.

Managing Innovation

Innovation management is the ability to stimulate and apply useful new ideas. An innovative company has five fundamental characteristics:

1. High degree of management trust
2. Active flow of ideas
3. Few organizational levels between executives and customers
4. Explicit idea management processes that people adhere to
5. Ability to recruit and retain talented managers who:
   - Delegate decision making
   - Involve others in developing ideas into actions
   - Routinely envision the future based on intimate market knowledge
   - Do not rely on the board alone for significant new ideas
   - Take a balanced view of risk.

Managing the Regulatory Environment

In some industries "case making to regulators" is an important supporting capability. Because convergence blurs traditional industry boundaries, companies must be able to describe the competitiveness of their market focus in economic terms that regulators can relate to.

CHARACTERISTICS OF A "CAPABLE" ORGANIZATION

Relatively few companies are world class in all of these capabilities, which are strongly learning based and oriented more toward knowcos than physcos. As a result, it is highly likely that knowco leadership will create the convergent world.

Convergent companies that will achieve these capabilities will be defined by 10 characteristics. They will be:

1. Customer centric
2. Uninhibited by legacies of success or failure
3. Pragmatic with regard to technology
4. Project oriented

5. Flexible with regard to resources
6. Networked effectively across internal boundaries
7. Designed to continually evolve both offers and business models
8. Knowledge based
9. Virtually vertically integrated
10. Expert at partnership.

EFFECTS ON ORGANIZATIONS

Employees need to know the company's business model in order to manage change successfully. Because employing e-business strategies and technologies frequently changes the business, managing change requires open communication and employees' willingness to accept and promote change.

In the convergent snapshot, true democratization of the business case for change emerges. Innovation is the key to developing successful new offerings that are technology hybrids of converging industries.

Embedding innovation into the company and into the individual learning environment makes possible the evolution of the business model and helps the company adapt to the constantly changing environment. In such an environment, managing change becomes everyone's responsibility, individually and collectively.

The convergent company's change vision, or focus, must be clearer than the traditional company's because so much of the business is intangible. The speed of innovation and change makes communicating the change vision in this arena a critical imperative. In other words, as John Chambers, CEO of Cisco Systems has pointed out in an article in *Fortune* magazine (May 24, 1999), to successfully communicate the change vision, "You've got to evangelize the concept."

That same article points out the differences between CEOs and e-CEOs. While CEOs of traditional companies are cordial, e-CEOs are brutally frank. Traditional CEOs are fast moving; e-CEOs are faster. Traditional CEOs hate ambiguity; e-CEOs thrive on it. Traditional CEOs are clearly focused; e-CEOs are intensely so. Traditional CEOs encourage; e-CEOs evangelize. Traditional CEOs are alert; e-CEOs are paranoid. Both traditional and e-CEOs are paragons of good judgment.

With constantly evolving product and/or service offerings, companies may need to shift their corporate structures and the responsibilities within those structures. Doing so allows the company to better meet customer needs. Simultaneously, companies must restructure their compensation, recognition, and reward policies. A convergent company may choose to reward staff not on sales booked, but on customer evaluations.

If employees are expected to provide innovation and to drive change as part of their day-to-day activities, they must do so within an environment that supports flexibility and discourages working groups, departments, or divisions from maintaining the status quo.

However, realignment of rewards may not be enough to retain the best talent. With the demand for cutting-edge innovative skills increasing every day, companies must create work environments that foster individuality within team frameworks.

Companies must manage cultural change proactively to anticipate employees' changing needs and must consider that those needs will extend beyond recognition and rewards to include such areas as medical benefits, savings plans, investment opportunities, training, work-life balance, and schedule/work hours.

Enabling technology helps maintain the culture and capture the skills an organization needs as it shifts and adjusts within the Internet economy. For example, Web-based recruiting and screening can help lower costs and improve recruiting efficiency.

Utilizing employees to assist in the electronic screening process accomplishes two goals. First, it allows employees to evaluate the human capital potentially being brought into the company. Thus, employees can protect their "investment" in the company. Second, it creates buy-in to the hiring process. As a result, employees have a vested interest in seeing the recruits they select succeed in the company. However, streamlined recruiting processes are only one aspect of successful recruiting. Employees must have the right skills and fit appropriately with the company's culture.

EFFECTS ON PEOPLE

Individual employees must continue to keep pace with the evolving business model by taking an active role in determining that their current skills are aligned with company needs. After this assessment, an employee may decide to change or shift his or her skill set to help satisfy a need elsewhere in the company.

Training must be readily available for individuals who need to change skill sets. With innovation as a hallmark of the convergent world, employees must be encouraged to learn new concepts and practices in order to further the company's goals.

In the convergent world, a company's employees may work very closely with business partners to create and facilitate new products and/or services or product/service bundles. The organizational integration characteristic of convergence may make a company's employees feel more "mobile" or more confident that they can leverage their skill sets elsewhere.

A good way to keep employees on board is to constantly involve them in recreating the change vision. E-business can be extremely empowering to those who understand the concepts well. If employees feel directed rather than empowered, the company risks employee defections.

That being said, "sharing" loyal company staff with business partners gives them more opportunities to try new ideas while furthering corporate relationships with supply- and demand-chain partners. This can be a useful way to fulfill individuals' creative needs, while improving the company's status. Allowing key employees to work in intellectually stimulating client environments is something law firms, consulting firms, and other organizations have done for years, though in ways less fluid than current suggested approaches.

END OF THE RAINBOW

The challenge for traditional companies in this ultimate state is recruiting and retaining valued employees. Large corporations are already finding it hard to hire excellent IT staff on America's West Coast. Increasingly, the new generation of programmers prefer to trade salary for stock options in an e-business start-up and risk one or two business failures. With stock options, they reason, only one success is necessary.

In Silicon Valley, loyalty is to the Valley as a concept, not to any one company. As industries fragment (snapshot three) and converge (snapshot four), individuality and individual power rises. Highly networked individuals in loose associations (partnerships from an earlier age) could become the dominant model for the business of the future—the successful knowco.

9

Managing Risk
in E-Business

Throughout this book, we have argued that in order to create customer value in the twenty-first century, and in turn provide corporate revenue and growth, a company needs to change its business model and engage in e-business. Major changes include: bypassing existing distribution channels to sell directly to customers; bundling products and services in new ways; integrating the value chain tightly with business partners; outsourcing applications and business processes; and reengineering industrywide processes.

However, the transition to an e-business operating model brings with it a number of risks. We have touched on the notion of risk in our chapters on how companies are affected by each snapshot within the e-business landscape. This chapter focuses on those risks in greater detail.

RISKS WITHIN E-BUSINESS

Some risks are new: implementation of and support for new products, services, and markets; security concerns around the use of public networks; and tax and legal issues surrounding the Internet, for example.

Existing risks are also heightened by a move to e-business. Among these are: maintaining appropriate controls and governance over core business processes; business continuity planning in a 24×7 environment; and developing appropriate employee skills.

Although risk is traditionally seen as a negative, the upside of risk is opportunity. Without engaging in business risk, companies cannot take advantage of opportunities and will not flourish in the e-nabled world of twenty-first century business.

A RISK MANAGEMENT MODEL

A proper risk management strategy is key to assessing the risk/opportunity ratio. Companies undergoing significant changes related to entry into the e-business environment need a framework and methodology for managing their risks. This framework helps them take the risks that lead to reward, mitigate necessary risks, avoid unnecessary risks, and properly allocate risk management resources.

To properly manage the risks of engaging in e-business, company executives must work with a common language, common approaches, and a common understanding of the company's goals and objectives. So that resources can be properly allocated, risk management for e-business requires a systematic approach that allows for timely identification and assessment of risks.

Given a company's strategic objective, a particular risk can be characterized in one of three ways: hazard, uncertainty, or opportunity. After analyzing the degree of acceptability, the magnitude, and the reward associated with the risk, management then chooses the appropriate risk option.

Management can accept, control or mitigate, or transfer the risk. Having made this decision, management then monitors the risk and its response and feeds that back into a constant review of strategic objectives.

COMMON E-BUSINESS RISKS

We have identified 15 e-business risks:

1. Strategic direction
2. Competitive environment
3. Dependence on others
4. Security
5. Reputation
6. Culture
7. Technology
8. Governance
9. Project management
10. Operations
11. Legal and regulatory
12. Human resources
13. Business process controls
14. Tax
15. Currency.

Figure 9.1   E-Business Risks: View #1

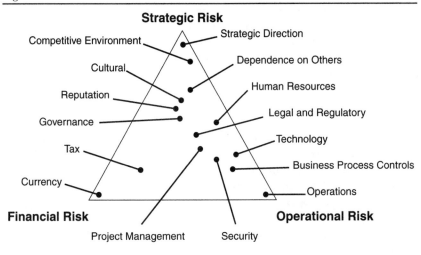

These risks can be mapped in one of two ways. First, we can position each individual risk along a triangular map with three major categories—strategic, financial, and operational risks—occupying the three corners (Figure 9.1). The other way to map the 15 risks is across the four e-business snapshots (Figure 9.2). All of these risks are present to one degree or another in all four of the snapshots. In Figure 9.2, the degree of risk is weighed on a scale of 1 to 4. A level one risk has a low probability of occurring and a small effect on the company if it does. A level two risk is

Figure 9.2   E-Business Risks: View #2

	Channel Enhancement	Value-Chain Integration	Industry Transformation	Convergence
Strategic Direction	3	3	4	4
Competitive Environment	1	3	4	4
Dependence on Others	2	4	4	4
Security	4	4	4	4
Reputation	2	3	4	4
Culture	1	3	4	4
Technology	2	3	4	4
Governance	1	3	4	4
Project Management	1	3	4	4
Operations	1	4	4	4
Legal & Regulatory	1	3	4	4
Human Resources	1	2	3	3
Business Process Controls	2	4	3	3
Tax Issues	4	4	4	4
Currency Issues	4	4	4	4

high probability, but small effect. Level three is low probability, but significant effect. And level four is high probability with significant effect.

The relevance of each risk category with respect to e-business, regardless of which snapshot a particular company occupies must be understood. The remainder of this chapter is devoted to a detailed discussion of each of these risks.

Strategic Direction

Success of e-business initiatives is directly affected by the company's ability to develop a strategic plan and to work to that plan. Even in the infancy of e-business, a company's strategic plan can make or break the company if channel conflicts occur. To reduce the risk of failure due to lack of existing infrastructure, the strategic plan must identify the major e-business growth initiatives for all areas of the company.

The strategic plan in support of e-business should be able to identify gaps in existing practices. Gap solutions and benefits should be carefully developed using, whenever possible, both qualitative and quantitative means. Benchmarking against competitive practices may provide one means by which a company can evaluate the impact of a strategic plan. Well thought-out performance measurements based on best practices and designed to ensure the plan's success can reduce the risk of failure.

The issues facing a company considering sell-side channel enhancement plays can be considerable, and the risk associated with leadership's failure to comprehend the strategic implications, to develop a sound plan, and to sufficiently sponsor change are significant. Fortunately, the risk impact associated with buy-side channel enhancement is relatively low and so, not surprisingly, many large enterprises will start their e-business journey here.

The implications of unsound strategic planning in an e-nabled value chain are heightened because of increased exposure to failure as more players are brought into the extraprise.

Industry transformation often involves discarding traditional business models. This move should not be taken lightly. The risk of failure here, caused by lack of executive sponsorship and discontinuity of strategic direction, is relatively high.

From an e-business perspective, it is critical that the strategic plan identify the major components required in an enterprisewide IT infrastructure. This network will allow the company to forge ahead with its e-initiatives. Additionally, potential e-business partners should be identified at this stage to maintain the company's outward focus.

E-business initiatives will pose a greater risk of failure if a company embarks on a haphazard progression toward maturity. When time or financial or manpower resources preclude an enterprisewide rollout, the rollout should occur in logical stages.

For example, if sales and customer service are not coordinated prior to beginning a major overhaul of the supply chain, high risk will impact some of the currently invisible value chain elements that will be integrated.

The ability to demonstrate a strong return on investment is another important driver of e-business initiatives. Often, the total cost of such initiatives is very difficult to capture and initial IT implementation outlays may be deceptively low. A company should be careful not to overlook the opportunity cost of erroneous e-business decisions, or of not taking any action at all.

Competitive Environment

As the competitive environment relative to e-business heats up, companies are eager to leverage the possession of real-time information. Therefore, while the timeline for the strategic plan should be geared toward minimizing misdirected effort, it should not be so drawn out that competitive advantage is compromised.

Implementation delays pose significant risk to a company racing to obtain first-mover advantage. Investments in a fail-safe implementation, ensuring appropriate resources and resource redundancy, and involving multiple delivery providers are ways to reduce this risk.

On the one hand, if a company is the first mover, it may be able to leverage the absence of a competitor. On the other hand, if the company is naturally a follower, it must understand that, in the world of e-business, few isolating mechanisms exist.

Barriers to entry are minimal. Additionally, learning curves are becoming shorter and only subject to a company's ability to develop or otherwise attract the expertise needed to maintain its vital business functions. These compressed learning curves allow companies quickly to match or exceed competitors' offerings. The result is a selling environment where pricing and availability advantages are temporary and where the risks associated with losing traditional competitive advantage are substantially increased.

Establishing business partnerships leads to creating collaborative planning agreements, facilitating exchange of real-time data, and constructing extraprises. In the past, when a supplier managed inventory through EDI with Wal-Mart, the technology lock-in represented a competitive advantage as potential partners of competitors wishing to gain similar vendor economies faced significant switching costs.

Today, with extranets and relatively cheap Internet EDI solutions, the difficulty of connecting reliably is not a barrier to supply-chain partnering. As a result, the risk of losing technology-driven competitive advantage, as a leader of an extraprise is much higher.

As more companies exploit the inherent advantages of e-business, the competitive risk within previously stable markets increases. Customer loyalty is becoming a primary concern of existing companies combating leaner and more flexible new entrants.

Increasing competition results in companies searching the far corners of the globe for new customers. Global product offerings require a worldwide network for product distribution and after-sales support.

At the same time, customer expectations are increased accordingly. A wide number of product offerings and immediate availability have become the standard in many industries, and established companies face an increased risk of customers fleeing to the competition.

Dependence on Others

As companies in search of business partners extend their processes beyond their four walls, a shift in the balance of power occurs that presents new risks. Previously guarded processes are now handled completely outside the company. These processes run the gamut from purchasing to distribution, manufacturing to general ledger.

Although well-thought-out increases in outsourcing dependencies should not expose the value chain integrator to greater points of process failure, the variance in control mechanisms between organizations could increase operational risks.

For example, a major automotive manufacturer that grants control and decision rights to a local bank to which employees electronically submit their expense reports over an Intranet must consider the increased risk of this dependency. This broader allocation of decision rights made possible by e-business technology must be controlled to ensure the realization of outsourcing benefits.

So many third parties are getting involved with providing e-business services that companies now face a plethora of outsourcing options. However, the management philosophy required to accommodate the presence of outside influence in basic business management activities is considerably different from that employed in most companies today. Successful value chain integration requires collaborative relationships where external providers are often responsible for monitoring basic operational barometers, such as inventory level or shipping activity, and for taking the required actions to sustain that component of the business.

Risk management throughout a value network requires controls that meet the mutually agreed upon requirements of dependent partners, and which are executed across partners without the barriers common to relationships in typical supply chains today.

To develop business relationships to this level of mutual control, suppliers and/or customers in the value chain must be electronically linked through real-time information-sharing networks. Partners must have access to formerly proprietary or confidential internal information and must be trusted to act on behalf of the other party's best interests. Managing dependency risks will require changes to corporate architectures to guarantee that decision rights, performance measurements, and rewards are aligned properly.

Another component of dependency on others that companies must manage is a decrease in one's ability to solve problems alone. As a safeguard against some types of availability/distribution disruption, a company may choose to maintain a select network of suppliers to assist in extraprise management.

Value chain consortiums may even go so far as to issue periodic quotas to all business partners for various activities. These actions provide extraprise members with fall-back positions in the event one supplier experiences difficulty. But they take away some of the leverage a company could exercise over a sole supplier. This is yet another example of the increased risk that comes with the gains of collaboration.

Security

In e-business, trust cannot be established in the absence of effective security. Security is attained by creating an appropriate technical architecture and surrounding processes to provide identification and authentication, authorization, nonrepudiation, privacy, and accountability.

Automated channel connections with customers alone represent a substantial increase in the systems and information risk to the would-be e-business. Add to that the type of information-based collaboration required for value chain integration, and the potential security risks associated with e-business leadership increase exponentially.

The essential elements of risk management for e-business are embodied in the technology deployed to ensure the exclusivity and validity of Internet-enabled communication.

Reputation

Few things are as fleeting or intangible as corporate reputation. This is certainly true on the Internet. As recently as five years ago, who could have foreseen the emergence of competitors "without walls?" Yet today, companies have pushed the envelope of e-business by sustaining business activities through a network of virtual warehouses. The most successful of these virtual companies have established solid reputations in a fraction of the time it has taken traditional companies to do the same. And the very success of these organizations has had a negative impact on the reputation of traditional companies that have, perhaps, been less quick to adapt than they could have or should have been.

Managing business under these conditions is certainly a new challenge to many companies. The issues facing companies as they embark on e-business initiatives are well documented. But managing customer expectations is equally challenging. Fulfilling these expectations goes a long way toward determining a company's reputation. Thus, the customer connection attained through the Internet has become the focal point of risk management in this area.

Furthermore, it is crucial that companies manage expectations with regard to customer demographics. While the younger generation is generally comfortable with on-line business, an older generation remains skeptical. The learning curve for customers needs to be managed on the lowest level; Web pages must be navigable by the novice without sacrificing the functionality demanded by the expert.

Companies need to manage their Web-based content as judiciously as they might manage business negotiations with their top customers. They must completely eliminate irrelevant, uninteresting, or objectionable content. Standard Web-design rules should apply, as many companies forget to address basic ease-of-use issues. Even now, many Web sites bury critical information below five or more link levels.

Other issues involve animation and slow-to-load graphics that often take away from the content of the page and limit the company's ability to make a strong impact on the visitor through its selling message. Including older graphics and time-dated material also detract from the effectiveness of a company's Web page.

Given that many Web sites have extraordinary usage numbers, it is also important that companies run a sufficient number of test scripts to avoid errors visible to the customer in the form of failed order submissions or undeliverable e-mail.

Even today, some global companies have Web sites that are unfriendly to one or another brand of browser. Not testing a site's content against at least the most popular browsers is discourteous to the customer (and only slightly worse than testing, discovering there is a problem, and going ahead anyway).

Culture

E-business brings with it cultural change of the highest magnitude. Users are subject to a learning curve where obsolescence is the only constant. Company employees will need significant amounts of training and support as they learn how to do their jobs in an e-business world.

In value chain integration, employees need to act on behalf of the entire extraprise. Customers also need to adjust to an electronically driven environment, where sales are closed with a point-and-click signature and the transaction medium is virtual. They need to understand how to extract value from this new channel, and their perceptions will drive company efforts to build loyalty through the intelligently manipulated interfaces of the Internet, rather than through personal relationships and interactions.

Global languages and customs must be understood as companies expand their boundaries overseas. Take, for example, a global pharmaceuticals company that goes to e-nabled indirect procurement. Contracts with external parties must include methods to monitor and assess performance, measure quality, and coordinate decision-making information. Internal performance monitoring and control will change as decisions move from employee to the procurement organization, which can now be held more closely accountable for company performance. Job design will be affected as the role of the purchasing department changes from operational to strategic.

Extended organizational boundaries, so suppliers can access information on sales and schedule replenishment, move other decisions outside the company. This requires changes in performance measures and rewards for purchasing professionals who manage these relationships effectively.

Unless company leadership is committed to an enterprisewide change of some magnitude, all of these factors could stunt the success of the e-business initiative before it even gets under way.

Technology

The challenges of implementing technology have not changed with e-business. But if e-business is to be successful, companies must address the multitude of troublesome details that make technology cumbersome and rigid.

"My computer has frozen!" Obviously, network support is a critical factor in any successful IT project. Poor performance and lack of reliability hampers efficiency and effectiveness. Network systems need to be robust enough to provide safeguards against failure. Additionally, when multiple front-end systems are linked to a single enterprisewide back-office system, hardware and software compatibility become critical. Interfacing programs are complex, and typically only a few people in the organization understand them. Because of the complexity of e-business solutions, support needs to be available and plentiful.

"I don't know how to use this function." This complaint underscores the importance of user training. Too often, systems are thrust on employees without appropriate learning opportunities, which dooms a system to a lifetime of inefficiency and limited productivity before it even gets off the ground. Training is perhaps the single most important

factor regarding the rollout of any new system. Too often, training is also the first element to be cut or eliminated when time or money constraints become an issue. In the case of global companies where transactions occur in a host of payment forms under varying regulatory rules, user ability to leverage the system's full capabilities is paramount.

The speed with which a system becomes obsolete is another technology risk a company needs to manage. Periodic network updates are normal and necessary. However, frequency of the updates must be balanced against time and cost. The technology level of the system must be sufficient to support the ongoing "e-nitiatives" for each primary functional area.

E-business also cries out for system standardization. A multitude of front-office systems each require interfacing programs to communicate with other users who do not share the same software. This lack of compatibility is often the most significant hurdle a company must clear before it can begin working in an environment in which information is available in real time.

Finally, but perhaps most importantly, is the issue of security. A system that is hacked can not only expose a company to ridicule, but can also harm its customers and business partners, thereby destroying trust.

Governance

Managerial guidelines for governing e-business processes can be ambiguous. A less-than-optimal organizational structure can lead to territorial conflicts. Establishing appropriate organizational drivers and defining roles and responsibilities are important if e-nitiatives are to be successful.

Task ownership should be balanced between central leadership and cross-functional development teams. Conflicts between departments can undermine the team's success if left unattended.

Lack of internal audit skills also leads to difficulties relating to governance. It is important that auditing personnel understand e-business legal and security requirements.

Due to the heavy reliance on business partners in most e-nitiatives, organizations should include their partners in governance discussions. Open communication is the best way to prevent misinterpretation.

Documentation should be shared and open items placed on the table for discussion. Poorly controlled outsourcing relationships can be avoided if partners are made aware of outstanding issues.

Protecting intellectual property must also be addressed. At a minimum, employees should be aware of the importance of documentation in an effort to reduce the risk of infringement on intellectual property rights.

Project Management

Corporate leaders must be the drivers of any type of initiative if it is to succeed. Unless a company has commitment from the top needed for enterprisewide culture change, any strategic initiative is doomed to failure, especially in the case of e-business initiatives.

Following buy-in from top management, the project team must then maintain the effort. Poor project leadership and lack of communication between groups leads to e-nitiatives that are not completed on time or on budget or that fail altogether. As simple as this sounds, losing focus in these areas is often a harbinger of things to come.

Problems with integration are another hurdle. Legacy systems often cannot be mapped forward in their entirety, resulting in hours of manual rekeying or elaborate data translation scripts that encourage inaccuracy before the new system is ever engaged.

Utilizing data standards helps in reducing this risk, as does employing middleware capable of bridging across-platforms. Left on their own, different departments or divisions often employ completely separate "best-of-breed" solutions to satisfy their data/interfacing needs.

But the need for conformity among new enterprisewide solutions is a big concern. Project management needs to address the requirements of each department if corporatewide buy-in is to occur.

Another central element in proper project management is managing geographically separate groups and/or systems. Lack of coordination across locations hampers overall system efficiency and prevents the company as a whole from leveraging all benefits of the proposed system. Using automated process control functions is one way to manage some of the risk under these circumstances.

Operations

Although it may seem that most e-business initiatives today are driven by a need to streamline the procurement processes, opportunities abound within operations to achieve gains through business partnerships. These opportunities are largely a result of operations-related efforts such as just-in-time manufacturing and third party product/component providers. Each of these requires a company to depend on outside suppliers to satisfy production needs on demand.

One e-business challenge in the operations area is the availability of technical expertise. As e-business moves from the first movers to early adopters, finding human resources to chaperone these initiatives is becoming more difficult. Development of in-house capabilities can be dangerous if left to just a few individuals; these "experts" may be priming themselves to leave the company for a more lucrative position elsewhere.

Companies need to develop adequate backup resources and contingency plans. Using aggressive testing plans and identifying potential failure points is crucial. Lack of appropriate safeguards could be lethal. For instance, eBay's share value fell 18 percent after three site failures in five days in early 1999.

As with any e-nitiative, forward planning needs to take into account scalability, particularly in operations, because rapid growth rates attributed to e-business can tax even the most robust production environment.

Additionally, change controls are needed to ensure that operations risks are raised within the context of the organization's direction. E-nitiatives are not just an IT issue; they are also pieces of a strategic direction that must be supported equally across all areas of the company.

Legal and Regulatory

Many of the legal aspects of e-business are still poorly defined. Court rulings and government legislation still pending will shape the way e-business evolves. Accordingly, companies must be thorough in ensuring that their actions comply with the most recent legal and regulatory guidelines.

Companies are trying to reduce their exposure to legal liability, regulatory sanctions or fines, and damage to their reputations. By creating a consistent global look and feel, companies hope to standardize their presence in the e-world. However, this task is difficult in light of complex interacting and conflicting jurisdictions, particularly on a worldwide level.

Establishing an on-line policy compliance framework is one standardization process currently being pursued. Unfortunately, even existing frameworks can be open to interpretation. For example, what may be considered objectionable content in one corner of the world may be acceptable in another. The clash of laws and cultures over free speech and privacy is not easy to resolve. No simple solution to these challenges is on the horizon.

Lack of clarity in contract law is also a risk. Companies wanting to reduce the risk of deceptive trade allegations or class action suits are at a disadvantage by not knowing all the rules in all the territories in which they trade or wish to trade.

Other disputes result from interpretations regarding intellectual property rights. The challenge? How can companies remain compliant with various international privacy laws and transborder data-flow issues such as encryption restrictions and policies, as they struggle to protect intellectual property and guard against cyber-fraud?

An important legal issue regarding reputation involves how name and brand identity is protected on the Internet. Internet regulations in this area are in their infancy and still evolving. Since many view the World Wide Web as public domain, copyright infringement rules are difficult to interpret and even more difficult to enforce.

Because minimal mechanisms are in place to shield a Web page from piracy, companies need to be cautious as to what material they make available on their Web sites. IDs and passwords are employed to track users, but such minimal protection measures will not totally stop harm or loss of reputation.

Human Resources

The primary function of the human resources department in the e-nabled company is to manage expectations relating to changes in role and job responsibility. Human resources needs to help establish direction to minimize the impact that e-nitiatives can have during periods of flux where roles are not clearly defined.

A loose organizational structure can help alleviate fears related to the new allocation of roles. Senior business champions must be identified and encouraged to commit managerial-level support to projects and provide some outward appearance of confidence and stability.

Human resources must also serve as the driver for continual education. As roles expand, employee versatility becomes more significant and necessary. E-nitiatives have a far greater chance of success when the correct project management processes, structures, and skills are in place.

Retaining skilled workers is already a priority in many companies. Personnel with specific skill sets for managing e-nitiatives can be difficult to find. Recruiting and aggressive retention strategies are being utilized to minimize the problem caused by lack of skills in critical areas. Also, human resources departments are finding creative ways to promote their companies and keep employees happy in the face of fierce competition for e-skilled employees.

Business Process Controls

Many of the normal business controls that apply in traditional business environments are equally applicable to e-business. Employing regular and reliable backup procedures are an important daily activity. Because in the e-nabled world, lost or inaccurate data affects the entire extraprise, the level of awareness about managing these risks needs to be raised accordingly.

Process integrity is also under scrutiny as companies look closely at the way they manage their businesses. E-business can not be treated as merely a front-end solution. Furthermore, e-business is not an IT-driven solution; rather, it is the result of a corporatewide commitment to a new way of doing business. The importance of input and support from all areas of the company can not be understated.

Accountability in the e-nabled world combines policies of trust with responsibility. Establishing business rules to delegate processes to operational levels assists companies in assigning ownership and clarifying lines of responsibility for employees.

Tax

The variations in worldwide tax laws are another ambiguous issue. One illustration involves the question regarding tax laws related to Web-server location. As one possible solution, Europe and the United States are considering implementing a point-of-consumption policy regarding Internet transactions.

Possible near-term opportunities for tax optimization include locating e-nabled shared-service functions in low tax régimes, in particular where an in-country economic value-add, rather than just a service for a fee, can be demonstrated. The amount of savings possible is, as always, a matter of negotiation with the relevant tax authorities.

Currency

An e-business must be able to deal in multiple currencies, to monitor exchange rates continuously to facilitate purchase/payment transfers, and to respond quickly to changing financial situations. Global cash management will be a new challenge to companies whose e-business initiatives take them overseas for the first time. On a basic level, companies will need to be able to obtain cash to facilitate global business initiatives. They will also need to select operating currencies to maintain financial stability. Companies will need to grasp the variance of foreign currency valuation and leverage tax shields within a global context.

E-BUSINESS RISK MANAGEMENT FOCUSES ON TRUST

E-business is all about changing the form of traditional relationships among companies, their customers, their distribution channel partners, and their suppliers and vendors. E-business technology provides all of these players with more information about each other. The key to mitigating e-business risk, therefore, is to develop the closest, most trusting relationships possible with all of the various players at each step of the process of delivering value to end customers.

ELLEMTEL UTVECKLINGS AB

Ellemtel Utvecklings AB, based in Stockholm, Sweden, is owned by Ericsson, the telecom infrastructure supplier, and Telia, the principal telecom operator in Sweden. Ellemtel's mission is to evaluate new telecom technologies, products and services, and to operate a high-speed network connecting industrial and public research centers and universities in the greater Stockholm area. Ellemtel wanted an easy-to-use, easy-to-administer system for secure services and trials on the network infrastructure, and flexible pricing for video broadcasts to a closed user group based on actual use rather than a flat rate. First they identified key trial activities: secure electronic mail and Web services, and encrypted documents and video multicasting. They implemented data classification and a security policy on a TriStrata Security System, enrolled trial users, and trained a system administrator. Then the company implemented a seamless integration of the TriStrata System with flexible IP-multicasting of an encrypted video stream to a user group, and a security log to account for actual use of services. All trial activities were fully secured with no negative impact to performance.

Trust is fundamental to all of these relationships. With trust, objectives can be achieved and opportunities realized. Trusting relationships are those in which:

○ Customers and business partners are assured that they can rely on the business processes that underlie the e-business transaction.

○ Customer information is leveraged to develop a stronger relationship without undercutting the customer's privacy or subjecting the information to unauthorized disclosure.

○ New channels are created while suppliers' and business partners' intellectual property rights are protected.

○ Brands and reputations are built and protected against intrusion by hackers.

10

Navigating Change: Becoming an Extraprise-Ready Company

In the fully e-nabled business future, customers will no longer buy simple products from simple companies. Instead, they will buy intricately constructed product and service bundles from equally intricately constructed extraprises. The extraprise will consist of network master or hub organization, a set of tightly integrated supply-chain partners who make up the extraprise value chain, a group of companies that provide outsourced business processes or applications, and companies that build and manage the network backbones. Finally, and most important, there will be a company that owns the customer connection, either the network master or some kind of e-intermediary—a facilitator or an aggregator. Companies that exist today, if they survive into the era of total e-business, will increasingly move toward filling only one role within the extraprise: network master, outsourced process or application provider, value chain partner, network backbone provider, or customer-connecting company.

Many companies, especially those that provide standardized products or services to the extraprise value network (commodity products and components, network services, outsourced processes or applications), will participate in many networks. Network masters, however, will be the master of only one network. Customer-connecting companies may connect to the customer for one particular network or may aggregate the products of many networks and feed them into a customer base.

Whatever role a company hopes to fill in the e-nabled business world, in order to be extraprise ready, that company will have to show other companies that it has the organizational and human infrastructure, as well as the technology, to be a valuable business partner.

The benefits delivered by promising technology often fall short or come late, but research shows that the failure to manage people is often the driver of business failures. People can and often do effectively block the success of major technology integration efforts. Not surprisingly, a majority of executives have repeatedly held that their biggest challenge with respect to large technology initiatives, including ERP and now e-business, is change management.

Heightened competition and significantly reduced financial/technological hurdles create the kind of urgency that greatly assists the initial steps of change, those involving management alignment. The first steps are relatively straightforward, and visionaries now have the evidence to get the ball rolling even within change-averse organizations.

From that point forward, the barriers are primarily associated with change management, an area where great leaders feel challenged but also justified in attacking with fervor. The Internet does not change these people barriers. The ability to manage change is still a litmus test for business success, whether or not an "e" is attached.

But in the extraprise-driven world, the complexity of orchestrating activities outside the company walls makes the change-management challenge even greater. When we talk about extraprise resource planning as an end state for the integrated value chain, people-complexity reaches its zenith. This chapter, then, is about becoming an extraprise-ready company, that is, about successfully navigating the change associated with e-business transformation within companies and within and across industries.

CHANGE BARRIERS

Typically, managers face five major difficulties to delivering the major benefits associated with transformational change. Unfortunately, e-business has a significant compounding effect on each one. In plotting a strategy to overcome these barriers, companies must understand the specific impact of e-business for each type and plan accordingly.

Organizational Scope

Cross-functional change is particularly difficult. Change across large, complex organizations is even more difficult. Change across collaborating organizations—an extraprise value network team—is perhaps the most difficult of all.

Additionally, geographic scope adds complexity and the challenge of cultural differences. E-business, especially in instances of value chain integration and greater states of industry maturity, implicitly involves the collaboration of partners and customers across geographic and cultural divides. Despite these difficulties, new entrants have managed to leapfrog into this collaborative state.

The key to their success may be the e-nablement of change management tools supported by Internet communications and applications.
While obstacles to executing the tools of change certainly exist, a technology e-nabled group of partners with an e-business infrastructure in
place may be better positioned to facilitate these efforts than a company
trying to effect internal change without such capabilities.

Evidence from the automobile industry just-in-time (JIT) model,
Wal-Mart, and now Amazon.com and others suggests that it can be easier
on a seat-by-seat basis to communicate beyond the walls of an e-nabled
company than it is for some traditional companies to communicate within
their own walls. The most successful business-to-business marketers have
defined the state-of-the-art in external communication. Their "trick" is to
leverage customer-focused models in the partner-to-partner portion of the
extraprise.

Change Complexity

Complex change is hard for people to handle. Their ability to change
can be tested beyond their limits. E-business change associated with
movement across the landscape challenges the minds of strategists, never
mind those of individuals fully involved in a company's operations.

Although the competitive landscape is simple in theory, the underlying complexity of intercompany collaboration is not for the fainthearted.
The change associated with achieving progress ahead of competitors may
represent innovation that is beyond the boundaries of an organization's
thinking. Without a vision of the future, great uncertainty exists about the
outcomes of any e-business change program.

Political Resistance

Successful change depends on the resolve of leaders at all levels. Resolve
entails understanding the impact of e-business on competitive strategy,
people, processes, and technology. The more power bases that need to be
confronted, the greater the political challenge and the greater the test of
leadership resolve.

While a leading company, a Wal-Mart or a Ford, may be able to require supplier compliance, the vast majority of companies are not that
powerful. In the future, extraprise partners may in fact have such power,
but in the near term, gaining commitment from multiple external power
bases is intensely challenging.

Resistance is high wherever change creates perceived losers. Value
chain integration reallocates profits throughout the network of participants. Whole companies may be subsumed in the process, and others
may lose a significant portion of their core businesses. Gaining commitment from perceived or actual losers will be very difficult.

The key to successfully implementing an extraprise will be gaining commitment from those who can drive change, and convincing potential partners that it is time to cut losses and aggressively pursue alternative positions in the value chain.

To ensure compliance and to tangibly reward efforts that support company objectives, transparent performance measures must be applied to personnel who choose to remain. Only when employees, as well as the shareholders, feel linked to the venture's success will that success be sustainable.

Cultural Challenge

Change is difficult when new ways of working challenge such cultural assumptions as, "That's not the way we have succeeded in the past." In its technology-centric method of application, its customer-value-centric view of business, and its reliance on collaboration, e-business poses a strong challenge to existing cultural assumptions.

Change Capability

Organizations that have not succeeded in past change efforts are less likely to succeed in e-business. Because they adhere to past values and ways of doing business, existing leadership and management may not be able to foster change effectively. It may even be necessary to rethink the company's structure and the company's role in the value chain. Some companies may find it easier to break into separate companies as a method of kick-starting change within various business units.

For an e-business value chain, change capability must be determined on a segment-by-segment basis. Selection of extraprise partners may hinge on their ability to change. A company's success may be determined by its ability to communicate its change capability through actions visible to the leaders of current and potential partners.

AN ORGANIZATIONAL CHANGE MANAGEMENT APPROACH

The tools of change management are not rocket science. Leadership, communication, training, planning, incentive systems, and the like seem simple, and, to the unwise, less important than other more exciting areas. But these tools can be used as levers, and, when applied correctly, can remove great obstacles with a minimum of effort. Conversely, improper application of these levers can have significant negative effects on change initiatives.

We believe that making a company *technologically* ready to become a useful member of an extraprise is the easy part. The difficulty is making the company *organizationally* ready. Successful change managers recognize the complexity of the challenge and adopt a structured approach to applying the tools that facilitate rapid change.

A company must take eight steps to show potential extraprise partners that it is ready, willing, and able to do business in an e-nabled world. Performing these steps in strict sequence is not required, and many can go forward concurrently:

1. Create a high-level vision for the company's e-business effort.

2. Develop strategies that make the company a natural extraprise partner.

3. Build commitment throughout the value chain; establish a cross-functional team focused around customer needs and desires.

4. Manage people's performance; establish performance measures and appropriate rewards and incentives (set the parameters for the e-business balanced scorecard).

5. Develop a culture that supports collaborative e-business; establish a common framework and terminology everyone can agree to; and educate the entire work force about e-business.

6. Design the extraprise organization; begin talking to customers about their needs and to suppliers about how jointly to establish extraprise working teams.

7. Develop leadership focus on e-business.

8. Target and deliver business benefits.

Step 1: Establish a Vision

Companies must understand why they are getting into e-business. Is e-business an offensive or defensive play? What role will the company play in the ultimate e-business panorama—a customer-connecting company, a value network master, a network partner within many networks, or a provider of outsourced processes, applications, or network services? The closer a company is to the ultimate customer, the greater its chances for differentiating itself and its products or services.

One way to frame an e-business vision is to ask and answer three interlocking questions:

1. If the end-state e-business world were to appear today, fully formed, where would the company fit?

2. If the company does not own the customer connection today, given its culture and organizational structure, is it realistic to believe that it can attain the customer connection in the future?

3. If the company cannot attain the customer connection, can it attain a greater value-adding position by "moving up the food chain" closer to the ultimate customer by disintermediating current intermediaries, or by using core competencies to create new intermediating opportunities?

The e-business change vision must be a coherent and powerful statement of what the extraprise can and should be at some future time. The time frame, varying from one to five years, will differ depending on the industry in which the extraprise will operate. This vision expresses both a general direction and a more specific destination. A well-formed vision:

○ *Stretches:* A good vision challenges the organization to move outside its comfort zone in order to take risks.

○ *Inspires:* A well-expressed vision motivates employees by increasing clarity and by involving them in leadership's view of the future.

○ *Directs:* A vision directs the organization internally, thereby enabling it to choose the future it wishes to create.

○ *Aligns:* A vision aligns diverse organizational elements toward a common goal.

Step 2: Develop Extraprise-Ready Strategies

Developing an extraprise-ready change strategy is a cyclical process involving assessment, strategy formulation, planning, and the determination of rolls and governance. The process is often repeated two or three times in a change life cycle in increasing detail. More than in the past, the speed of e-business change compels companies to review their strategies frequently. Also, constant marketplace pressure increases the speed at which the cycle must be completed.

A review of strategy typically involves using readiness assessment, change configuration, and history assessment tools:

○ A *readiness assessment tool* assists in gaining an understanding of the people-related risks of a particular change and of where to concentrate change management efforts.

○ A *change configuration tool* assists in selecting the best route to delivering change and should uncover the choices available for implementation, as well as methods for gaining business benefits most quickly.

○ A *history assessment tool* assists in understanding how past change programs have performed. It should show what has failed or succeeded in the past, and why. This tool should provide insight into what must be handled differently this time to ensure success.

A successful plan must harness the value from assessment and strategy work. Typically, plans address key changes, support requirements, and program management. Plans must include how and when to implement key changes from the new organization, how and when to act in the domains of change vision, leadership, communications, involvement, and training, and how and when to set up and manage the program team.

Defining the change strategy may seem onerous, but truths learned through the experience emerge that can provide perspective helpful in managing complexity.

○ Commitment to full deployment need not be a prerequisite to starting implementation; in practice only a critical mass of champions is required.

○ Change programs are not unique; they have important similarities. Learning gained from previous change programs can be applied.

○ Carefully phased and sequenced action programs often have a higher probability of lasting success than frenzied, big bang changes.

○ Organizations currently appear to have a two-year attention span when it comes to making substantial change progress before another equally compelling need emerges.

○ The best plans are developed from two directions—backward from the vision and forward from the starting block.

○ As an athlete's fitness increases with exercise, companies undergoing successful change seem to increase their capacity for more change.

○ When change overload sets in, employees tend to work on changes or problems that are most easily solved, and on those most in their immediate control.

Step 3: Build Commitment

Change can be achieved through commitment or compliance. Building commitment is usually the worthy, but expensive, goal of change. Companies should not pay for more commitment than they actually need.

However, because the key constraint on any would-be extraprise leader is the lack of control over potential partners, the price of commitment is often unavoidable.

As a result, it is important to address a few key questions:

○ Do we need commitment or compliance?

○ How much commitment is required?

○ From whom is commitment required?

○ What are the likely causes of resistance?

○ Are individuals able to cope with personal change productively?

Armed with the answers to these questions, a company can better determine which tactics to use. Figure 10.1 illustrates some of the various tactics for gaining commitment and ensuring compliance.

Luckily, e-business technology provides unique methods of executing communications plans aimed at gaining commitment. In the same way, companies using tools that facilitate a "market of one" can target change-management communication for the "audience of one." Intranet and extranet project sites and usage patterns of visitors to those sites can be used to measure communication performance and to streamline communication distribution.

Figure 10.1   Gaining Commitment; Ensuring Compliance

Internal Compliance Tactics	Extraprise-Wide Commitment Tactics
• Change Information Systems	• Build Teams
• Reduce Headcount	- Project Teams
• Change Organizational Structure	- Work Group Teams
• New Meeting Structure	• Manage Stakeholders
• New Workplace Design	- Understand Needs
• New Administration Process	- Face-to-Face Meetings
• Change Sign-Off Process	• Communicate Change
	- With Stakeholders
	- With Project Teams
	• Transfer Knowledge and Skills
	- New Ways of Working
	- Change Skills
	• Manage Resistance
	- Understand Causes
	- Engage Resisters

Step 4: Manage People Performance

Performance management is about extracting behavior from measured performance. A tangible link exists between a company's goals and the performance metrics it uses to motivate actions. In the best case, the high-level goals transparently communicate throughout the extraprise the required changes in workers' activities.

But there is generally too much separation between strategic goals and day-to-day activities. As a result, it is necessary to carefully consider the methods used to motivate the work force in the current state, and then to modify performance measures appropriately to ensure compliance with new goals. Remember the old business adage: "That which gets measured, gets done."

Performance measures must, at a minimum, be easily understood, and, in the best case, readily accepted by those subject to them. Acceptance of measurements is greatly enhanced if there is a cascading system of metrics, that is, one in which a manager's metrics are directly dependent on the team's performance.

Effective incentives ensure that employees' personal compensation is directly tied both to their own measured performance and to the company's outcomes. For example, a bonus structure that is split between a personal scorecard and the company's performance (perhaps by shares or options) enlists support and discourages "gaming the system" (whereby employees are focused on maximizing personal reward with no concern about what the organization actually needs them to do).

Using e-nabling technology, employee performance measurement can, more than ever, be automated. By its very nature, e-business embodies interactions between partners and customers. As a result, much of the burden of developing performance measurement systems may be avoided by integrating the capability as a collateral feature of the core technology supporting e-business.

Step 5: Develop an Extraprise Culture

Culture is the combination of values and beliefs that provide direction and energy to what people do each day. Culture is visible all around the company in artifacts and manifestations such as performance standards, icons, myths and stories, rituals, traditions, use of language, and the way relationships are encouraged to develop.

Values and beliefs are the deeply seated underpinnings that influence individual and organizational behavior every day. For example, they influence the way people are rewarded or the way they are encouraged to take risks—seeking forgiveness afterwards, for example, or asking permission before. Values and behaviors need to match market needs and be capable of evolving as these needs change.

E-business can enhance culture by establishing virtual communities of interest developed to support a change program. FAQ bulletin boards, intranet/extranet sites that provide consistent and well-maintained informational content, and knowledge management tools all support culture formation.

If the company is to become an e-business, developing internal e-business capabilities is the most transparent method of communicating corporate intent and of bolstering cultural change.

Framework and terminology are key to any major change effort. Those who are given the task of determining the company's e-business strategy should be speaking with, not around, each other.

Too often, company leaders who are saying the same thing argue about correct terminology—about, for example, the difference between e-business and e-commerce or about whether an opportunity is a reintermediation or an intermediation.

While we believe precise language is important, if these arguments become differences without distinctions, they are useless. The bottom line is this: The company needs to be able to make rapid decisions about important strategic matters, and to do this everyone has to use the same dictionary.

Education is key to successful cultural change. Education is not the same as training. As a company moves into e-business, it will still run many of its day-to-day operations in a non-e-nabled way. But over time, more and more of its processes and operations will become e-nabled. That's why every member of the company needs to understand both the concepts behind e-business, as well as the company's strategy for using e-business. Education about e-business has three components:

1. *Spreading the word.* E-business should become part of routine corporate communication. Every regular communication vehicle should include something about e-business.

2. *Sharing knowledge.* As corporate leaders learn more about the uses and value of e-business, their knowledge must filter down to everyone else in the company.

3. *Creating e-communication.* E-business is about a new way of communicating. To make e-business real, the company needs to use e-business tools to communicate internally.

The need for communication is why e-procurement is such a useful first e-business step: So many individuals within a company procure goods or services that doing it electronically drives home the e-business message.

At the end of the day, e-business is about more effectively meeting and satisfying customer needs or desires. Even if most of a company's e-business focus is on back-end processes—the reduction in cycle time, improvement in accuracy, and reduction of costs, overheads, and head count—customers will benefit in terms of speed and cost.

Step 6: Build the Extraprise Community

Organizational design is crucial for companies facing e-business challenges. Organizational design elements, including the reporting structure, roles, performance measures, work groups, and integrating mechanisms, must be designed to respond to those challenges.

E-business-related challenges include changing global economic factors, customers who are more demanding, changing work force expectations and regulatory environments, a globalizing marketplace, global competition, and the continuing emergence of new technology and business models.

Typically, companies have to address two vital organizational design issues: enterprisewide (corporate center and business unit design) and unit level (work unit and individual position design). But the e-business also has to think of the design issues confronting the extraprisewide value network, or even those of value chains that seem totally different but that will ultimately converge.

Companies looking for partners with which to work in value networks are not interested in bilateral relationships. Rather, they are looking for many partners with different core competencies and skill sets with whom to create multilateral relationships.

Step 7: Develop Extraprise Leadership

Academics, consultants, and corporate leadership frequently talk about who should lead a company's e-business efforts.

According to one school of thought, the CIO should be the e-business leader because e-business is basically a technology effort and because in order to make e-business work, the Web technology must interface cleanly with the company's internal enterprise software.

According to another school of thought, two "process" leaders should head the e-business effort: the head of sales and marketing for the customer-facing, revenue-generating e-commerce programs, and the chief financial officer (CFO) for the cost-reducing back-end supply chain streamlining and e-procurement efforts.

A third camp, to which we belong, believes that e-business is essentially a strategic issue, and that the leadership of a company's e-business effort should rest with the leader of company strategy.

Regardless of the specific choices of leadership team structure, the goals are the same: setting direction, demonstrating personal resolve for change, and influencing others to give their support and commitment. Change leadership is at the center of successful change. In a recent survey of 450 companies, Organizational Aspects of IT Special Interest Group (OASIG) (a U.K. government-supported group concerned with the organizational aspects of IT) found that only 24 percent had change leadership in place before change efforts were initiated.

Change leadership is not the same as project leadership. Confusing the two leads to change failure. Change leaders are change agents concerned with the holistic elements of the change and not the day-to-day activities that are changing. Successful change requires a clear contract between project and change leadership.

Step 8: Deliver Business Benefits

The challenge of delivering sustained benefits is considerable. A successful change effort requires not only developing a value proposition and business case, but also defining how benefits will be quantified throughout the project's life. It is important to establish terms of reference that make clear the business case, and to set direction so all participants understand what they must deliver, when, and at what cost and risk. Sustaining the benefits requires an ongoing effort that must be motivated through sound performance measurement and evidenced by credible benefits outcome measurements.

Benefits should be attached to project milestones to make clear what will be delivered, by whom, and when. Change-load assessments are helpful in establishing whether an organization's people can assimilate change. The change-load assessment process identifies temporal overlaps in change requirements, illustrates the need to make tough choices about the timing and level of planned change, and provides an important input to the overall change strategy.

In most cases, benefits do not magically appear when the change "goes live." In reality, as Figure 10.2 illustrates, performance often dips in the run up to going live, recovers to break even over a period of time, and then begins to move up toward the performance target.

However, many times going live improperly becomes the goal, especially in protracted projects where energy and commitment wane. As a result, one goal of the benefits case development should be to identify early wins—"low-hanging fruit"—that can be used as leading indicators and motivators. Identifying these opportunities and capitalizing on

Figure 10.2   Fluctuations in Performance

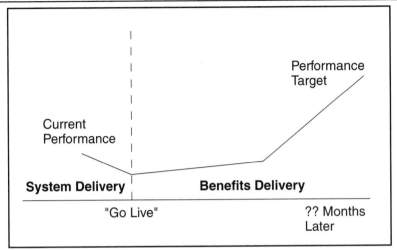

them according to schedule goes a long way toward maintaining focus on the change and on realizing benefits.

For a new channel, measurement of e-business success seems simple. But the net benefit must include the costs of channel cannibalization. Benefits realized may be the aggregate of several effects, among them increased market share and margins and decreased costs. But the most important measure is maintenance of customer loyalty. In the e-nabled world, many existing companies are subject to customer base erosion caused by new entrants and opportunistic competitors.

HOLISTIC E-BUSINESS ORGANIZATIONAL CHANGE MANAGEMENT

The success of any e-business change effort hinges on implementation of a comprehensive eight-point plan (Figure 10.3), timing and coordinating activities, using appropriate supporting tools, and applying best practices.

The scope of an e-business change program for sell-side channel enhancement is similar to that of a major IT integration change effort, such as introducing ERP. However, plans supporting value chain integration include efforts spanning value chain partners and require a substantially different implementation strategy.

Company leaders should share roles in value chain integration. Partner participants should be involved in formulating the change vision and strategy. Efforts to build commitment should extend to all participants. Companies must design a value chain culture, develop company-specific

Figure 10.3   Eight-Point Plan for Success

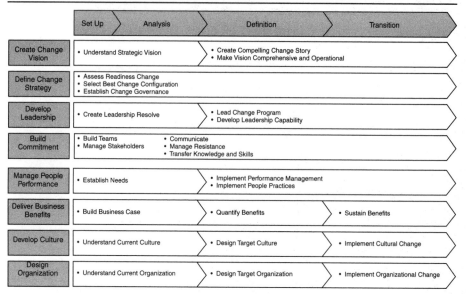

performance measurements, and identify benefits specific to value chain participants.

Leapfrog strategies that include newly formed or yet-to-be formed partnerships and transforming value chain teams that have not worked closely in the past further compound the difficulty of change. In many ways, completely new organizations have a change advantage over existing organizations in successfully executing these strategies. New companies do not carry the baggage of individual company histories and thus can truly focus on coordinating value chain partners.

E-business change is a business-centric activity. It is not technology process improvement driven by the CIO. Rather, when successful, it is a CEO-driven strategic change. Achieving successful e-business change requires solid leadership and the execution of a well-thought-out change plan that directly supports the improvement of processes and the implementation of technology.

11

An Analytical
Framework for E-Business

Since about 1997, financial markets—especially in the United States and Western Europe—have conferred a huge market price premium on e-nabled companies. Much to the distress of long-established bricks-and-mortar companies, some Internet-based startups (some would say up-starts!) that have exploded onto the scene in the last few years have attained immediate billion-dollar market valuations.

If they have any earnings at all, many Internet-based enterprises— most of which are business-to-consumer companies—have price to earnings ratios (P/Es) in the hundreds. While financial markets demand that bricks-and-mortar companies show steady profit growth in order to maintain valuation and a modest p/e, an announcement by an Internet company that it has one million new subscribers, even if those subscribers have not actually purchased anything, can send a stock soaring. The game appears to be about eyeball share more than actual market share.

However, bricks-and-mortar company executives cannot simply lament the unfairness of current equity market psychology. They need to look at how becoming an e-nabled company can truly enhance their ability to generate revenues and reduce costs, thereby increasing profits, and, ultimately, share price.

Traditionally, investors' expected future cash flows determine a company's market value. Therefore, most companies need to be persuaded by a compelling business case before committing to the time, financial cost, and organizational change necessary to move to an e-business environment.

The new rules of the e-business game mandate that such a business case be radically different from the norm. The case for e-business must satisfy both the chief financial officer (CFO), who will be integrally involved in managing the change, and the CEO, who is concerned with the larger view of the company's overall prospects.

NEED FOR A BUSINESS CASE

The purpose of the business case is not merely to justify an investment to the CFO and other corporate leadership. A proper business case develops the baseline hoped for or anticipated results against which the entire change effort can and should be measured.

The business case should cover the financial and nonfinancial performance metrics against which to measure the e-business implementation. These metrics must guide management of the implementation of all projects that fall within the e-business program.

The CFO is the architect and, in the best companies, the navigator of the organization's financial future and supply chain. The CFO sets targets for the company's supply- and demand/distribution-chain-focused activities, ensuring that the company's operational managers are moving in the same direction.

THE BUSINESS CASE FOR E-BUSINESS

Can a compelling case that justifies the premium offered in today's market for so-called dot.com stocks really be made for becoming an e-business? We believe the answer is yes, but not with traditional financial analytics. A business case based on discounted cash flow (DCF) and net present value (NPV) usually argues against a change to e-business.

What, then, should one base such a case on? We believe the e-business case can only be supported by a more pro-active set of financial analytics, one that takes into account the uncertain environment that e-business has itself created. In addition, such a business case can only be made using financial analytics that work on the supposition that an improvement in customer value inevitably leads to a parallel improvement in shareholder value.

Take, for example, the traditional approach to valuation. In e-business, valuation is not about running accounting numbers. Companies are coming to realize that knowledge of customer needs and desires can be more valuable than physical assets. In e-business, knowledge replaces inventory and machinery. Relationships with other businesses up and down the value chain replace the management infrastructure needed to make myriad one-off purchasing and sales decisions. And the rapid transfer of knowledge across corporate boundaries replaces conventional face-to-face communications.

In short, five characteristics of e-nabled companies explain their increased market value. E-nabled companies:

1. Rapidly capture market share from bricks-and-mortar competitors

2. Focus on customer relationships, thereby maintaining and in some cases increasing customer loyalty

3. Leverage not only their own core competencies but those of their upstream (in the supply chain) and downstream (in the demand distribution chain) business partners as well, forming a tightly linked value network

4. Can expand more easily due to the speed with which leadership makes and communicates decisions

5. Increase shareholder value through e-business branding and through the way they communicate this value to the financial markets.

Therefore, e-business enhances the value proposition for both the customer and the company. The result? An increase in overall stakeholder value.

Increased Revenue/Decreased Costs

E-business increases revenue in three ways. First, it provides access to new markets and additional segments of existing markets. Forrester Research expects that e-business market share will grow to 9 percent of the overall economy by 2003 and that the e-business channel will replace some other market channels.

Customers' growing computer literacy is redefining the market. By using the Internet to obtain more and better information about products, services, and prices, they are putting new pressures on companies. Early adopters of e-business technology grew rapidly, even in industries where growth was minimal (the Amazon.com effect).

Today, however, much of that early adopter advantage has dissipated. In fact, cost reduction will be the largest e-business opportunity for current and future companies. For example, e-business slashes transaction costs for both nonproduction- and production-related materials. Lower purchasing costs, shorter cycle times, tighter manufacturing cycle times, prenegotiated agreements, minimized inventory levels, and vendor-managed inventories all help companies cut costs. Service and logistics costs are also dropping, as are overhead costs, which can be reduced and ultimately eliminated through electronic purchase requisitions, purchase orders, payments, invoices, and bill presentations. Increasingly accurate transactions also lower transaction auditing expenses, reduce expedited manufacturing and shipping to correct incorrect or late orders, and improve accounts receivable cycle time.

Why Companies Cannot Wait to Become E-Businesses

The potential gain from moving to an e-nabled business environment is high. The upside risk—the risk of participating—is low but not nonexistent. E-business requires an investment in technologies, some of which are still unproven. Companies may also encounter some minor distractions to core business processes and incur a relatively high cost for change management.

But the downside risk—the risk of not participating—is high. Nimble Internet-only companies are grabbing market share from giant companies that are tethered to a bricks-and-mortar world. The "coolness" of Internet technology and the ease-of-use factor are eroding traditional customer loyalties. Bricks-and-mortar companies are perceived increasingly as less agile than fully engaged e-businesses.

The stock market has validated the e-business value proposition even in the absence of tangible profits. Clearly, companies that choose to ignore e-business are at risk.

The bottom line: E-business is about speed, flexibility, and relationships.

AN E-BUSINESS ANALYTICAL FRAMEWORK: CUSTOMER VALUE AND COMPETITIVE CAPABILITY

It is useful to view both customer value and competitiveness as equations:

$$\text{Equation 1: Customer Value} = \frac{(\text{Service}) \ (\text{Quality})}{(\text{Price}) \ (\text{Time})}$$

$$\text{Equation 2: Competitive Capability} = \frac{(\text{Agility}) \ (\text{Reach})}{(\text{Time-to-Market})}$$

E-business improves all of the variables in these equations by enhancing customer value and competitiveness.

Customer Value Variables

The e-business value proposition for the customer consists of four variables: service, price, quality, and fulfillment time.

Service Goes Up.   A customer realizes the full value of a company's offering through its service. E-business increases the level of service by providing personalized and accurate customer information, with better tracking and performance measurement.

E-business provides six capabilities that improve customer service: interactive and personalized customer communications; speed and accuracy; enhanced ability to track and measure capability; instantaneous, 24×7-communications; a customer-driven business model; and finally, instantaneous customer communication that allows the company to re-bundle product and service elements to meet customer-defined optimum value, otherwise known as customer delight.

Price Goes Down.   Price is what the customer pays the company for its offering. E-business can sometimes reduce the price customers pay because such devices as volume aggregation, auctions, the decoupling of product offerings, and pay-per-use payment models increase the transparency of company pricing. At other times, however, prices do not go down. In all cases, however, the "market of one," where products are priced individually for each customer, keeps e-business pricing flexible.

E-businesses can price more effectively because of their better understanding of their customers' buying behaviors and of the level of real-time local demand. Also, e-businesses are able to customize offerings by rebundling related services and products—often from a number of different companies—into attractive "baskets."

Quality Goes Up.   In e-business, quality refers to more than just goods or services. Quality also refers to the customer's experience interacting with the company. E-business improves and customizes that experience by providing the customer better information on products and services and by enabling customers to form communities.

As transactions become standardized and automated, e-nabled companies can focus more of their organizational resources on managing the hands-on rather than the transactional aspects of the customer relationship. By being able to communicate instantaneously with the customer, e-businesses can use e-mail to provide "free" value-added services, such as notifying customers about preventive maintenance or other product enhancing subjects.

Fulfillment Time Goes Down.   Fulfillment time is the period from initial order to delivery. E-business reduces fulfillment time because direct order/configuration reduces order-entry errors; content-based products and services can be delivered on demand; and e-nabled businesses have streamlined production processes.

E-business helps companies improve their internal business processes, thereby reducing fulfillment time. E-nabled companies use automated order-to-payment and streamlined purchase initiation processes. Delaying product differentiation to a point as close to the customer as possible reduces production/configuration time. So does just-in-time production. Networked and outsourced shipping enables well-timed product departures and optimizes time en route.

Competitive Capability Variables

The e-business value proposition for the company consists of three variables: agility, reach, and time to market.

Agility Goes Up. Agility is the ease with which a company is able to change strategic direction quickly and smoothly, and to provide customers with what they want, even if that is not a standard product or configuration.

A well-crafted e-business infrastructure promotes scalability, that is, the ability to add volume quickly without overwhelming the system. This in turn leads to flexibility in mergers and acquisitions and quick reconfiguration of the virtual value chain. Better marketing information supports real-time resource reallocation.

Reach Goes Up. A company's reach is its ability to connect to potential customers in new markets. An e-business can use a virtual sales force to reach global markets with product information while targeting new demographics within current markets. It can also leverage its brand across several dissimilar industries. For example, grocery retailers in the United States and Europe are adding products ranging from financial services to gasoline.

Time to Market Goes Down. Time to market is a product cycle beginning with design and concluding with revenue recognition. E-businesses participate in collaborative product design, often over great distances. In addition, as companies link tightly with their supply-chain partners, they engage in collaborative R&D, concurrent engineering, and other methods to reduce the time to market.

VALUE DRIVERS AND E-BUSINESS

Value-based management examines how a company performs against seven value drivers. Figure 11.1 illustrates how the seven value drivers should align in order to give a company competitive advantage. The seven value drivers and their definitions are:

1. Revenue Growth. At what rate is the business's top line growing?

2. Operating Margin. What are the costs to serve the customer in terms of sales, general, and administration (SG&A) to deliver each dollar of revenue?

3. Working Capital. What does the company need to carry in terms of inventory and/or more receivables to satisfy customer needs? How much credit are suppliers willing to provide?

4. Capital Expenditures. The incremental capital investments a company must make to reach and service customers or to produce products.

5. Cash Tax Rate. The tax rate in cash terms the company must pay on profits as a percentage of revenue.

6. Cost of Capital. The discount rate applied to future cash flows based on the company's capital structure.

7. Competitive Advantage Period. The amount of time during which the company expects to sustain growth in operating profits and shareholder value.

An appropriate e-business strategy can help companies improve many of these value drivers. By enhancing an organization's customer-value proposition and competitiveness, e-business actually drives shareholder value (Figure 11.2). As the figure illustrates, the overall effect of e-nabling a business is to improve all of these value drivers. (Not every value driver acts against every one of the customer value and competitive capability variables. Their effect, for example, on cost of capital is neutral. The end result, however, is a net positive impact on shareholder value.)

Figure 11.1   Aligning Value Drivers to Achieve Competitive Advantage

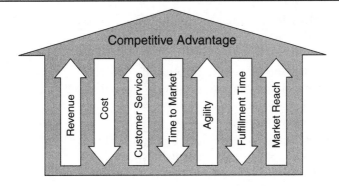

Figure 11.2　Driving Shareholder Value

Selected Value Drivers	Customer Value Proposition Elements				Competitive Capabilities			Net Driver Effect
	Service	Price	Quality	Fulfillment Time	Agility	Time to Market	Reach	
Revenue Growth	●	●	●	●	●	●	●	●
Operating Margin	●		●	●	●		●	●
Working Capital			●	●	●			●
Capital Expenditures					●	●	●	●
Cash Tax Rate					●			●
Cost of Capital								
Competitive Advantage Period	●		●	●	●	●	●	●

● Signifies an improvement in the value driver

Net Shareholder Value Impact

Value Driver: Revenue Growth

E-business enhances customer value and competitiveness in the following ways to increase revenues:

○ Services. Expanded and improved customer service increases customer loyalty. Companies then gain a larger share of the customer's dollars and extend the length of the customer relationship.

○ Price. E-business can price more rationally by using auctions and dynamic pricing models.

○ Quality. Improving the quality of the customer interactions increases current customer satisfaction and makes offerings more attractive to potential new customers.

○ Fulfillment Time. Reduced order fulfillment and customer-buying time (searching, selection, and purchasing) increases overall customer value. E-business also accelerates overall time to market, adding real value.

○ Agility. Increased agility increases a company's flexibility and ability to execute opportunistic strategies and actions, respond to changing competitive conditions, and defend its markets.

○ Reach. Expanded market reach means better access to more customers on a global scale.

○ Time to Market. Reduced time to market extends product or service life cycles and increases the number of new products or services available.

Value Driver: Operating Margin

E-business enhances customer value and competitiveness in the following ways to increase operating margins.

○ Service. Web technology reduces the cost of serving customers. On-line information is available 24 hours a day, seven days a week. Customers can use self-service features, participate in on-line chat communities, receive electronic notification of product updates and preventive maintenance schedules, and register their products electronically. The company and its value-adding partners can share information with customers in real time.

○ Quality. Collapsed supply chains made possible by e-nabling technology increase quality at every point in the value chain. Companies also lower their cost of delivering high quality by minimizing inaccurate order-processing information and by electronically linking order processing, production, suppliers, order fulfillment, and logistics.

○ Fulfillment Time. Reduced fulfillment time results in less inventory, and, therefore, fewer costs.

○ Agility. More rapid integration of acquisitions and a greater ability to redeploy existing resources reduces operating costs.

○ Reach. Extended reach via electronic channels leverages the company's existing brand and marketing investment across a greater potential audience.

Value Driver: Working Capital

E-business enhances customer value and competitive capability in the following ways to decrease working capital.

○ Quality. Minimizing errors in order processing and demand planning reduces safety-stock requirements.

○ Fulfillment Time. Reducing order fulfillment time decreases the amount of inventory held across the supply chain.

○ Agility. Sourcing from a large base of potential suppliers results in reduced working capital needs and better credit terms.

Value Driver: Capital Expenditures

E-business enhances customer value and competitive capability in the following ways to improve asset utilization.

- ○ Agility. Redeploying assets in response to changing market conditions creates greater fixed asset efficiencies. Sourcing inputs, finished products, and complementary products and services from the marketplace rather than producing them internally reduces overall capital expenditure needs.
- ○ Time to Market. Decreased time to market and increased reach drives more and better asset utilization.

Value Driver: Cash Tax Rate

E-business enhances customer value and competitive capability in the following way.

- ○ Agility. Globally diversifying its value chain reduces a company's overall global tax burden. Shared service, typically back office, functions can be easily distributed to low tax regimes.

Value Driver: Cost of Capital

E-business has an effect on the cost of capital only in that a company's "e-ness" increases its share price (and decreases its cost of equity). However, this effect may be transient.

Value Driver: Competitive Advantage Period

E-business enhances customer value and competitive capability in the following ways to lengthen the competitive advantage period.

- ○ Service. Innovative customer service differentiates a company's offering and helps to sustain and extend its competitive advantage.
- ○ Quality. High-quality customer interaction increases the psychological cost to the customer of switching.
- ○ Fulfillment Time. Improving time to service and synchronizing with customer schedules also increases the psychological cost to the customer of switching.
- ○ Agility. Increased responsiveness to changing market conditions, competitive offerings, ability to unbundle and rebundle offerings and to configure products and value-added services in an

infinite number of ways reduces the likelihood that products will become obsolete.

○ Time to Market. Rapid product introductions reduce competitors' potential to leapfrog a company's offerings.

○ Reach. Greater reach provides a company with earlier recognition of competitive threats and provides opportunities to respond appropriately.

E-BUSINESS POSITIONING

An e-business can assume one of three positions: standing still, following, or leading. Standing still is not an option for rational managers.

Figure 11.3   E-Business Stagnation

Customer Service	• Lose existing customer service advantages • Potential cause for customer defections
Price	• Increased because of commerce penalties due to pass through charges
Quality	• Perception of quality reduction due to comparative lack of value-added services • No real change to quality
Fulfillment Time	• Same • Noncompetitive long term
Agility	• Noncompetitive long term
Time to Market	• Noncompetitive long term
Market Reach	• Loss of customer intimacy results in shrinking market reach • Impacted by customer's extended reach

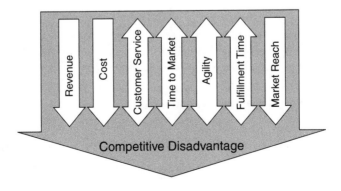

Figure 11.4   E-Business "Followership"

Customer Service	• Significant capability to increase customer service/intimacy
Price	• Reduced by cost efficiencies passed through to the customer
Quality	• Somewhat increased due to customer self-service
Fulfillment Time	• Decreased to internal process theoretical minimum
Agility	• Increased through standardization of data formats and interoperability
Time to Market	• Decreased through knowledge management and extended access to information throughout the company
Market Reach	• Increased • Defense of current reach likely

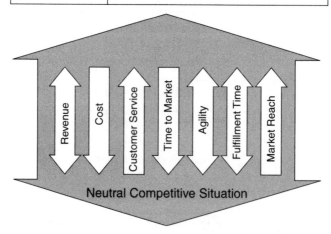

Following may protect short-term position but cannot ensure long-term advantage. Only leading will produce long-term advantage. Figure 11.3, Figure 11.4, and Figure 11.5 illustrate these three positions.

CASE STUDY: A RADICAL APPROACH

The chairman of a global high-tech solutions provider asked some very probing questions about a proposed $1 billion investment in e-business. His team's "simple" objective was to transform the traditional, vertically organized company into a radical new customer-centric organization.

Figure 11.5   E-Business Leadership

Customer Service	• New dimension in customer care • Achieve intimacy • Retain loyalty
Price	• Significant decrease • Source of competitive advantage for entire value chain
Quality	• Increased through standardized customer interface and automated processes
Fulfillment Time	• Drastically increased • Source of customer loyalty
Agility	• New strategies enabled
Time to Market	• Greatly enhanced • Long-term advantages gained in the short term
Market Reach	• Rapid geographic increase • Incremental penetration of "markets of one" served by competitors as market segments

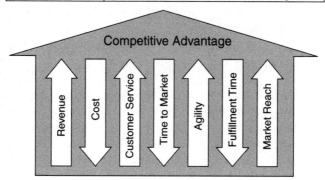

Most senior management viewed the proposal a no brainer, particularly since their major competitors were following similar paths. However, the business was driven by hard economic value-added (EVA) numbers, and the CFO had made promises to Wall Street.

The justification to the board for the e-business investment was a fluffy concept of "enhanced customer value." It simply didn't stack up against EVA.

Closer investigation revealed four seemingly intractable problems:

1. The DCF numbers simply didn't work. E-business could not be justified in terms of traditional cash flow.

2. The "enhanced customer value" proposition could not be easily supported in financial terms.

3. The CFO did not know how to communicate effectively to Wall Street the proposed e-business investment package.

4. In the heart of the business operations, rumblings were already starting about how e-business would affect delivery of key performance indicators (KPIs), and the resulting management bonuses.

The solution was to adopt a radical new approach, not only for the business case, but also for ongoing program management of the e-business implementation. A whole new set of financial management principles was introduced into the business focused on a customer-centric e-business view of the world. The approach consisted of five parts:

1. A clear shareholder value driver focus, from both a company and customer perspective

2. An even clearer focus on the "seventh driver," sustainable long-term competitive advantage

3. New financial analytics that accommodated the inherent uncertainties of the e-business world

4. An investor relations program in sync with the company's underlying e-business strategy

5. An integrated and consistent framework for successfully managing the ongoing e-business program.

The long-term result for the CFO was a sea change in financial management for the entire company. Investment allocation processes were overhauled. Major changes in planning and budgeting processes were initiated. Performance metrics were turned on their heads. And a communication blitz got the message out to both institutional and individual investors.

TIPS AND PITFALLS

Corporate leaders around the world are facing the same situation as that confronting our hypothetical CEO and CFO in the foregoing case study. Like them, all company leaders need to heed the following warnings and suggestions:

1. Be open; think outside the box of generally used financial analysis techniques. E-business requires a whole new set of ground rules.

2. Consider the views, motivations, and expectations of *all* stakeholders when considering e-business developments. E-business is surely showing that focus on customer value and relationships

with other players throughout the value chain can lead to enhanced, long-term shareholder value.

3. Look outside traditional organizational boundaries to find all of the places where e-business creates value.

4. Think about ongoing e-business benefit execution, not just up-front evaluation. The role of the CFO is not just to be the architect of the up-front plan, but to be the navigator of the company's course as he or she executes that plan.

5. The future currency of business will be information and knowledge as much as or more than physical assets.

Appendix

The E-nabled Value Chain: A Detailed View

E-business has the potential to change the way companies undertake activities and processes all along the value chain. With an e-nabled value chain companies can transact business in a faster, leaner, and more flexible manner.*

This appendix relates how companies can use e-business technology to redesign the processes within six parts of the value chain: marketing, product development, sales performance, materials procurement, logistics/distribution management, and customer service provision. The segment of the value chain dealing with the actual production of goods is not part of our discussion, except when that production is outsourced.

Figure A.1 illustrates a standard value chain for a products-oriented company with the first step, Perform Marketing, highlighted. At the beginning of each subsection we return to this value chain graphic, highlighting the part of the value chain being discussed.

Figure A.1   Standard Value Chain: Performing Marketing

Perform Marketing	Develop Products	Perform Sales	Procure Materials	Produce Products	Manage Logistics
Manage Customer Service					

---

*This appendix provides a list of e-business opportunities a products-oriented company may implement to e-nable the value chain. This list does not include the universe of opportunities but provides a significant foundation upon which to build an e-business presence.

207

PERFORM MARKETING

Marketing generally has three main business objectives: gaining market share by attracting new customers, increasing customer retention, and obtaining the best value for each marketing dollar spent. Figure A.2 illustrates these objectives, along with critical success factors and the ways to e-nable the marketing effort.

Strong and effective marketing campaigns attract new customers, energize them, and persuade them to purchase products and/or services. The e-nabled company reacts quickly to changing market conditions and has the ability to "push" relevant information directly to the customer's desktop.

Marketing executives should realize their greatest profits by selling actively to their current customers because the cost of acquiring a new customer far exceeds the cost of selling to an existing customer. The e-nabled company can quickly test and deploy new pricing strategies without expensive republishing efforts, access on-line research and knowledge bases that maintain significant information about competitors, and put their name and product information in new areas for customers to see.

Wherever possible, organizations look for ways to optimize their marketing dollars to reduce overall expenditures. The e-nabled company can continuously monitor and capture customer feedback at a low

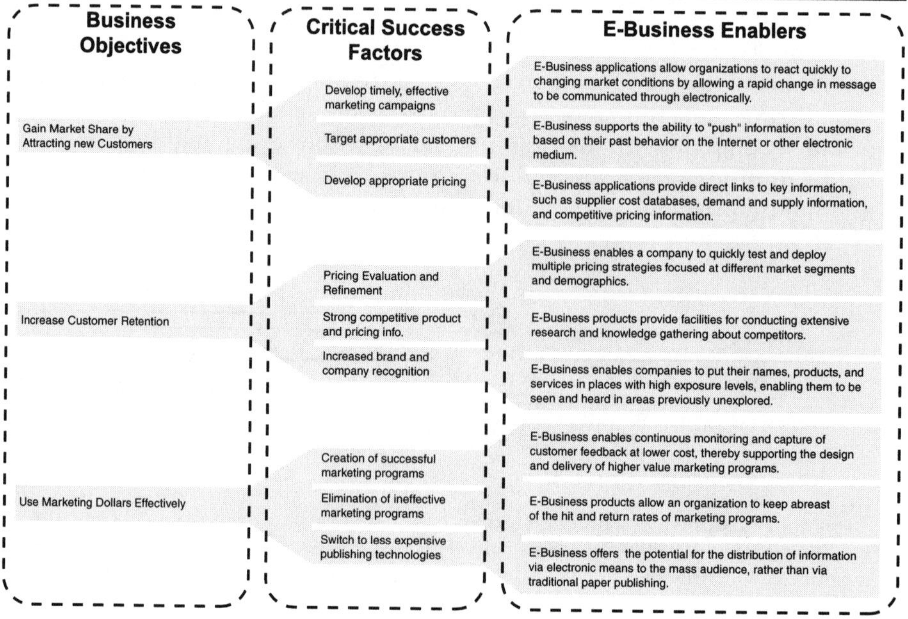

Figure A.2   E-nabling Marketing: Objectives and Critical Success Factors

cost, keep abreast of the "hit" and "return" rates generated by marketing programs, and distribute information electronically.

In a typical company, marketing affects six major business processes. Managerial processes include understanding customers and markets; developing marketing strategies and plans; and managing products and services. E-business supports not only information gathering, but also, and most significantly, developing and maintaining pricing, planning and managing the sales channels, and advertising and promoting products.

Developing and Maintaining Pricing

Developing and maintaining pricing is initiated by the introduction of a new product or sales channel, or by the need to maintain pricing over time, perhaps because of a change in a competitor's pricing strategy. Marketing professionals can take a number of steps to help them develop pricing. They can, for example, survey competitive products, determine the true cost of creating the product, and gauge the demand for some products and supply of others.

As external market factors change, the price an organization can charge for its products may also change. Being able to react competitively to changing market factors can mean the difference between the continued vitality of a product and its demise. Determining the proper price, especially for a new product, is critical to revenue and profitability.

The e-nabled pricing process is illustrated in Figure A.3.

Pricing information databases have transformed the pricing update process. With these databases, prices can be instantly updated and disseminated throughout the extraprise. They have the potential to replace the traditional price sheet or pricing catalogue.

In addition, with on-line pricing modules, multiple pricing schemes can be held in a single repository allowing different pricing models to be used for different customers and customer types. Four e-nabling functions support this process:

1. Pricing inquiry
2. On-line order management
3. Product configuration
4. Customer history.

The benefits of this technology are lower costs and reduced cycle time. Directly publishing pricing information electronically reduces or eliminates the cost of creating price books and other hard copy documentation. A central repository to maintain all pricing information also

Figure A.3   E-nabled Pricing Process

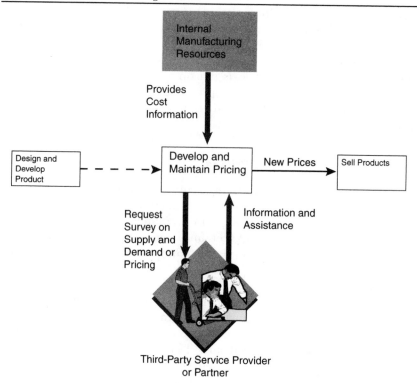

Third-Party Service Provider
or Partner

reduces costs. Changing prices quickly and posting those changes instantly to field staff and customers reduces cycle time, and assessing the impact of price changes also becomes easier.

Two e-nabling technologies support this process:

1. On-line price updates
2. On-line order management.

These technologies also transform a company's ability to assess price determinants and to monitor pricing. By posting their pricing catalogues on-line, vendors can assess supply and demand by interacting with customers on the Internet. In addition, customers in an electronic world are more likely to communicate pricing information to suppliers electronically.

Five e-nabling technologies make this possible:

1. On-line catalogues
2. On-line feedback and user surveys

3. Web site hit information

4. On-line competitor pricing information

5. Electronic links with supplier ERP systems.

In addition to reduced cycle time, benefits include improved accuracy by enabling a company quickly to determine costs electronically via direct links with suppliers or multisupplier catalogues.

Planning and Managing Sales Channels

Planning and managing sales channels is initiated when an organization either needs to determine how best to present its product to the market, or to review and maintain channels after a channel plan has been established. Normally, companies perform initial brainstorming to identify potential sales channels.

A company may decide that it wants to market its products directly to the public, that it may want to use distributors to distribute the product throughout the marketplace, or that it may want to use value-added resellers to sell the product. Once the channels are determined, the company must execute the channel plan, setting up the appropriate resellers or distributors or creating an internal marketing process. The company continuously monitors the channel, tracking sales results and order flow. Revisions to the channel plan and strategy may result in the addition or removal of channel partners.

The e-nabled sales channel planning and management process is illustrated in Figure A.4.

E-business transforms implementation of the channel plan because once a company determines its plan for sales channels and those channels

Figure A.4   E-nabled Sales Channel Planning and Management Process

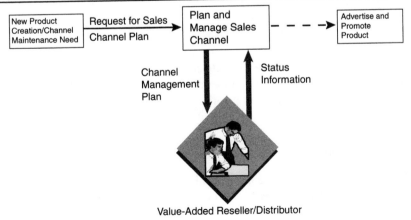

Value-Added Reseller/Distributor

are established, it may provide e-nabled tools to facilitate efficient inter-action with demand chain partners. The company may also provide marketing materials and product information and monitor sales leads received and sent through those channels.

Demand chain partners can then easily provide feedback on the tools, as well as new marketing information for future use. In addition, the company may bypass some traditional channels and use automated channels such as the Internet to market their products and services.

Four e-nabling technologies allow companies to do this:

1. Sales force automation tools
2. On-line access to ERP systems from the field
3. FAQs and Tech Tips in on-line knowledge bases
4. On-line marketing materials.

The benefits include increased customer satisfaction, cycle time reduction, and better operating effectiveness.

These technologies increase customer satisfaction because distributors and value-added resellers feel linked up with the e-nabled extraprise. They reduce cycle times because information flow to demand chain partners is close to real time. They enhance operating effectiveness because new automated channels emerge that allow the organization to market without the cost or hassle of traditional relationships.

A transformation occurs in the monitoring and maintaining of sales channels because once they have been established, the organization monitors sales channels to make sure they are achieving productivity goals. This includes monitoring the desired sales volume, lead follow-up response time, and percentage of leads closed. Two e-nabling technologies make this possible:

1. Sales force automation software
2. Sales tracking software.

The benefits of this transformation include customer satisfaction and operating effectiveness. It also enhances customer satisfaction because a company can ensure that its channels are following up promptly on sales opportunities. It improves operating effectiveness because companies can rapidly reorganize poorly performing sales channels and create additional ones.

Advertising and Promoting Products

Advertising and promoting products is one of the key processes in marketing. During this process, companies create advertising campaigns, distribute promotional materials to channel partners, and organize promotions. The marketing department may use an outside agency or internal department to plan, develop, and execute advertising campaigns.

During this time, companies may use customer focus groups to judge the effectiveness of campaigns and to gauge customer reaction to products and advertising. They may conduct customer surveys to determine the worthiness of a campaign and distribute marketing materials and advertisements to channel partners.

The e-nabled advertising and promotion process is illustrated in Figure A.5.

E-nabling technologies transform the processes of identifying customer drivers, conducting focus groups, and collecting data. Companies use this information to tailor campaigns to customer demands and market standards.

Figure A.5   E-nabled Advertising and Promotion Process

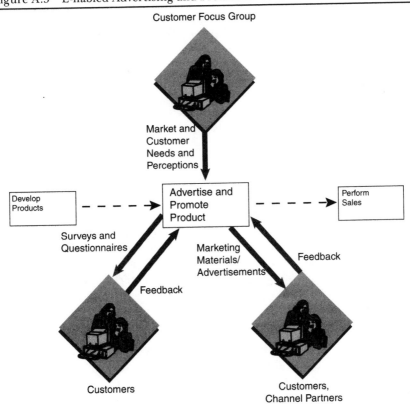

Four e-nabling technologies make this happen:

1. On-line surveys and questionnaires
2. Electronic meetings and focus groups
3. On-line feedback forms
4. On-line chat forums.

The benefits of this transformation are improved accuracy (companies stay in tune with continually changing customer needs); 24×7 convenience; ease of use (the interactive medium encourages use); and high value/low cost.

Campaign rollouts are transformed because once the plan has been determined and the actual advertising and promotion campaigns created, the advertising and promotion can be rolled out electronically. For example, companies can use Web sites to launch new products, taking advantage of Internet search engines that point interested customers toward the Web site.

Companies can use push technology to send automatically special promotional information and products to a potential customer's personal computer (PC). Five e-nabling technologies allow this to occur:

1. Web sites
2. Push technology
3. Search engines
4. Web site banner advertising
5. Electronic download sites.

The benefits of e-nabling campaign rollouts are cost reduction, improved accuracy, and revenue enhancement.

An inexpensive electronic publishing medium and the ability to target interested customers quickly reduce cost. Accuracy is improved by the speed with which campaigns can be updated and modified. Revenue is enhanced by increased customer visibility over a wide geographic spread because of the global reach of electronic technologies.

DEVELOP PRODUCTS

Typically, developing products (Figure A.6) involves three main business objectives: to bring products to market more quickly; to reduce product development costs; and to improve new-product success rates. Figure A.7 illustrates these objectives, along with critical success factors and the ways to e-nable the product development effort.

Figure A.6   Standard Value Chain: Product Development

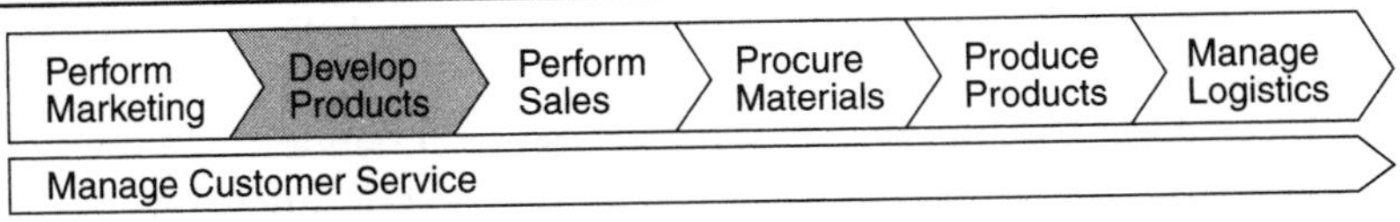

| Perform Marketing | Develop Products | Perform Sales | Procure Materials | Produce Products | Manage Logistics |

Manage Customer Service

To achieve competitive advantage and pioneer status for new innovations, products must be brought to market as quickly as possible. The e-nabled company can quickly and efficiently capture design and market information from the customer, "the market," and market research companies. Equally, access to designers, suppliers, and outsourcers speeds up coordination throughout the product development cycle. Finally, the e-nabled company can conduct virtual client product testing.

Clearly, price is one of the key issues in successfully launching a new product. Consequently, it is essential to drive down costs wherever possible. The e-nabled company can use on-line research and on-line communication with suppliers and outsourcers to access specifications, quotations, proposals, and design changes. Additionally, the e-nabled company has access to a wider range of suppliers and outsourcers, thereby ensuring competitive quoting.

Figure A.7   E-nabling Product Development: Objectives and Critical
                  Success Factors

Business Objectives	Critical Success Factors	E-Business Enablers
		E-business enables process via access to on-line market research; customer information for the design process can be gained from existing data or via on-line direct questioning.
	Faster Access to Research Information	
	Design and Production Process Shortened	E-business provides on-line access to designers and suppliers; fast access to client testing is available through virtual customer product analysis.
Bring Products to Market More Quickly	Better Turnaround Times with Suppliers and Outsourcers	E-business offers on-line access to suppliers and outsourcers.
	'Best' Research Achieved Using Fewer Resources	E-business enables cost-effective on-line research; scope is increased and manpower input reduced.
Reduce New Product Development Costs	Competitive Supply and Outsource Costs	E-business enables communication and coordination with suppliers; also wider access drives down prices.
	Specification Production Design and Design Change Work Eased	E-business eases configuration and design process via on-line access to suppliers and outsourcers: specification, design, and change to design are dealt with quickly and at lower cost.
	Fast Transfer of Feedback and Info	E-business enables continuous monitoring and capture of customer feedback at lower cost, thereby supporting the design and delivery of new higher-value product offerings.
Improve New Product Market Success Factors	'Deep and Wide' Market Research	E-business supports deeper and wider market research which ensures a better understanding of customer wants.
	Enhanced Accuracy of Product Design	E-business enhances accuracy of product design through enriched collaboration between design and virtual product testing.

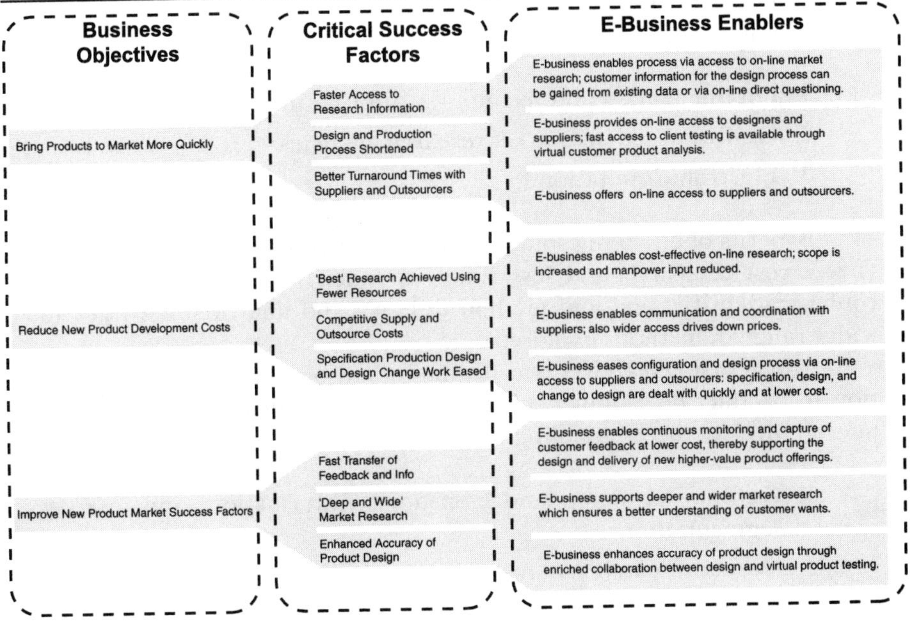

The e-nabled company can reduce the risks associated with product launches. It can continuously capture a high volume of client information and feedback; exploit significantly deeper and wider market research; and achieve higher accuracy through third-party collaboration.

The activities associated with developing new products involve five major business processes. Each process can be e-nabled.

Researching Products and Services

The product research process aims to establish the market need for a new product. The process is typically initiated with a new product idea or concept from marketing. It begins by determining the market research that is required and involves an external market research agency that chooses the research method to be used. Once a suitable research method has been sourced, the research material is prepared and the external agency is commissioned to conduct the market research.

The company reviews the results of the market research and, if satisfactory, an external agency typically conducts market testing of the new concept. Results of these tests are used to make a go/no-go decision about developing the new product.

The e-nabled product research process is illustrated in Figure A.8.

Electronic questionnaires and electronically facilitated customer focus groups, home placement, or market testing necessary for a company to decide whether to develop a product transforms the methods for sourcing research. This transformation involves three e-nabling technologies:

1. On-line market and technology information
2. On-line access to market research agencies
3. Electronic quotation.

Benefits of e-nabling sourcing research methods are cost reduction (lower cost of search and less time expended); cycle time reduction (quicker identification and method design); and improved accuracy (a wider range of methods explored).

The actual research is transformed when potential consumer reaction to product developments is captured electronically. This transformation involves three e-nabling technologies:

1. On-line customer and consumer information and market segmentation
2. Market research systems
3. Interactive market encyclopedia systems.

Figure A.8   E-nabled Product Research Process

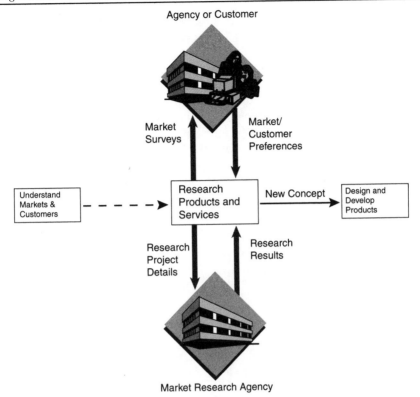

The benefits of transforming research are improvement in accuracy (a wider scope of research at less cost) and cost reduction (less manual effort in conducting market research).

Market testing is transformed when digitized products can be distributed and all product test results collected electronically. Two e-nabling technologies allow this to occur:

1. Virtual market research
2. Virtual focus groups and questionnaires.

The benefits of transformed market testing are cycle time reduction (improved speed at lower cost) and improved accuracy (more accurate data collection and no rekeying of results).

Designing and Developing Products

The product design and development process begins after a few concepts have been tested and a decision has been made to develop a new product. This process typically involves working closely with external design agencies and suppliers to develop prototypes.

Suppliers and partners may participate in the design of subassemblies and components, while design agencies may be contracted to assist with overall design. This stage of product development may also require working closely with regulatory agencies to ensure compliance and approval. The final design feeds into the phase of new-product development in which manufacturing processes are established.

Figure A.9 illustrates e-nabled product design and development.

Figure A.9   E-nabled product Design and Development

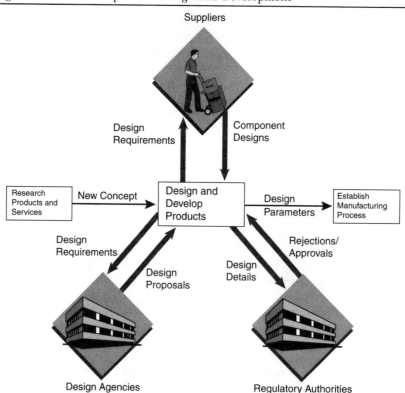

E-business technology transforms communication with designers, suppliers, and regulatory agencies. This transformation involves three e-nabling technologies:

1. Detailed product brief and concept communication
2. Electronic quotations from agencies and suppliers
3. On-line links with regulatory agencies.

Benefits of e-nabling these communications include cycle time reduction (timely communication and accelerated regulatory feedback and decision making) and cost reducing improvements in accuracy.

Concurrent engineering is transformed as well. Concurrent engineering is the iterative process matching material and component capabilities with the original product brief. Market research and testing during this phase may lead to design alterations. Three e-nabling technologies assist here:

1. On-line communication for revisions
2. Electronic quotations for revisions
3. On-line "what if" costing scenarios.

Benefits of e-nabling concurrent engineering are improved accuracy and cycle time reduction. Clear and regular communication e-nabled throughout this part of the process for product development helps companies meet timing, cost, and quality objectives.

Establishing Manufacturing Processes

The aim of this process is to establish the manufacturing processes required to produce the new product. The company obtains the final design of the new product from the product design process and evaluates it against its production capability.

This process helps companies identify requirements for new capital equipment, components, and external services. Potential suppliers of required materials and services are identified and evaluated. Successful production trials lead to an agreed on design and commissioning of the production process, and the new product is manufactured.

An e-nabled manufacturing process is illustrated in Figure A.10. In this process, tooling and outsourcing are transformed by electronic channels that can be used to request assistance, to source capital equipment, or to search for third-party producers.

Figure A.10   E-nabled Manufacturing Process

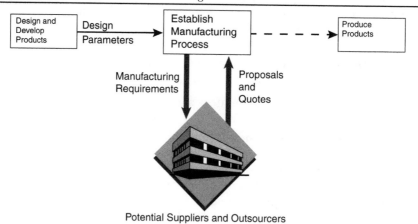

Three e-nabling technologies assist this effort:

1. Electronic specifications for requests for quotes (RFQs)
2. Electronic quotations
3. Electronic proposals.

    The benefits of e-nabling tooling and outsourcing are cycle time re-duction (a wider range of sources may be consulted at reduced cost and time); cost reduction (reduction in time for sourcing allows a wider range of suppliers to be consulted, potentially reducing purchase cost); and im-proved accuracy (queries and classifications can be dealt with quickly and accurately).

Managing Product Configuration

The aim of this process is to maintain and manage the master configura-tion details of the final product design. Within this process, companies identify product component suppliers, obtain prices, and update master records. Where necessary, they communicate the master configuration details to extranet partners. An e-nabled product management configu-ration process is illustrated in Figure A.11.

    Costing and listing components and confirming data externally are the activities that this process transforms.

    Once the final product development is complete, logistics, fi-nance, and purchasing need to update their systems with product

Figure A.11   E-nabled Product Management Configuration Process

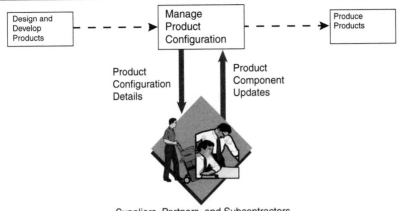

Suppliers, Partners, and Subcontractors

codes, component codes, and costings. This can be done in concert with supply chain partners supported electronically.

Three e-nabling technologies assist here:

1. On-line product information and configuration

2. On-line parts and pricing lists

3. Electronic quotations.

The e-nabling of the costing and listing of components leads to reduced costs and cycle time and improved accuracy. A wider range of sources consulted may reduce cost and time, while on-line queries and classifications are dealt with quickly and accurately.

Managing Product Introduction

This process involves working with the marketing group on all activities crucial to a successful product launch. The company may engage an external marketing and advertising agency to run the launch program and may obtain feedback from consumers and/or customers who have reviewed the initial product design. An e-nabled product introduction management process is illustrated in Figure A.12.

Three activities—arranging the launch, distributing and launching the product, and reviewing development success—are transformed in the e-nabled company.

Arranging the launch requires extensive communications with supply chain partners concerning promotions, advertising, and the launch

Figure A.12   E-nabled Product Introduction Management Process

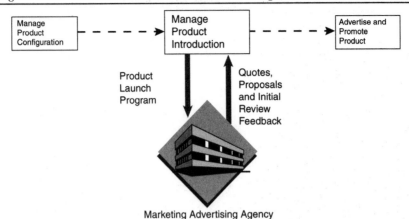

Marketing Advertising Agency

itself. Agencies may require specific product samples or mock-ups. Two e-nabling technologies support these efforts:

1. Electronic product information
2. Electronic promotion information.

The benefits of e-nabling this activity are improved accuracy (a common understanding of critical success factors is established) and reduced cycle time (many parties communicate efficiently).

Prior to launching a new product or revised product, companies must run down the stocks of current products to be replaced. Electronically communicating the information for launch of a new product improves needed stock turns. On-line promotion and launch communication is the e-nabling technology that assists this activity.

Benefits of e-nabling this activity are cycle time reduction (communication is more efficient) and improved accuracy (companies receive direct input into marketing efforts from the product development process).

Initial product design may need to be altered following customer, consumer, or other feedback. In addition, companies must constantly fine tune the product development process. On-line consumer feedback e-nables this activity.

The benefits of e-nabling the process of reviewing development success are improved accuracy (companies obtain timely and accurate feedback that they then use to review product sales) and cost reduction (feedback is easier to collect).

PERFORM SALES

In a company producing a product, performing sales (Figure A.13) generally involves three main business objectives: growing sales revenue, reducing cost of sales, and increasing customer retention. These objectives, their key success factors, and ways the sales process can be e-nabled, are illustrated in Figure A.14.

The overriding goal of the sales organization is to grow revenue. With increasing competition in a global marketplace, customers have more options than ever before. The mission of the sales force is to retain those customers and capture new ones.

An e-nabled sales force continually monitors and captures customer information at lower cost, thereby increasing its ability to manage the customer relationship and eliminating geographical sales boundaries that have in the past constrained a company's ability to develop global product offerings tailored to a market of one. By supporting effective communication with demand chain partners, the e-nabled sales force leverages the sales capacity of these partners.

Reducing cost of sales is critical in a competitive marketplace characterized by ever shrinking margins. While revenue growth is the goal, reducing the cost of sales also helps to ensure maximum profitability.

The e-nabled sales force is empowered by customer self-service for inquiries, presales information gathering, and some automated sales. Sales personnel can focus on developing high value-added relationships with customers that have complex needs or that make large volume purchases.

The growing trend toward commoditization in many industries places a great emphasis on customer retention. Additionally, the costs associated with winning new customers are far higher than those required to retain existing customers.

The e-nabled sales force supports 24 × 7 access to sales service, service tailored to individual customer needs, and enhanced information sharing.

Sales activities occur in six main business processes. Those associated with tracking sales and managing customer accounts are managerial. E-business may improve those processes by supporting information gathering. The most significant e-business effect, however, is on operational processes: managing leads, selling products, and entering and tracking orders.

Figure A.13   Standard Value Chain: Performing Sales

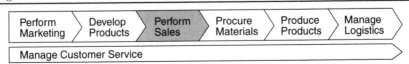

Figure A.14   E-nabling the Sales Process: Objectives and Critical Success Factors

Business Objectives	Critical Success Factors	E-Business Enablers
		E-business enables the timely and accurate distribution of sales leads to the appropriate sales resource or channel partner. Follow-up action may be scheduled and progress status tracked to ensure that all leads are dealt with promptly.
	Follow-Up Sales Leads Promptly and Efficiently	
Grow Sales Revenue	Extend Reach and Range of Sales Activities	E-business offers the opportunity to eliminate geographical sales boundaries and develop product offerings tailored to a market of one—worldwide.
	Exploit Opportunities to Cross-Sell and Up-Sell	E-business offers the opportunity to guide customers through alternative product configurations, product add-ons, and optional extras. The customer is able to explore without feeling pressured to buy.
	Reduce/Eliminate Administrative Activities	E-business enables customer self-service for most sales inquiries including product information, configuration options, pricing options, and order status information.
Reduce Cost of Sales	Focus Sales Resource on High-Value Opportunities	E-business enables customer self-service for all activities relating to sales of simple low-value commodity products enabling high-cost sales resources to focus on sales of high-value complex solutions.
	Shorten Sales-Cycle	E-business enables the customer to quickly make a 'buy decision' by providing convenient accessibility to all neccesary information.
	Provide a Responsive Service to High-Value Customers	E-business offers the potential to provide key high-value customers with immediate, 24 x 7 access to sales, and after-sales service information.
Improve Customer Retention	Personalize Sales Service to Major Customers	E-business enables the tailoring of sales support service to individual customer needs; major customers are guided towards the products and services compatible with their current and anticipated needs.
	Build Closer Customer Relationships	E-business promotes closer relationships with customers by enabling the potential to share information on future product development and customers' demand forecasts.

Managing Leads

Marketing activity generates sales leads that are collected, logged, and mapped to the appropriate marketing campaign as a measure of its success. Subsequent to review, they are passed on to the appropriate sales person or demand chain partner. Each lead is tracked to ensure follow-up and to monitor status and outcome.

Figure A.15 illustrates the e-enabled lead management process.

E-business transforms four activities within the lead management process: receiving sales leads and documenting opportunities, assigning sales leads, scheduling callbacks, and updating lead status.

Physical world or electronic marketing may generate electronic inquiries. At the time of capture, these may be mapped to the relevant activity using information the prospect provides. Full details are captured and logged for assigning and tracking.

This transformation involves two e-nabling technologies:

1. Electronic lead capture and logging
2. Electronic lead triggers.

Figure A.15   E-nabled Lead-Management Process

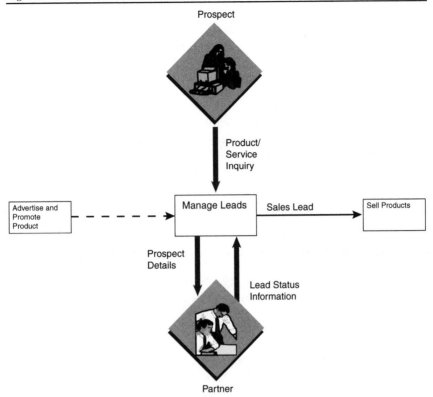

Transforming the receiving and documenting of leads results in the following benefits: cost and head count reduction (handling of sales leads and administrative activities are automated) and improved accuracy (all leads are captured, logged, and tracked).

Automating the assignment of sales leads controls the activity by facilitating distribution of leads to appropriate internal sales professionals or demand channel partners.

Sales territory business rules may be built in, ensuring that leads are distributed accurately. Customer profiles and other relevant sales support data may be attached to each lead. Three e-nabling technologies support this activity:

1. Electronic sales lead distribution
2. Electronic customer profiles
3. Channel management rules.

E-nabling the assignment of sales leads improves accuracy (all leads are accurately distributed to the relevant sales channel together with supporting information); reduces costs (overhead associated with manually sorting and communicating leads is eliminated); and enhances operating effectiveness (distribution of leads among sales channels is tracked for measuring and monitoring effectiveness of sales channel strategy).

Callback scheduling, together with alerts for each assigned lead, can be automated, ensuring that leads will be followed up in accordance with agreed service levels. In the event a lead has gone uninvestigated, the lead management system initiates alerts and automatic escalation. In some cases, leads may then be automatically reassigned to another sales professional or demand chain partner.

This transformation involves two e-nabling technologies:

1. Automated schedules
2. Customer profiles.

Automating the callback scheduling activity improves customer satisfaction (responses are timely and efficient); reduces cycle time (follow-up is timely, ensuring that opportunities are processed efficiently); and improves accuracy (all leads, especially requested callbacks, are followed up).

A centrally managed automation of this function ensures that all sales channels simultaneously update leads at preagreed intervals. Reminders and alerts may be issued, updates requested, and information captured in a standard format to maintain consistency and ease of analysis.

This information may be used to develop and maintain a consolidated sales forecast across a wide-ranging sales channel strategy.

This transformation involves three e-nabling technologies:

1. Electronic request-for-status updates
2. Lead status tracking
3. Consolidated sales forecasting.

E-nabling the lead status updating activity reduces costs (high manual overhead in tracking lead status is eliminated) and improves accuracy (effective collection of lead status enables more accurate sales forecasting and measurement of marketing activity effectiveness).

Selling Products

A lead from the managing leads process typically initiates this process. As soon as lead managers determine the prospect's needs and provide

Figure A.16   E-nabled Product Sell Process

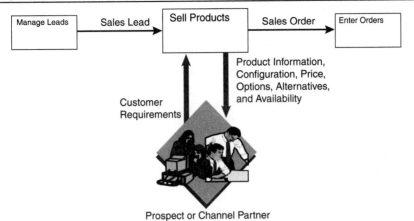

Prospect or Channel Partner

product information, a suitable product/solution is configured and a quotation prepared. If the product is available, a shipment date is communicated. Opportunities exist to cross-sell or up-sell to other related or superior products. Both the direct sales force and demand channel partners perform activities within this process.

Figure A.16 illustrates the e-nabled sale of products.

An e-nabled selling organization completely transforms solution proposal activities. This single step automates the seven manual steps of the selling products process. Of course, the electronic channel may not be appropriate for all types of products and all sales situations. But it offers a low-cost, convenient route for most straightforward purchases and for repeat orders.

Through automation, customer needs are analyzed and mapped to product types, providing supporting product information. Electronic configurators assist the customer in choosing options, and parts-and-price lists help to provide quotations for each configuration.

Customers can investigate various price/performance configurations and check on product availability. The customer may also be guided toward optional extras and/or superior product configurations, thereby maximizing cross- and up-selling opportunities.

Sixteen e-nabling technologies support the transformation of this function:

1. Step-by-step question and answer
2. Behavior-based marketing and promotions
3. Characteristic-based product search
4. Target marketing by customer type

5. Electronic product catalogues

6. Real-time customer-specific pricing

7. Customer-specific marketing

8. Customer-specific product filtering

9. On-line product configurators

10. Real-time product/option availability

11. Cross-sell engines

12. Up-sell engines

13. Fax service integration

14. E-mail service integration

15. Credit card validation

16. Freight, tax, and shipping calculations.

An e-nabled solution proposal activity increases customer satisfaction (the customer is able to explore a variety of options at his or her leisure in a personalized environment); reduces cost and head count (costs are reduced by eliminating overhead for manual steps relating to handling low-value sales; head count is reduced by freeing the sales staff to focus on high-value big-ticket sales and on customer relationships); improves margins (the cost of handling high-volume, low-cost products is reduced); and reduces cycle time (customer self-service applies to all stages, from analyzing need and identifying product, to creating a quote, and order entry).

Entering Orders

The arrival of a customer order—typically in the form of a fax or other hard copy—initiates this process. Personnel check and validate, and, if acceptable, enter it into a computer-based order-logging system. Once inventory is checked, a shipment date can be set. The customer is then sent an order confirmation, together with the planned shipment date. Any errors and/or omissions on the order need to be addressed before the order is communicated to either the production group or outbound logistics. Finance is notified when orders are shipped so invoices can be sent. Figure A.17 illustrates an e-nabled order entry process.

This single automated step transforms the order validation/confirmation process by replacing the five manual steps typically required to enter, validate, and confirm a customer order. Although the sales process takes care of much of product/needs determination, the product and solution information from that process is necessary to complete order entry.

Figure A.17   E-nabled Order-Entry Process

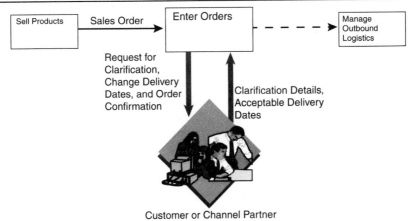

Customer or Channel Partner

In the event the sales/order entry process is combined, product catalogues and electronic price lists help the customer select an appropriate solution.

Entering product/model information is a natural extension of selecting a product. Customers confirm the products/models they select and the prices, review delivery options, and choose how they will pay. These choices are entered into the computer, available inventory and manufacturing schedules are queried, and the customer receives confirmed availability and shipment information together with an order confirmation.

This transformation involves 10 e-nabling technologies:

1. Customer profiling
2. Relationship marketing
3. Shopping cart
4. On-line catalogue
5. On-line price lists
6. Product configurator
7. Product ordering
8. Solutions (needs analysis) functionality
9. On-line available-to-promise
10. On-line order confirmation.

E-nabling the order validation and confirmation activity improves customer satisfaction, reduces operating cost and head count, lowers processing cost, improves accuracy, and cuts down on cycle-time.

Customer satisfaction and hence customer retention is increased through increased visibility for the customer and through improved accuracy and cycle time. Accuracy is improved by automated checking and order configuration, thereby eliminating errors. Cycle time is reduced by customers' entering the orders themselves, eliminating backlogs, and by integrating with outbound logistics partners.

Head count and operating cost reductions are achieved because low-ticket and repeat orders are handled through electronic channels, resulting in the elimination of manual order entry process steps. Lower costs for processing low-value orders maximizes margins.

Tracking Orders

The arrival of a customer inquiry, usually by telephone, initiates the order tracking process. Personnel then use the order confirmation number to retrieve order status information that is communicated to the customer. Figure A.18 illustrates an e-nabled order tracking process.

This single automated step transforms the order entry process by replacing the four manual steps previously required to determine and communicate order status information to the customer. Order confirmation information can take several forms. Usually, an order identification number is tied to each order.

The ability to receive accurate and timely status or order information at any time—from order receipt to manufacturing, through distribution and shipment—is a best practice. While consumers also demand accurate and timely information, in a reseller environment accurate shipment information has implications for billing and revenue recognition.

Figure A.18   E-nabled Order-Tracking Process

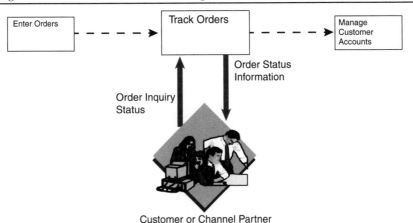

Order Inquiry Status

Order Status Information

Enter Orders

Track Orders

Manage Customer Accounts

Customer or Channel Partner

This transformation involves two e-nabling technologies:

1. Order confirmation number
2. Order status.

E-nabling the provision order status improves customer satisfaction, boosts accuracy, reduces cycle time and head count, and lowers operating cost.

Customer satisfaction and hence customer retention is raised because of increased customer visibility and improved accuracy and cycle time. Integration with manufacturing and logistics systems boosts accuracy. Customer self-service, which allows 24×7 instant gratification, reduces cycle time. Eliminating manual steps reduces head count and operating costs.

PROCURE MATERIALS/SERVICES

Procuring materials and services (Figure A.19) involves three business objectives: improving supplier performance, reducing cycle time and transaction costs for indirect procurement, and reducing total acquisition costs for purchased materials and services. Figure A.20 illustrates these objectives, the critical success factors for achieving them, and the ways in which indirect procurement can be e-nabled.

Supplier performance is key to manufacturing success. Ever-shorter lead times, combined with the need to reduce costs associated with inventory, demand speed, accuracy, and timeliness throughout the entire supply chain. E-business supports and e-nables new strategic relationships, provides cost-effective and flexible information sharing, and supports new automated mechanisms for collecting and feeding back supplier performance data.

The unit price of indirect procurement represents a significant portion of the overall cost base for large companies. Streamlining the procurement process while reducing unit costs can reduce costs. E-business eliminates virtually all handoffs and delays by linking the point of requisition to the approved supplier, automating approval and authorization policies, and facilitating corporatewide and potential intercompany aggregation of indirect material requirements.

Figure A.19   Standard Value Chain: Procuring Materials/Services

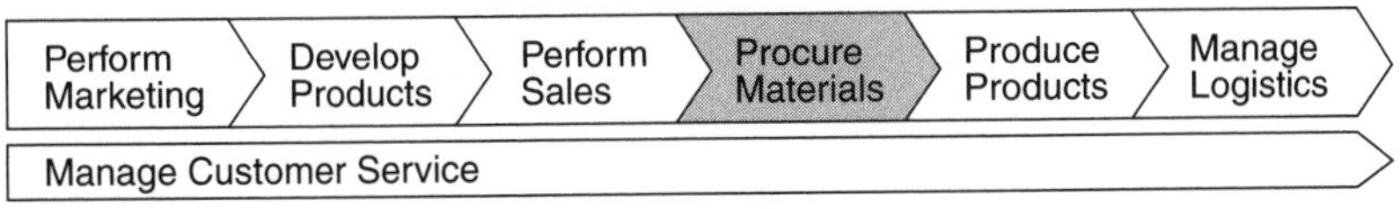

Figure A.20   E-nabling Procurement: Objectives and Critical Success Factors

Business Objectives	Critical Success Factors	E-Business Enablers
	Integrate Key Suppliers into the Organization	E-business enables cost-effective collaborative relationships with key suppliers through sharing operational data on materials management. This may be extended to collaborating with suppliers on new product development.
Improve Supplier Performance	Provide Accurate and Timely Information to Suppliers	E-business enables the sharing of information relating to demand forecast. Suppliers are better able to plan ahead and meet required performance criteria.
	Measure Performance and Provide Feedback	New strategic relationships with suppliers enabled through e-business offer new metrics and mechanisms for managing the continuous assessment of suppliers and providing feedback.
	Automate Process, Eliminate Non–Value-Adding Elements	E-business enables the elimination of the majority of hand-offs and delays normally associated with MRO procurement by providing a direct link between the users and the suppliers.
Reduce Cycle-Time and Transaction Cost of Maintenance, Repair, and Operations Procurement	Enforce MRO Procurement Policies	Electronic MRO eliminates the costs associated with maverick purchases by cost-effectively enforcing the use of approved suppliers together with policies on authorizations and approvals.
	Aggregate MRO Requirements	E-business enables corporate-wide, and also potentially intercompany, aggregation of MRO requirements to enable cost savings from suppliers.
	Identify and Assess Complete/ Potential Supply Base	E-business enables both cost-effective and time-effective search across a wider spectrum of suppliers to identify and qualify suitable suppliers.
Reduce Total Acquisition Costs of Purchased Materials & Services	Select Appropriate Suppliers	E-business facilitates the cost-effective, timely, and thorough investigation of supplier credentials before instigating a commercial relationship.
	Secure Competitive/ Preferential Terms	E-business creates the opportunity to develop longer-term strategic win–win relationships with suppliers, offering the prospect for negotiating preferential terms.

Relentless price pressure in many industries has caused companies to continually strive to obtain lower prices from suppliers. E-business facilitates cost-effective and powerful searching and managed "virtual communities" of prequalified industry suppliers and e-nables new, win-win relationships with key suppliers.

Four main activities are associated with procurement of materials and services: developing sourcing strategies, selecting suppliers, ordering materials and services, and appraising and developing suppliers. Managerial activities include those associated with developing sourcing strategies and appraising suppliers. E-business enhancements to information gathering support these activities. But e-business mostly impacts selecting suppliers and ordering materials and services.

Selecting Suppliers

Normally, receipt of an approved purchase requisition for which there are no currently approved suppliers initiates the supplier selection process. The aim of this activity is to identify potential suppliers and research their credentials to establish their suitability.

Depending on the type of product, this can be both time consuming and costly. It may involve sending out an invitation to tender (ITT)

and then collecting and analyzing responses. In some cases, thoroughness may be compromised to meet urgent requirements.

A short list of suppliers is then sent an RFQ containing proposed terms and conditions, and, after some negotiation, one or two preferred suppliers are chosen and added to the approved supplier list used by those conducting the order materials and services activity.

If the requisition is for a stock item, a blanket order is placed with the supplier to cover forecasted inventory requirements. For many companies, this process may be invoked too often, as most procurement is repetitive, and there is a trend toward longer-term relationships with a smaller number of key suppliers.

Figure A.21 illustrates an e-nabled supplier selection activity. Four specific activities within selecting suppliers are easily e-nabled: identifying suppliers, researching suppliers, establishing pricing agreements, and issuing blanket purchase orders.

If companies are to take advantage of additional cost savings, they must continually identify new vendors. E-business allows access to a

Figure A.21   E-nabled Supplier Selection

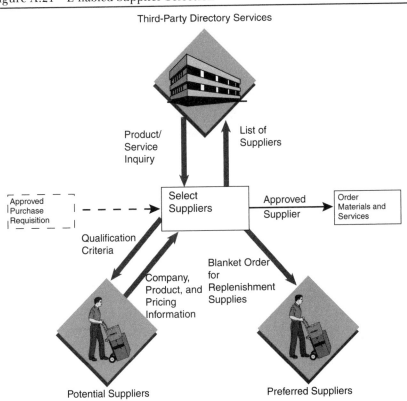

Third-Party Directory Services

Product/
Service
Inquiry

List of
Suppliers

Approved
Purchase
Requisition

Select
Suppliers

Approved
Supplier

Order
Materials and
Services

Qualification
Criteria

Company,
Product, and
Pricing
Information

Blanket Order
for
Replenishment
Supplies

Potential Suppliers

Preferred Suppliers

global supplier base. In addition, it creates the potential for a virtual marketplace, an electronic community of interest based around a particular industry or, perhaps, a specific product type. These may be managed communities consisting of prequalified and certified suppliers.

Four electronic capabilities support the identification of potential suppliers:

1. Electronic marketplace
2. Search engines
3. On-line industry directories
4. Electronic product catalogues.

E-nabling this activity improves accuracy and reduces cycle time, head count, and cost.

Electronic searches locate potential suppliers more quickly, reducing cycle time. They also require fewer resources to perform wider searches, reducing head count and cost. In addition, well-maintained electronic directories, together with managed virtual communities, result in quick identification of relevant suppliers.

Companies research suppliers to gain a complete understanding of their profiles, including delivery histories, quality programs, current customers, and financial standing. E-business facilitates this by providing immediate access to four important research tools:

1. Specialist market research
2. Specialist search engines
3. Specialist information directories
4. On-line industry directories.

E-nabling this activity reduces cycle time and head count and improves accuracy. Immediate access and powerful search facilities offer the opportunity to reduce cycle time and head count. High speed and low cost mean that accuracy and thoroughness are not compromised.

With these tools in place, companies can issue electronic RFQs to a short list of suppliers, and interested suppliers can submit electronic pricing proposals. For long-established strategic suppliers, this complex information exchange may be based on several scenarios of projected demand estimates. This exchange is e-nabled by two technologies:

1. Electronic communication
2. Electronic quotation management.

E-nabling this activity respectively reduces cost and cycle time by electronically capturing pricing and other information used for automated analysis and by using electronic communication to reduce process complexity.

Companies can provide suppliers who are issued blanket purchase orders direct and secure electronic access to inventory levels and usage patterns. This step is e-nabled by three technologies:

1. Electronic replenishment
2. Electronic communication
3. Electronic forecasting.

E-nabling this activity reduces cost (less overhead is required to keep suppliers up-to-date with changing information) and improves accuracy (instant communication of changes in demand forecasts is possible).

Ordering Materials and Services

Companies order materials and services in three different ways: replenishment, ad hoc buying, and indirect procurement. Each involves a slightly different set of activities.

Replenishment. Inventory replenishment is typically initiated by analysis of the sales forecast to determine forecasted MRP requirements. Representatives from sales, production, and logistics perform this activity jointly. As a result of this analysis, the company forms estimates for inventory levels of raw materials and finished goods. If it determines that a new item needs to be stocked, a blanket order is established with a suitable supplier.

Whereas forecast planning normally determines the replenishment of existing stock, in this case a "call off" order is issued to the preferred supplier. The order status is tracked, and the logistics department is notified of an impending delivery. Figure A.22 illustrates an e-nabled replenishment activity.

The e-nabling transformation that occurs is referred to as vendor-managed inventory (VMI), which is based on sharing demand forecasts, current inventory levels, and logistics information with suppliers. Using VMI, the preferred supplier can automatically determine inventory requirements, self-manage replenishment activities, and communicate shipment notices.

Figure A.19 illustrates only the procurement portion of the overall material management operation. VMI is achieved utilizing four e-nabling technologies:

1. Electronic VMI
2. Electronic demand forecasting

Figure A.22   E-nabled Replenishment

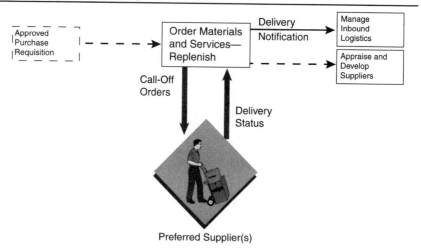

Preferred Supplier(s)

3. Advance electronic shipment notice

4. Electronic invoicing.

E-nabling this activity reduces cycle time, head count, and cost, and improves accuracy.

Sharing information reduces cycle time, allowing suppliers to plan better and to deliver to forecast demand. Eliminating manual steps reduces head count, and reducing the cost of inventory results in significant savings. Sharing information in a timely fashion improves accuracy and reduces the likelihood of inaccurate and/or incomplete deliveries.

Ad Hoc Buying.   Ad hoc buying typically refers to single purchases of items that indirect procurement does not cover but that are unrelated to direct production. Receipt of an approved purchase requisition for the item(s) in question initiates this activity.

The first step is to find a qualified supplier. This involves searching for potential suppliers and issuing RFQs. Pricing, terms and conditions, and lead times are used to select a supplier. A purchase order is created and issued, and the delivery status is tracked. The logistics department is notified of the impending delivery.

Depending on the nature of the requisitioned item, this entire process can be both time consuming and costly. Figure A.23 illustrates an e-nabled ad hoc buying process.

E-business enables the buyer to use electronic procurement to perform all the steps in the procurement process more efficiently. Electronic

Figure A.23   E-nabled Ad-Hoc Buying Process

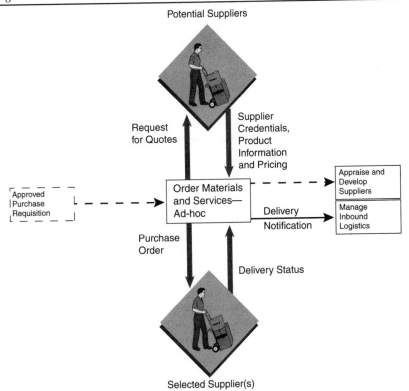

search engines, together with virtual communities of suppliers, help locate suitable suppliers quickly.

The buyer may then explore the suppliers' electronic product information, configure different options, and obtain pricing availability information. Electronic ordering eliminates the need for purchase orders.

These steps are e-nabled in eight ways:

1. Electronic searches
2. Virtual communities
3. Product catalogues
4. Product configurators
5. Quotation management
6. Electronic ordering
7. Product availability
8. Electronic tracking.

E-nabling this activity reduces cycle time, head count, and cost, and improves accuracy.

Electronic searches reduce cycle time because they enable potential suppliers and required products to be identified more quickly. Electronic searching also requires fewer resources to perform wider searches, thereby reducing head count and cost. Using well-maintained electronic directories, together with managed virtual communities improves accuracy.

Indirect Procurement. Indirect procurement is the buying of nonproduction related supplies. In the United States, it is frequently referred to as maintenance, repair, and operation (MRO) buying; in Europe it is more frequently referred to as nonproduction requirement (NPR) buying.

Initially, an indirect procurement requisition is submitted for approval. If the requisition is for the replenishment of items from a current supplier, a "call off" order is issued to that supplier.

If, however, the requisition is for a first time purchase or purchase of a single item, a suitable supplier must be identified and product

Figure A.24   E-nabled Indirect Procurement

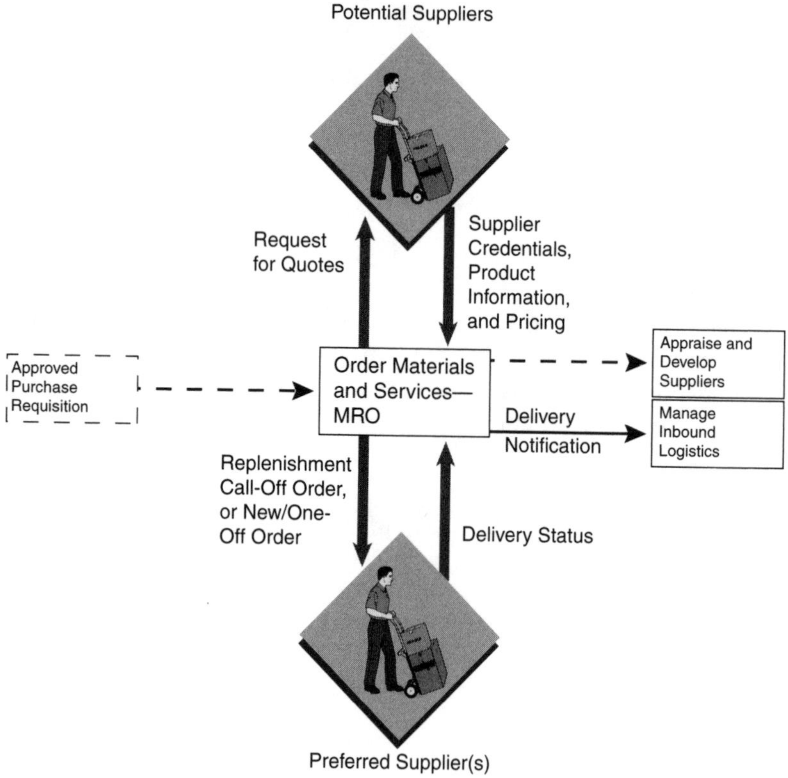

information and quotation obtained before the order is placed. Delivery status is tracked, and the logistics organization is notified of an impending delivery. The entire process can be time consuming and very costly relative to the value of the item. Figure A.24 illustrates an e-nabled indirect procurement activity.

Electronic indirect procurement connects the point of requisition (that is, the individual who identifies the requirement) with the preferred supplier. Once the procurement authority selects and certifies the preferred supplier, product catalogues, configurators, price lists, and availability information is electronically retrievable at the point of requisition. Approval and authorization procedures, normally time consuming and costly, are preconfigured into the electronic indirect procurement process to ensure they conform to policies.

Throughout the corporation and potentially among companies in the network, seven e-nabling technologies can be used to aggregate indirect procurement requirements to support price negotiations with suppliers:

1. Electronic product catalogues
2. Product configurators
3. On-line price lists
4. Electronic ordering
5. Product availability
6. Electronic delivery tracking
7. Automated approvals and authorization policies.

E-nabling the indirect procurement activity set reduces cycle time, head count, and cost, and improves accuracy. Eliminating hand offs and delays reduces cycle time and head count. Moving from a manual to an electronic process also reduces costs and keying errors, leading to improved accuracy.

MANAGE LOGISTICS/DISTRIBUTION

Managing logistics (Figure A.25) typically involves three business objectives: minimizing internal and external logistics costs, reducing inventory, and increasing the value that logistics activities deliver to the company

Figure A.25   Standard Value Chain: Managing Logistics/Distribution

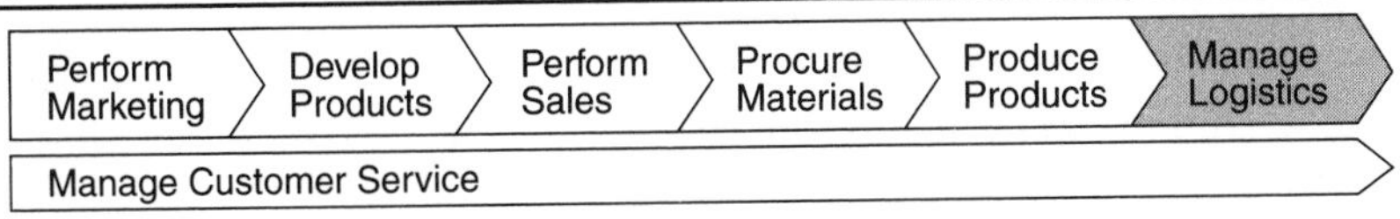

Figure A.26   E-nabling Logistics/Distribution: Objectives and Critical Success Factors

Business Objectives	Critical Success Factors	E-Business Enablers
	Streamline Internal Processes for Transportation	E-business enables electronic booking and appointment confirmation with an organization's freight carriers. Advanced ship notices and quality control information can help automate manual warehouse processes.
Minimize Internal and External Logistics Cost	Minimize Freight Costs	E-business supports improved carrier scheduling, load planning, back-haul planning, and freight rating with low cost, timely information to enable better transportation execution.
	Collaborate with Suppliers in Planning	E-business offers a vehicle for the rapid information exchange required by vendor-managed inventory, co-managed inventory, and collaborative planning, forecasting, and replenishment (CPFAR).
	Collaborate with Partners on Forecasts/Replenishments	E-business enables business partners to rapidly exchange the information (orders, forecasts, promotions, inventory, order status, production schedules, and supply-chain variances) necessary to globally optimize a multicompany supply chain.
Minimize Inventory Investment	Employ Flow-Through Strategies	E-business allows collection of time-sensitive information to support the precise scheduling and robust transaction functionality required by cross-docking, drop shipment, and direct-to-store shipping programs.
	Reduce Cycle Times	E-business allows many time consuming steps such as logging receipts, logging quality information, telephoning carriers, and scheduling supplier receipts to be automated or eliminated.
	Maintain High Order Fill Rates and 'On Time' Shipments	E-business enables the communication of timely, exception-based status messages that allow delivery guarantees and intervention to avoid late shipments.
Increase Value Added	Provide Value-Added Products Processes and Services	E-business information supports mass customization and the synchronization required to assemble, consolidate, and apply special packaging, and to integrate multiple suppliers in a short lead time environment.
	Delight Customers with Timely, Accurate Order Status and Info	E-business supports a wide variety of order status info particularly in-transit inventory visibility allowing customers to delay allocations/schedule better. E-business allows electronic Available to Promise and due date quoting with constraint-based supply-chain planning.

and its customers. Figure A.26 illustrates these objectives, the critical success factors for achieving them, and ways logistics can be e-nabled.

The main goal of logistics is to deliver the right product at the right time at the lowest possible cost. E-nabling the effort results in low-cost and timely information, and, through electronic exchange, automates such labor-intensive processes as telephoning carriers, comparing freight rates, evaluating backhauls, and scheduling pick up and delivery.

E-business also supports more effective optimizing of freight rates, one of the largest supply chain expenditures. E-business enables better planning of full loads and backhauls that results in reduced freight rates.

E-nabling technologies provide the logistics operation with the rapid communication capability necessary when replenishment planning is outsourced. As best practices evolve and companies move from VMI to comanaged inventory, and finally to collaborative planning, forecasting, and replenishment, information exchange among partners increases.

Companies are increasing their focus on improving cycle times and on reducing inventory. Collaborative planning, using rapid and low cost electronic exchange of information, optimizes the entire multicompany chain. Flow-through strategies such as cross-docking, direct-to-store shipping, and drop shipments, improve supply chain velocity, which then improves inventory turns.

The e-nabled logistics operation transforms or eliminates many manual processes. Business can provide logistics information quickly, cutting time and inventory out of the distribution process.

Customers are demanding more and faster delivery of products, services, and information. High fill rates and on-time shipments are critical to customers as inventory buffers disappear throughout the supply chain. Value-added processes and services are becoming increasingly important as mass customization combats industry commoditization.

The e-nabled logistics operation allows customers to access order status, available to promise, and due date quotes that improve customer satisfaction.

Three main activities are associated with logistics: managing inbound logistics, managing the warehouse, and managing outbound logistics.

Managing Inbound Logistics

The objective of the inbound logistics process is to receive required goods into the business. Materials must be available at the right time, but inventory levels cannot be too high.

Notice of an impending receipt from purchasing or the arrival of goods on the receiving dock triggers the inbound logistics activity. Inbound logistics can involve transport order placement, scheduling, delivery appointments, and receiving. It can also involve the timely and cost-effective verifying of the quality/quantity of raw materials and purchased finished goods and components received into the warehouse.

Receiving docks and crews must be scheduled. Incoming material must be verified against the purchase order. Some parts may require quality inspection. Inbound logistics' primary communication and information flows are with supply chain partners (delivery scheduling), the warehouse (notice of goods received), finance (verification of receipt prior to payment to supply chain partner), and purchasing (what was received and what was rejected).

Figure A.27 illustrates an e-nabled inbound logistics management process. Vendor-managed inventory, receiving inbound materials, and confirming quality are each transformed by e-business. Vendor-managed inventory is the application of e-business and strategy to replace two steps of the inbound logistics process (along with several in procurement). Under VMI, the supply chain partner maintains the appropriate inventory level.

This has broad application in high technology and many other industries because of high volumes and repeat business. The company can outsource replenishment of certain material categories. To make these programs succeed, participating companies should focus on timely flow

Figure A.27   E-nabled Inbound Logistics Management Process

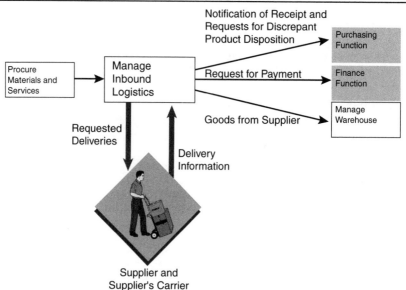

Supplier and
Supplier's Carrier

of information and clear communication of forecasts and schedules, and especially on highly accurate inventory.

Head count and cost reduction, cycle time reduction, and operating effectiveness are among the benefits of VMI. Fewer buyer/planners are needed to plan replenishment, reducing cost and head count. Cycle time is reduced because it takes less time to replenish inventory, and information is substituted for inventory. Operating effectiveness is increased because stockouts are less frequent, which contributes to a smoother, more orderly operation flow.

The automation of the receiving process through advanced ship notices (ASNs) e-nables the receiving of inbound materials. ASNs facilitate the readiness of docks, equipment, and personnel. Verification steps, such as ensuring that all received items have a valid purchase order number, can be performed in advance.

Advance ship notice information includes parts, quantities, PO number, and pallet contents, which assist receiving personnel to verify receipt. Two e-nabling technologies support this effort:

1. Advance ship notices

2. Electronic dock assignment notices.

E-nabling receiving activities reduces head count and cost, trims cycle time, and improves accuracy. Eliminating the data entry associated with receiving, telephone scheduling of deliveries, cross-docking disruptions, and demurrage charges reduces head count and costs.

More effective scheduling and synchronizing of receiving dock activities reduce cycle time and allow greater throughput and lower inventory levels. Reducing the substantial error rate associated with updating internal systems with packing slip data in various supplier forms improves accuracy.

The process of confirming quality is transformed because quality details, such as specs, properties, statistical process control (SPC) results, inspection results, and material safety data sheets, can be electronically transmitted to the supply chain partner to update the quality system. The e-nabling technology supporting this enables the electronic transmission of quality information.

E-nabling quality confirmation reduces head count (direct electronic updates eliminate manual activities) and improves accuracy (entry of quality information is automated).

Managing the Warehouse

Managing the warehouse involves providing fast-moving products, value-added services, and high accuracy levels. A notice from inbound logistics that some material is ready to be put away initiates this process. The responsibilities of managing the warehouse include storing and internally deploying raw materials, components, and/or finished goods before shipping them to the demand-side partner or to the customer.

Activities includes pallet staging, product put away, cycle counting, creating priorities and grouping picks, picking, replenishment of picking bins, final packaging, packing, pack list generation, load building, and pallet staging.

Warehouse and distribution centers also must perform reverse logistics—activities such as rewarehousing, reclassifying product, and processing scrap. The primary communication and information flows are to/from demand-side partners and customers (special requirements and customization), supply-side partners (shipment status), and outbound logistics (notice of goods to be shipped).

Figure A.28 illustrates an e-nabled warehousing process. E-nabling this process transforms two activity sets: cross-docking and special packaging and pallet configurations.

Cross-docking is defined as moving goods to bypass a step of "normal" storage. Manufacturing cross-docking involves moving finished goods directly from the production line to the delivery truck, bypassing finished goods storage. Distribution center cross-docking occurs when product is moved directly, or staged briefly, from the supply truck to the delivery truck.

Figure A.28   E-nabled Warehousing Process

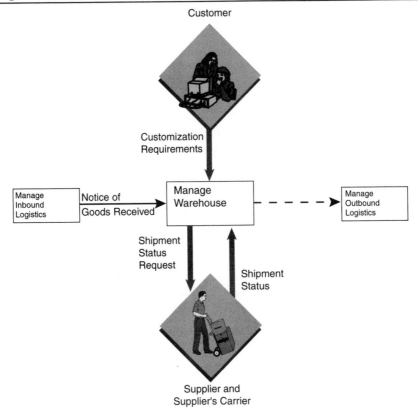

Cross-docking requires precise scheduling of deliveries and shipments. Even ASN information may not be timely enough. To maximize the benefits of cross-docking, the inbound carrier should electronically provide up-to-the-minute shipment status. Cross-docking can be opportunistic (when, for example, one substitutes freshly received inventory for stored) or planned (when, for example, one anticipates inbound shipment and schedules outbound shipment accordingly).

In either case, e-business technology supports the rapid information exchange required for an electronic view of material flows. Four e-nabling technologies support cross-docking:

1. Electronic shipment status
2. ASNs
3. Electronic delivery schedules
4. Electronic booking and appointment confirmation.

E-nabling cross-docking improves customer satisfaction by reducing lead times to customers and reduces cycle time by moving inventory through the warehouse or distribution center faster and increasing the velocity of the entire supply chain.

Because of e-nabled special packaging and pallet configuration, logistics activities are becoming a crucial tool for differentiating products and protecting margins. Customers are demanding mass customization services such as assembly, kitting, consolidation, special packaging, labeling, and multivendor integration services.

Frequently, these services can only be defined immediately prior to shipment. Just-in-time delivery of these services is also logical, given such issues as allocating inventory and minimizing handling.

Electronic communication of the customer's desired value-added services is the lowest cost and most effective method of getting the necessary information on time. The customer can transmit these requirements to the enterprise so warehouse flows are not disrupted. Product moves from picking and special value-added processing, to shipment staging in a predictable, scheduled flow.

E-nabling technology makes it possible to electronically transmit the following information:

○ Special assembly/kitting requirements
○ Special packaging specs
○ Special labeling
○ Pallet configuration layouts
○ Multivendor integration requirements.

E-nabling special packing and pallet configuration improves customer satisfaction by enabling mass customization services and packing, and revenue growth, by making it possible to charge premium prices for such high-value-added services.

Managing Outbound Logistics

Managing outbound logistics is the final group of steps in the logistics process. Its primary objective is to provide goods to the customer on time at the lowest possible cost. A notice that some goods have been picked and are available for shipment usually initiates the process.

In outbound logistics, loads are built, routed, and "offered" to one or more carriers. Multiple phone calls are usually required before a carrier "accepts" the load. A vehicle and a shipping dock are allocated at the appointed time. Sometimes a delivery appointment must also be arranged.

Finally, status must be frequently reported while the goods are in transit. Although some companies maintain their own delivery fleets, most outsource some or all of the actual transportation operations. The primary communication and information flows are to/from demand chain partners or customers (delivery schedule and status), carriers (status of deliveries), and finance (requests to pay freight bills).

Figure A.29 illustrates e-nabled outbound logistics. E-technologies transform the following three activities: scheduling delivery to the customer dock, confirming booking and appointment, and messaging delivery status.

In an era of increasing synchronization among demand chain partners, e-business links can be used to inform them of a requested delivery time and location, and to confirm the slot at their dock. With e-nabling technologies, the following information can be forwarded or received electronically:

Figure A.29   E-nabled Outbound Logistics

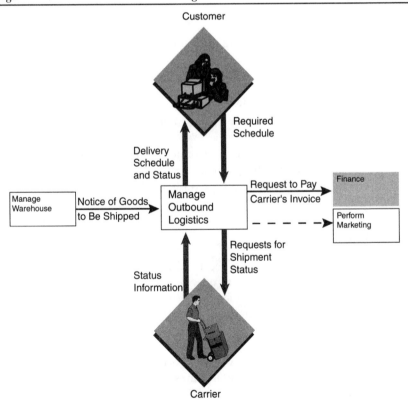

○ Delivery slot request

○ Customer confirmation of dock assignment.

E-nabling the activity reduces head count by improving dispatcher productivity and improves accuracy by avoiding delivery schedule misunderstandings.

With e-business, companies can automate booking and appointment confirmation. Load plans and routing models can be transmitted to preferred carriers. If one preferred carrier rejects the load or fails to respond, it can then be offered to the next preferred carrier.

The carrier's confirmation that it will take the load is also electronically transmitted back to the company. By using a load-control center—a companywide transportation planning and execution system—the transformation potential is further magnified. Load-control centers use e-business technology to acquire necessary information from carriers.

In an e-nabled booking and appointment confirmation activity, five pieces of information can be transmitted electronically:

1. Transportation inquiries
2. Load plans/offers
3. Confirmations/acceptances
4. Truck assignments
5. Pickup appointments.

E-nabling this activity reduces head count (e-business combined with a load-control center can increase loads per dispatcher by 500 percent) and lowers cost (effective comparison of transportation alternatives using e-business can reduce freight costs by 5 to 15 percent).

Customers and suppliers often need to know who has the goods, where the goods are, and when the goods will arrive. E-nabling delivery status messaging allows more sharing of data and, therefore, provides all partners with greater supply chain visibility. Full order information can be transmitted to carriers. Carriers who track their vehicles can then provide status at the item level.

Moreover, by comparing the status with the due dates from the order, carriers can provide suppliers and customers with at-risk deliveries and other supply chain variances. This gives customers powerful decision support information, whereby they can replan and minimize any dissatisfaction.

With exception-based status messages, suppliers can consider alternative methods for current as well as future shipments. In an e-nabled effort, five bits of information can be transmitted electronically:

1. Sales orders
2. ASNs
3. Order status and location
4. Projected delivery time
5. At-risk deliveries.

E-nabling this activity increases customer satisfaction (timely and accurate order status allows customers to plan better, particularly when the customer uses delayed inventory allocation, postponed final assembly, consolidation, and cross-docking); reduces head count (electronic status messaging helps avoid the time-consuming three-way communication between suppliers, customers, and carriers); and improves accuracy (actual delivery times are more precise, which supports better carrier performance).

MANAGE CUSTOMER SERVICE

Generally, managing customer service (Figure A.30) is guided by three main business objectives: increasing customer satisfaction by improving the timeliness and quality of service; reducing the cost of delivering service; and growing services revenue by offering value-adding service offerings in increasingly competitive markets. Figure A.31 illustrates these three business objectives, their critical success factors, and ways to e-nable the provision of customer service.

The processes associated with customer service are handling inquiries and service requests, providing service, and measuring customer satisfaction. All can be transformed through e-nabled information exchange.

Handling Inquiries and Requests for Service

The arrival of a customer inquiry or service request initiates this activity. While companies can respond to simple inquiries immediately, in the case of complex inquiries or service requests, they must validate the customer as current and then elicit, capture, and log the details of the inquiry.

Figure A.30   Standard Value Chain: Managing Customer Service

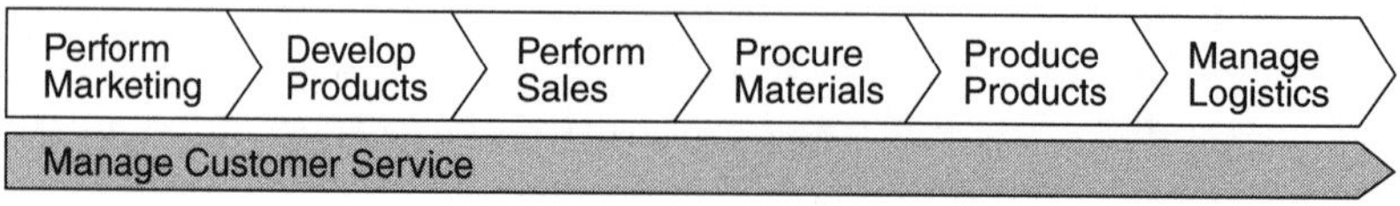

Figure A.31   E-nabling Customer Service: Objectives and Critical Success Factors

Business Objectives	Critical Success Factors	E-Business Enablers
	Ensure Accuracy and Completeness of Data	E-business enables capture of inquiries and service requests directly from the customer; intelligent electronic agents ensure accuracy and completeness of information.
Improve Timeliness and Quality of Service	Deploy Appropriately Skilled CSR	E-business supports the timely and accurate routing and escalation of service requests internally, and, if necessary, with external partners or third-party service providers.
	Equip CSRs with Accurate Support Information	E-business offers the potential for access to, and availability of, a wider network of information resources to aid accurate and speedy problem resolution.
	Leverage Partner Services Capabilities	E-business enables cost-effective collaborative service provision by reducing the overhead associated with information sharing and communication.
Reduce Cost of Service Provision	Outsource to Third-Party Suppliers	E-business enables communication and coordination with third-party service suppliers.
	Focus CSRs on Value-Adding Activities	E-business offers the potential for customer self-service on most simple inquiries and problems, thereby focusing CSRs on complex, value-adding activities.
	Design and Introduce New Service Offerings	E-business enables continuous monitoring and capture of customer feedback at lower cost, thereby supporting the design and delivery of new higher-value service offerings.
Grow Service Revenue	Offer Service Capability to Industry Partners	E-business supports effective collaboration with industry partners, thereby enabling the leverage of service capability to other Industry partners.
	Extend Reach of Service Provision	E-business offers the potential to provide and support service capability across a wider geographic reach, utilizing local field service agents as necessary.

The customer is provided with a confirmation number for use in future correspondence relating to the inquiry/service request. Inquiries are passed to an appropriately skilled CSR, who attempts to resolve the problem. The customer may also be routed and/or escalated to other CSRs, or to third-party service providers and partners. Inquiry resolution may require further communication with the customer to obtain detailed information. Service requests are routed to the appropriate service area, where the service provision process takes over.

Figure A.32 illustrates an e-nabled inquiry handling and service request process. E-nabling this process transforms three activities: receiving, authorizing, personalizing, and self-service; CSR assisted inquiry resolution; and routing and escalation.

Applying e-business offers the potential to replace the three manual steps involved in receiving an inquiry or service request, identifying and validating the customer, and capturing/logging the details. The benefits, of course, depend on the nature and complexity of the inquiry/request. The electronic channel may not be appropriate for all cases.

The customer signs on with a unique ID, which is automatically validated. He or she is then presented with a personalized service interface. Most straightforward inquiries such as documentation, product information, service request status, and basic problem solving, may be dealt with by self-service.

Figure A.32   E-nabled Inquiry Handling and Service Request Process

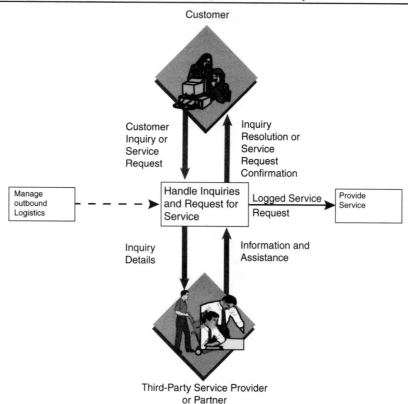

Customer

Customer Inquiry or Service Request

Inquiry Resolution or Service Request Confirmation

| Manage outbound Logistics | | Handle Inquiries and Request for Service | Logged Service Request | Provide Service |

Inquiry Details

Information and Assistance

Third-Party Service Provider or Partner

In the case of a service request, or a customer inquiry that cannot be satisfied with available information, the customer can submit the request/inquiry, together with any supporting information. In such cases, the customer receives a service confirmation for future communications relating to the request/inquiry.

The logged request/inquiry is then categorized according to the information entered by the customer, allocated a priority, and communicated to a CSR for action.

Thirteen e-nabling technologies support this step:

1. Product inquiries

2. General information

3. Service status

4. Fault reporting

5. Receipt point for complaint

6. Customer history

7. Customer configurations

8. Personalized service interfaces

9. Inquiry classification

10. Inquiry logging

11. Priority allocation

12. Call-enter integration

13. Diagnostic aids.

E-nabling this activity set increases customer satisfaction, reduces head count and cost, improves accuracy, and enhances revenue growth.

When customers can move faster through the inquiry process because of personalized and customized sites, take advantage of 24 × 7 service, and provide feedback to the company electronically, satisfaction is improved.

Head count and costs are reduced because CSR productivity improves, and CSRs are more free to focus on complex problems and value-added activities. Most straightforward inquiries and problems can be handled electronically with greater accuracy and at dramatically reduced cost and time.

Revenue growth opportunities arise from the company's ability to track customer inquiries and convert them into possible leads; its opportunity to capture information regarding customer satisfaction; its ability to gather and report service statistics quickly and accurately; and its ability to capture customer feedback electronically.

In certain cases, customers are unable to resolve their problem through the self-service facility. In these cases, CSRs analyze and resolve the inquiry. The CSR has access to electronic documentation, third-party suppliers, and diagnostic tools that help. The customer can be asked to submit further details through electronic channels, and the resolution may also be communicated electronically.

Eight e-nabling technologies support this process:

1. Product information and configuration

2. Parts lists

3. On-line documentation

4. FAQs and Tech Tips

5. On-line user manuals

6. Knowledge base of solutions

7. Customer configurations

8. Diagnostic aids.

E-nabling CSR-assisted inquiry resolution improves customer satisfaction by providing the customer a richer mix of media for communicating complex responses and, possibly, 24×7 availability. It improves accuracy because CSRs have immediate access to up-to-date third-party information.

Providing Service

Receipt of a service request from the previous process initiates service provision activities. The request could relate to repairing (break/fix), upgrading, installing, or deactivating a supported product.

In the case of installations or upgrades, the precise details of the equipment are established and any spares are obtained from spares inventory. Any service assistance from a third party is requisitioned and the request is expedited. In the case of a break/fix request, the problem is analyzed with further information from the customer where necessary. In some cases, the problem is routed/escalated to the appropriate internal experts or to a third party.

Once the company determines how to resolve the problem, it obtains parts and expedites the service request. A request is made to the finance department to invoice the customer and the service request is closed. The internal knowledge base is updated appropriately to aid in the resolution of similar problems in the future.

Figure A.33 illustrates an e-nabled service provision process. E-nabling this activity transforms four activity sets: analyzing service requests; routing and escalating; notifying customers of planned actions; and closing requests and updating knowledge bases.

CSRs are able to browse through a host of research agents and sources of information to help analyze and find an answer to the reported problem. In addition, in some industries, the analysis activity may be supported by remote interrogation of the equipment in question. This step is e-nabled through:

○ Product information and configuration

○ Parts lists

○ FAQs and Tech Tips

○ Knowledge base of solutions.

E-nabling this activity reduces cycle time by increasing the speed of inquiry resolution and by providing easy access to third-party information.

Figure A.33   E-nabled Service Provision Process

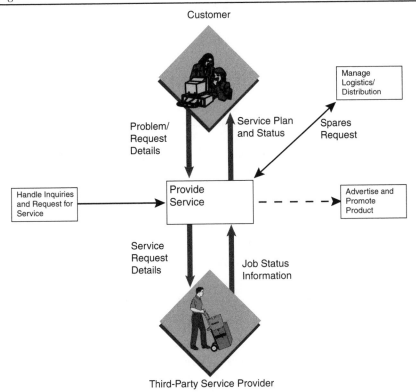

It improves accuracy because information is up-to-date. And it lowers the cost of analyzing problems by providing access to a wider support network. Such access allows less experienced CSRs to take on complex problems.

The logged service request may need to be routed internally to the appropriate CSR or, in some cases, externally to the appropriate third party. The third party can assist in resolving the problem or, alternatively, work with the customer to resolve the service request.

E-nabling routing decisions and execution involves:

○ Collaborative service

○ Transaction management systems.

E-nabling the system reduces cycle time by speeding up problem resolution and improves accuracy (relevant sources and expertise are quickly identified and deployed to resolve inquiries).

An e-nabled company can electronically notify customers about the status of a service request and schedule a service visit. This step is e-nabled by:

○ Service request status tracking
○ Service scheduling and planning.

E-nabling this activity increases customer satisfaction because the customer can be updated continuously and at low cost. If the service request was handled by an outsourced CSR, the completion notice and invoice are received electronically, and the resolution details are captured electronically and stored in the knowledge base.

E-nabling this effort reduces cost. Knowledge is easily captured, and the linked knowledge base improves invoice clearance.

Measuring Customer Satisfaction

Measuring customer satisfaction takes place in the background. It seeks to measure customer satisfaction with field service and call-center response and with product reliability. Companies use surveys and questionnaires to obtain customer views and ratings based on the customer perceptions, needs, and priorities in each of these areas.

They validate the information gathered in the surveys and questionnaires by conducting some customer interviews before the results are analyzed to understand trends and root causes. Measuring customer satisfaction is a crucial element in the design and delivery of customer service. The results are continuously fed back into other parts of the company.

Figure A.34 illustrates an e-nabled customer satisfaction measurement process. In this process, two areas are transformed: identifying customer needs and measuring service delivery and product reliability.

Customer needs and service expectations can be identified and collected electronically. This information can be used to tailor service levels and products in line with customer demand and market standards. Electronic surveys and questionnaires e-nable these activities.

E-nabling this effort improves accuracy, makes it convenient for customers to respond on a 24 × 7 basis, and, through an easy-to-use interactive medium, encourages response.

The company's ability to measure service delivery and product reliability is enhanced through electronic collection channels. This activity set measures customer satisfaction in three areas:

1. Field personnel's ability to deliver effective customer service. Customer satisfaction criteria are used as a benchmark to assess performance.

Figure A.34 E-nabled Customer Satisfaction Measurement Process

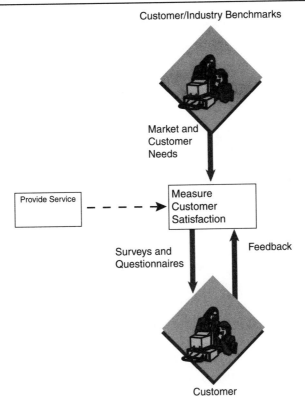

2. The call center's ability to deliver effective customer service. Customer satisfaction criteria are used to benchmark perfor- mance.

3. Product reliability and failure rates. These become the basis for product improvement efforts by product development personnel.

Electronic surveys, questionnaires, and customer feedback e-nable measurements.

E-nabling this effort improves customer satisfaction by providing an easy-to-use interactive medium and 24 × 7 convenience; reduces cycle time by increasing the speed of returns that help facilitate change; and improves accuracy by widening the geographic spread.

Index